Useless Etymology

Useless Etymology

Offbeat Word Origins for Curious Minds

JESS ZAFARRIS

Chambers

First published in Great Britain by Chambers in 2025
An imprint of John Murray Press

6

A CIP catalogue record for this title is available from the British Library

Library of Congress in Cataloging-in-Publication available

Hardback ISBN 978 1 399 80918 4
ebook ISBN 978 1 399 80920 7

Typeset by KnowledgeWorks Global Ltd.

Printed and bound in the United States of America

John Murray Press policy is to use papers that are natural, renewable and recyclable products and made from wood grown in sustainable forests. The logging and manufacturing processes are expected to conform to the environmental regulations of the country of origin.

John Murray Press
Carmelite House
50 Victoria Embankment
London EC4Y 0DZ

John Murray Press
123 S. Broad St., Ste 2750
Philadelphia, PA 19109

www.chambers.co.uk

John Murray Press, part of Hodder & Stoughton Limited
An Hachette UK company

The authorized representative in the EEA is Hachette Ireland, 8 Castlecourt Centre, Dublin 15, D15 XTP3, Ireland (email: info@hbgi.ie)

For anyone who has found a Wonderland, Neverland, or Narnia hiding inside a single word, but especially for Emily.

CONTENTS

PROLOGUE
Understanding Etymology

Hello.

Did you know that "hello" didn't become a standard greeting until the introduction of the Bell telephone in 1876?

It appeared a bit before that in a couple of records from the 1820s and 30s, but it wasn't commonly used—and it didn't quite mean the same thing. These records suggest that, if you were approaching a remote property, you would announce yourself by saying "hello" or "hello a house."

This early "hello" was a variation of the earlier and more common words "hallo," "halloo," or "hollo." These words were used to hail someone from afar, like when you were hunting and needed to call out to your dogs or fellow hunters, or when you had to shout to a coachman or ferryman to pick you up. Typical greetings, meanwhile, were often more along the lines of "well met," "hail," "good day," "good morning," and "good evening."

"Hollo" and "hallo" may originally come from an Old High German variation meaning "to fetch." The word "holler" is also a variation of "hollo."

The variation "hullo" appeared around the 1850s in literature, notably in Charles Dickens' *Oliver Twist* (1838), which was immensely popular at the time (and still is), also as a word for hailing someone from afar.[1]

[1] Charles Dickens, *Oliver Twist* (Cambridge, MA: Hurd & Houghton, 1874), 98.

Initially, Alexander Graham Bell proposed using the word "ahoy" as a telephone greeting.[2] But Thomas Edison suggested in a letter to an official responsible for introducing telephones in Pittsburgh that the word "hello"—which after all already meant calling to another party from a distance—be used instead.[3] The term became so deeply associated with telephones that, by 1889, central telephone exchange operators were known as "hello-girls."

Related: The word "hullaballoo" is based on "hollo" and was originally spelled "holloballoo" among similar variations. See Tobias Smollett's *The Life and Adventures of Sir Launcelot Greaves* (1762): "I would there was a blister on this plaguy tongue of mine for making such a hollo-ballo."[4]

On the fecklessness of pedantry

One surprising thing about the study of language and linguistics: The more you learn, the less pedantic you become and the more you revel in the glorious, rip-roaring chaos of iterative creativity.

Don't get me wrong, there are rules—so many rules. More and more rules every day. Just look at the off-kilter language of memes (see: meme). But we make up the rules as we go along, collectively and with cackling abandon. It's that collaborative artistry that makes the study of etymology so darn fun.

---

[2] Alexander Graham Bell, *Letters of Alexander Graham Bell*, ed. John K. Cowen (Cambridge: Cambridge University Press, 1990), 124–5.

[3] Thomas Edison, *The Diary and Sundry Observations of Thomas A. Edison*, ed. Paul Israel (New Brunswick, NJ: Rutgers University Press, 1995), 45–6.

[4] Tobias Smollett, *The Life and Adventures of Sir Launcelot Greaves* (London: John Murray, 1762), 102.

Useless Etymology exults in, peers beneath, and giggles at the words we use every day—the hidden meanings, shocking twists, and elaborate patterns to be found in our language. The words and phrases you'll find in this book are eclectic, to say the least, but they are collected here in a spirit of unslakable curiosity. Some were found in rabbit holes of my own making, while others were discovered on quests gifted to me by word enthusiasts who follow my etymologically adventurous blog, my TikTok channel, and my and Rob Watts' podcast *Words Unravelled*. (If you haven't already, check those out. Or if you're in the mood for something spicy, you could always pick up my previous book, *Words from Hell*, or any of the pieces I've been quoted or profiled in among the pages of *The New York Times*, *The Guardian*, *The Boston Globe*, and elsewhere.)

So, it's a book of factoids?

Yes and no.

Today many people use the word **"factoid"** to mean "a fun fact," a little morsel of interesting information—and this book does contain many, many such facts. So, yes, given that to most people the word "factoid" means "a fun fact," *Useless Etymology* is a book of factoids.

But, originally, factoid was not a word for a fun fact.

In fact, a factoid wasn't a fact at all.

The term was coined in 1973 by Norman Mailer in his novelistic biography of Marilyn Monroe to refer to supposed "facts" in magazines and newspapers that had no basis in fact but were there to manipulate the emotions of readers.[5] He

[5] Norman Mailer, *Marilyn: A Biography* (Boston, MA: Little, Brown and Company, 1973), 67.

used the suffix *-oid*, which comes from the Greek *eidos*, meaning "appearance" or "shape." So, for Mailer at least, a factoid was not a fact, but something that had the appearance or shape of a fact, even though it wasn't one.

So, you could say that the assertion that factoid means fun fact is a factoid because it has been repeated so often that it has become accepted as the actual, factual definition.

Because of factoid's original meaning and origin, William Safire—the writer behind the *New York Times* column "On Language"—has suggested the word "factlet" to represent a little piece of interesting information instead.[6]

"Fact" itself has also been on an intriguing etymological journey. Before the 1600s, a fact wasn't a fact as we know it today, but was instead an action, a deed, a "thing done"—or even a crime! It's a doublet with the word "feat."

"After the fact" was originally found in legal contexts, and here the "fact" was a crime.

Facts became facts as we know them today in the context of scientific empiricism. Rather than a belief, a fact was something that was proved in a mathematical sense or demonstrated by means of the scientific method. These were the original "feats" of science and empiricism that demonstrated "facts"—something shown by an action rather than imagined or supposed.

The lessons in this book are also classifiable as **"trivia"**: little bits of information that are of little consequence outside of being curiosities. You might call them "trivialities"—even though I, and I hope most of you, believe that words and their origins are not trivial and do matter a great deal.

Trivia is a Latin word, the plural of *trivium*. The related Latin word *trivialis* meant "common" or "ordinary." But the literal meaning of the Latin *trivium* is "a place where three roads meet."

---

[6] William Safire, "On Language: Factoid," *The New York Times*, August 7, 1983.

What does a three-way crossroads have to do with interesting morsels of mostly useless information?

The Roman Empire was famously connected by public roads, many of which still exist today, sometimes in much better condition than our contemporary asphalt roads. The intersections of these roads, especially three or more, were a great place for the public—or plebeians—from different places to meet, hang out, and trade goods. Thus, crossroads came to be known as distinctly public, common places where inconsequential or trivial things were said and done.

The "trivium" is also a term from Classical education representing the three arts of grammar, logic, and rhetoric. These were the fundamental areas of study before students began studying the more advanced topics of the quadrivium: arithmetic, astronomy, music, and geometry. "Quadrivium" is the older of the two terms, likely coined by the early medieval philosopher Boethius.[7] However, the idea of grouping these disciplines had been in use long before that and was outlined in the writings of Pythagoras and Plato. "Trivium" was coined a few centuries later, modeled after and paired with the quadrivium during the Carolingian Renaissance of the 8th and 9th centuries. Variations are still in practice in liberal arts contexts today.

The adjective "trivial" appeared in English as early as the 1500s, harking back to the idea of inconsequential news shared by common people but also the idea of fundamental educational disciplines. "Trivia" wasn't used in English until 1716, when John Gay published a book by that name about the streets and crossroads of London.[8]

---

[7] Johannes Fried, *The Middle Ages*, 3rd ed. (Cambridge, MA: Harvard University Press, 2015).

[8] John Gay, *Trivia: or, The Art of Walking the Streets of London* (London: John Nourse, 1716).

"Trivia" wasn't a common word for "fun fact" until 1902, when Logan Pearsall Smith published a series of books called *Trivia.*[9] Smith was known for his clever sayings and essays, and his *Trivia* books were full of interesting little observations about public life and human behavior—like what you might observe at a crossroads or on the street.

"Trivia" as a word for gamified fun facts began to crop up in university culture shortly thereafter, and then on the quiz shows of the mid-1900s. At that point, it was probably meant to be a double entendre, harking back to both the knowledge you would absorb studying the disciplines of the trivium *and* the informal news you'd get on the street corner. "Trivia" then got another huge boost in popularity in 1982 with the game *Trivial Pursuit*—which also alludes to the crossroads in the design of the board, in addition to being a game that tests your trivial knowledge (in every sense of the word).

Lexical links

"Trivia" is far from the only English word that emerged from the Latin *via*, meaning "way, road, path, highway, channel, course."

If something is **obvious**, it's clear and easy to see. So easy, in fact, that you might figuratively trip over it—and literally, too—because the word "obvious" literally means "in the way," or more precisely, "in front of you on the path or road" (*ob* "in front of, against" + *via* "way").

Impervious (*im-* "not, opposite of" + *per* "through" + *via* "road, way") describes something resistant to attack, literally because it cannot be penetrated or crossed. There is no way through it.

Something that happened **previously** (*prae* "before" + *via* "road") occurred earlier along your route or path.

[9] Logan Pearsall Smith, *Trivia* (London: Constable and Company, 1902).

To **deviate** (*de* "off" + *via* "way") is to literally stray from a course, and to be devious or a deviant is to stray from the (moral) path.

Voyage is a French evolution of the Late Latin *viaticum* "a journey," meaning a "journey" along a road.

To **convey** something is to carry it along with you or to carry it to someone else, and **convoy** is a collection of people and vehicles that go along their route together. Both are from the Old French *convoiier* "to accompany, escort," made up of *com* "with, together" + *via* "way, road."

An **envoy** is someone sent somewhere to represent someone else, and it's closely related to the word "invoice," which you use to request that someone send along payment. Both are ultimately from the Latin *inviare*, "to send on one's way," from *in* "on" + *via* "road."

What is etymology, exactly?

Etymology is the study of word origins.

As a discipline, it has been practiced for as long as anyone has thought to study why a word means what it means, and looks and sounds the way it does.

The word "etymology" itself comes from the Greek *etymon*, meaning "true sense" (and before that, *etymos* or "true"). The implication is that this is "the study of the truest sense" of words and their meaning. *Etymologia* was studied by the ancient Greeks, and it entered English as *ethimolegia* in the 14th century.

Etymology has long involved as much art as science. Before the printing press, spellings changed and meanings evolved with astonishing speed. (This is increasingly true, given how quickly dialects and modes of communication evolve in digital spaces.) The fact that the historical record was spotty at best only compounded the difficulties facing the wannabe etymologist.

But now that so much has been digitized, we have the opportunity to examine the changes to languages and meaning with more nuance than we ever could.

The "art" of etymology has remained, however. You'll find as much joyful examination of myth and explosive creativity as hard fact within these pages (although I will try always to tell you when a myth's a myth and a factoid's a factoid).

Every word has a story

Sometimes it's a short story.

For example, did you know that the word "corgi" means "dwarf dog" in Welsh? Isn't that adorable?

Sometimes it's an old story.

To "stellify" is to turn someone into a constellation or other celestial body. This word is more than 600 years old. It's found in the prologue to Geoffrey Chaucer's *The Legend of Good Women*, which was penned sometime in the 1370s or 1380s.[10]

And many other words in this book have roots and histories that predate Chaucer by millennia.

Sometimes it's a silly story.

Many words have unexpectedly naughty roots, and one of my favorites is the word "feisty." Nowadays, feisty means "lively, determined and courageous" or "touchy and aggressive," and usually refers to small, determined animals and people.

Before that, the word "feist" was an early 19th-century name for "a small dog"—which, of course, makes sense if you've ever met a small dog. But feist as a word for a small dog is a shortened version of the Middle English phrase *fysting curre*—that is, feisting cur. A cur is a dog, and "fysting" meant "stinking"

[10] Geoffrey Chaucer, *The Legend of Good Women*, ed. John H. Fisher (New York: Holt, Rinehart and Winston, 1964).

but literally "farting" or "breaking wind." Thus, to be feisty is to be like a stinky, farty little mutt dog. According to Sir Francis Grose's *Dictionary of the Vulgar Tongue*, which was published in 1811 and consists of heavily editorialized definitions, the meanings of the words "feist" and "dog" were conflated because high-class ladies would blame their gas on their little lap dogs. And, by the way, feisty shares a root with the word "fizzle," which was also originally a word for breaking wind.

Sometimes it's an enthralling story.

The word "mesmerize" comes from the name of a real person: Franz Anton Mesmer, a German physician responsible for the theory of "animal magnetism," which, combined with the practice of mesmerism, gave us modern-day hypnosis.

"Mesmerizers" or "magnetizers" were thought to be able to manipulate currents of the "magnetic fluid" within living things, to treat whatever ailed them.

Is etymology really useless?

Of course not. Etymology gives you superpowers.

It grants you the ability to guess the meanings and origins of words without ever looking them up. For instance, the word **"sustain"** is made up of two word elements that appear in hundreds of other words.

So, let's break it down.

Most of the time when you see a word that begins with *sus-*, you're looking at a variation of the Latin *sub*. And I bet you already know that words using *sub* usually have something to do with being "under" or "beneath" something else. *Sub* also has a few other meanings in some cases, like "after" or "up from below."

***sub*- word**	**literal meaning**
subterranean	under/beneath the earth
subconscious	under/beneath conscious thought
submerge	to put under (water/liquid)

Sometimes when you smash it up with other words, the *b* in *sub* is replaced with letters like *c*, *f*, *g*, *p*, or *s*—as in "sustain." This is called **assimilation**, and it happens with other prefixes (often Latin-derived ones) including *ad*-, *ab*-, *com*-, and *in*- as well. All these sometimes drop or change their final letter in order to more smoothly combine with other roots and word elements.

For example:

***sub*- word**	**literal meaning**
succeed	to move/come after (someone else)
suffer	to carry/be under (a weight or burden)
suggest	to bring up (an idea)
suppose	to put under (an assumption)

Other *sus*- words besides "sustain" include "suspect," "suspend," and "resuscitate":

***sus*- word**	**literal meaning**
suspect	someone under observation or consideration
	Latin *sub* + *specere* "look at, observe"
suspend	to hang from beneath something
	Latin *sub* + *pendere* "hang"
resuscitate	to summon back up again
	Latin *re*-+ *sub* + *citare* "to summon"

In Gen Z slang, "sus" itself is also short for "suspicious," although ultimately it's also from that same Latin prefix, plus the Latin root verb *specere*, "to look at." That's the same root as "suspect." Both imply something that makes someone look up from below. Initially, the Latin *suspicere* meant "to look up to" someone in admiration, but it was also a word for looking at someone mistrustfully—giving them some sneaky side eye—or looking up at something that doesn't seem quite right.

So now that we know about *sus-*, we know that the other part of "sustain" is *tain*.

You might recognize that this word element also appears in words like "contain," "retain," and "detain." It's from the Latin *tenere*, meaning "to hold."

So, our word "sustain" describes something supported or held up, either figuratively or literally. A roof will collapse if it can't sustain the weight of snow on it; food sustains your body by keeping it going.

Some noun forms of these words make the connection even clearer: "sustenance," "content," "retention," "detention."

***-tain* word**	**literal meaning**
sustain/sustenance	hold up (from underneath)
	Latin *sub-* "up, from under" + *tenere*
contain/content	hold together (in a space)
	Latin *con-* "with, together" + *tenere*
retain/retention	hold back
	Latin *re-* "back, again" + *tenere*
detain/detention	hold away from
	Latin *de-* "down, away" + *tenere*

And *tenere* is also in dozens of other words with different structures, like "tendon," "tenacity," and "tension."

Getting it now?

You might enjoy having this foundational knowledge propping up your perspective as you proceed through these pages. But if you've only skimmed this introduction, don't fear: All you need to enjoy each element of this book is contained under each word. Jump around, flip from chapter to chapter, or read it backwards. You'll find something to laugh or sigh or rage at on every page.

Sir Terry Pratchett wrote: "It doesn't stop being magic just because you know how it works."[11]

It's the same with words. Learning how they came to be—in all their creative, goofy glory—lends them wonder and power. The more you know, the more intentionally you can wield them as you express the clutter and joy and horror and hilarity of a universe well worth all the wordsmithing that comes with it.

[11] Terry Pratchett, *A Hat Full of Sky* (New York: HarperCollins, 2004).

Abbreviations used in this book

OE	Old English—the form of English spoken from the mid-5th century to the late 11th century.
OED	*Oxford English Dictionary*, 2nd ed. (Oxford: Oxford University Press, 1989)—the etymologist's bible
PIE	Proto-Indo-European—the reconstructed common ancestor of the Indo-European language family, spoken from around 4500 to 2500 BCE.
★	Used to signify a reconstructed word or root in an unrecorded language such as Proto-Indo-European or Proto-Germanic.

Note on transliteration: All languages written in non-Roman scripts (e.g. Greek, Sanskrit, Arabic) are given in transliterated (Romanized) form.

Part 1
The Oddities of English Etymology

Where Words Started and Where They Are Now

1

The Power of Perspective

Apparent Anachronisms

As we learned with "hello," the frequency with which we use words can warp our perception of their age.

If you hear a character in a period film that takes place before the late 1800s use terms such as ambivalence or escalate, that's anachronistic.

Then again, the Greeks used the word *kudos* much as we do today when congratulating people.

And indeed, English speakers have been saying **kudos** since the 1700s.

In Greek, *kudos* meant "glory," and it was adopted into English university culture by students who likely read it in works such as *The Iliad* and *The Odyssey.*

In these works, Greek heroes lived by the heroic code, embodying courage, physical strength, leadership, honor, and the acceptance of fate. Living up to this code meant distinguishing yourself through word and action, "being both a speaker of words and a doer of deeds,"[1] and supporting your allies and inconveniencing your enemies.

All of this added up to your balance of *kudos* and *aidos*—good reputation and bad reputation, or prestige and shame.

---

[1] Homer, *The Iliad* 9.417.

So, to give someone kudos is to credit them with an act of glory or prestige, as opposed to an act of *aidos*, a shameful show of cowardice or dishonor. It's interesting that we haven't normalized giving *aidos* to people who behave dishonorably in Modern English.

Legit as a shortening of legitimate (Latin *legitimare* "to make lawful," related to English "legal") dates to the late 1800s, as a shortening of "legitimate theater" in England's 1737 Licensing Act. Only high-end theaters were licensed to perform "legit," or "legitimate theater," while others were only allowed to present supposedly lower forms such as pantomime or melodrama.

Booze is recorded as early as the mid-1500s—though, if you consider its Middle English source, *bous* ("alcoholic drink"), to be the same word, it's even older than that. The word is Germanic in origin and perhaps came to English via Middle Dutch (*buse* "drinking vessel"). Booze and the variant *bouze*, originally cant words, gained additional popularity in the U.S. in the 1700s in both noun and verb form, perhaps in part thanks to a liquor importer who, coincidentally, was named Edmund G. Booz (see: aptronyms). "Cant" was originally a Scottish word for a slope or a slant, also related to "chant." In the 16th and 17th centuries, it became a word for either street slang or the figuratively "slanted" or insincere jargon of pretentious types, then ultimately became a noun, referring to terminology distinct to a particular group.

Yahoos are a race of "brutes" in Jonathan Swift's satirical 1726 novel *Gulliver's Travels*. In the wake of the novel's success, the term came to be applied to louts and hooligans of all stripes.[2] It became a supposed cry of excitement or thrill through the notion that hooligans might yawp something similar.

---

[2] Jonathan Swift, *Gulliver's Travels* (Basingstoke: Pan Macmillan, 2004), 288.

Another word that may be older than you'd expect is **synergy**.

Today, the word "synergy" is, to some, the quintessence of soulless corporate jargon, but its history unveils some curiously ancient and enlightening—forgive me—key learnings.

Synergy is a Greek-derived word whose components give it the literal meaning "working together" (Greek elements *syn-* "together" + *ergon* "work").

It's first found in religious contexts. Several New Testament books, which were originally written in Greek by the Apostle Paul, contain the Greek word *synergoi*. Depending on the version, it's typically translated into English as "fellow workers" or "laborers together"—that is, people who work synergistically: "We are fellow workers [*synergoi*] with God; you are God's cultivation, God's building."[3]

Beginning in the 17th century, this led to the use of "synergy" and "synergism" to describe the Christian theological principle that an alignment between human free will and the divine plan can lead both to salvation and to earthly achievements that are greater than one's individual labor would merit.

The takeaway: Collaboration (a Latin-derived word that also literally means "working together") is divine. We're starting to see why this word became a corporate cliché.

Another stepping stone on its journey to professional prosaicism was its use in toxicology beginning in the 19th century. Here, "synergy" describes instances when compounds work together to produce a more powerful effect than they would separately. The opposite of "synergy" in this context is "antagonism," when compounds work against each other and the effect is less powerful than what you would expect.

As is the case with many things in our business landscape, "synergy" began its corporate life in the 1950s.

---

[3] 1 Corinthians 3:9–10, NRSV.

Russian American mathematician and business strategist H. Igor Ansoff coopted the term in the 1950s and 1960s, particularly in his 1965 book *Corporate Strategy.* Ansoff famously developed the Ansoff matrix, a strategic product-marketing tool that is still in use today as a means of illustrating the balance of opportunity and risk in business decisions: "A natural companion to the competitive advantage is the synergy component of strategy. This requires that opportunities within the scope possess characteristics which will enhance synergy."[4]

It was also around this time that the Walt Disney Company published a whimsical image of its business strategy. Although it wasn't initially described as such by its creators, it has since been cited as one of the first and most iconic corporate synergy maps, cementing the term as one synonymous with cross-departmental collaboration.

So, it's incumbent on us, as the leaders of today's communications economy, to gauge whether "synergy" has been a net value-add to our lexical toolbox. What do we think: workhorse or 800-pound gorilla? Let's review our core competencies and circle back at the end of Q3 to discuss. (Sorry, sorry.)

Ye olde nonsense

Many of Shakespeare's words are older than you'd expect, but what of words that are younger than you'd think?

Modern businesses that attempt to look old-fashioned sometimes tack on the phrase "ye olde," as in "ye olde bakery" or "ye olde tavern."

This practice is essentially anachronistic nonsense.

---

[4] H. Igor Ansoff, *Corporate Strategy: An Analytic Approach to Business Policy for Growth and Expansion* (New York: McGraw-Hill, 1965), 194.

"Ye olde" didn't exist in Old or Middle English. Its first recorded use was in the 1700s, when people were trying to be deliberately old-timey, just like today.

Now, the word "ye" did exist in Old English. It was a second-person plural pronoun, and it was generally spelled *ge*. But what is often mistaken for "ye" in phrases like "ye olde bookshop" was in fact the word "the" spelled with the letter thorn (þ, Þ), which looks similar to the letter 'y' in scripts such as English blackletter, a calligraphic script used in England from approximately 1190 to 1300.

So, if you read "þe old apothecary" in such a script, you might easily think that it says "ye." Fast-forward a few hundred years and there are "ye olde" things all over the place.

Unsurprised? Let's escalate things a bit…

There are some words, like "hello," that are so ubiquitous now that their technological origins are no longer obvious.

For instance, the word **"escalate"** didn't exist before the invention of the escalator. Meanwhile, the word **"escalade"** didn't begin life as a brand name for a Cadillac SUV; it existed as early as the 1590s as a word for scaling fortifications with ladders. It's related to the word "scale," as in to scale a cliff. (It entered English via French, from the Italian *scalata* "climb with a ladder," from the Italian *scala* "ladder." (In Middle English, "scale" was, similarly, a noun meaning "siege ladder.")

The earliest working escalator was patented in 1892 by Jesse W. Reno and introduced as a novelty ride at Coney Island a few years later. He called it the "Endless Conveyor Elevator."[5]

[5] Jesse W. Reno, "Endless Conveyor Elevator," U.S. Patent 470,918, filed March 15, 1892 and issued March 8, 1892.

In the meantime, George A. Wheeler also patented a moving stairway.[6] Charles D. Seeberger, who bought Wheeler's patent, was the one to coin the term "escalator" when he trademarked it in 1898—which, by the way, means that the word "escalator" is a genericized trademark (see: proprietary eponym).

Seeberger landed on the word "escalator" by combining the earlier word "escalade" with the word "elevator." The verb "escalate" didn't come along until later. It isn't recorded until the 1920s as a back-formation of "escalator."

Oh, and speaking of elevators, the word "elevator" is probably *a lot* older than you think—like, the 1600s. At that time, it meant a person or muscle that lifts other things. In the late 1700s, this meaning was extended to inanimate technology to refer to the earliest wooden grain elevators.

And although "escalate" is a back-formation of "escalator," "elevate" is not a back-formation of "elevator"—it predates the word "elevator" by about a century. But "elevate" may be a back-formation of the word "elevation," which is recorded yet another century earlier.

On back-formations

But what is a **back-formation**? Many Latin-derived nouns that end in *-tion*, like "elevation," were adopted directly into English from French. Only then did we back-form them into verbs, making it seem as if there were English verbs corresponding to these fancy Latin/French nouns all along.

For instance, "evaluate," "regurgitate," "exploit," and "destruct" entered English *after* "evaluation," "regurgitation," "exploitation," and "destruction."

[6] George A. Wheeler, "Elevator," U.S. Patent 479,864, filed August 2, 1892.

"Resurrection" was adopted into English directly from Old French in the 1300s. But the verb form "resurrect" isn't recorded until the 1700s.

In fact, as recently as the early 1900s, "resurrect" was considered to be incorrect because the Latin root verb of "resurrect" is *resurgere*. So, if you're being prescriptive about Latin word-forming patterns, the verb form of "resurrection" should be "resurge."

Obviously, this changed because "resurrect" sounds like it pairs more logically with "resurrection." Still, though, because of that pedantry, the noun "resurgence" arose starting in the early 1800s, even though the standalone verb "resurge" is no longer as common.

Why does this happen?

One reason verbs are often back-formations in English is because, after the Norman Conquest in 1066, a whole lot of words entered English from French and Latin and, in some cases, were rearranged to fit existing structural rules in English.

Noun forms like those ending in *-tion* likely entered English first because languages often have need of nouns before they need specific verbs to go with them. Humans tend to want to be able to name things and concepts before the less tangible actions surrounding them get names. That's part of the reason that English has about three times as many nouns as verbs. So does French.

Eventually, though, we got around to making specific verbs corresponding to these nouns. We invent new words in this way all the time. Many of the words Shakespeare supposedly "invented" were existing words for which he changed the part of speech. A couple of his back-formed verbs include "negotiate" from "negotiation" and "metamorphose" from "metamorphosis."

Back-formations also happen with other parts of speech. For example, the verb **"sulk"** is a back-formation of the adjective "sulky," and the adjective **"grandiloquent"** is a back-formation of the noun "grandiloquence" (Latin *grandis* "big" + *-loquus* "speaking").

Here are a few more:

- The adjective "lazy" is older than the verb "laze."
- The noun "hesitation" is older than the verb "hesitate."
- The noun "editor" is older than "edit."

Sometimes back-formations can become word-forming elements and pieces of portmanteaus. For example, outside of the specialized context of poetry and music, "the__verse" is a common back-formation of **"universe."**

"Universe," which is made up of Latin elements (*unus* "one" + *versus "turn"*), has the literal meaning "turned into one." So "verse" literally means "a turning," but over time it has become a word-forming element meaning "world or realm." You can stick prefixes onto it to get words familiar to fandoms everywhere, like Buffyverse, Whoniverse, or Duniverse. According to the book *Brave New Words: The Oxford Dictionary of Science Fiction*, "verse" was first used in this way by Orson Scott Card, who referred to the universe of his novel *Ender's Game* (1985) as the Enderverse. However, I would argue that this usage of "verse" is much older than that, because philosopher William James coined the word "multiverse" in the 1890s.

Sometimes back-formations result in irregular variations of words. "Destroy" is ultimately derived from the Latin *destruere*, "to tear down, demolish" (*de-* "down" + *struere* "to build"), which literally means to "un-build." The Latin verb *struere* is also the root of all these words: structure, construct, obstruct, destruction, obstruction, construction.

So why does "destroy" have a different ending? It's all about the way these words traveled from Latin into English.

Destroy is by far the oldest word among those listed above. It came to English in the 1200s, and while it's originally from the Latin elements we've outlined above, its spelling is influenced by its Norman French form, *destruire*.

As is usually the case, the nouns—destruction, obstruction, construction—entered English first, before the verbs—structure, construct, obstruct—with influence from these Latin noun forms: *destructionem*, *constructionem*, *obstructionem*.

They all share *structus*, the past participle stem of *struere*. Latin also had verb forms of these words: *destruere*, *obstruere*, *construere*. But because English adopted the nouns first, we hung on to that "struct" part when creating the English verbs.

The verb "destruct" is a back-formation of destruction. But, because we already had "destroy," we usually say we "destroyed" something rather than we "destructed" it. In fact, "destruct" didn't appear in English as a verb until quite recently—in 1958—and the phrase "self-destruct" didn't show up until 1966 in the voiceover at the beginning of the TV show *Mission: Impossible*.

Sometimes back-formations are simply fanciful or humorous. For instance, "beforemath" (the situation before a significant event) is found in tongue-in-cheek contexts from the past century-and-a-half, as in this passage from a short story in a 1911 edition of *Collier's*:

> "But how about the aftermath?" inquired Mr. Wilson.
> "Oh," said Melvor with a shrug, "we haven't got anything to do with that. There's bound to be an aftermath. We'll do our part if we can avoid a beforemath."[7]

[7] *Collier's: The National Weekly*, 1911.

Etymological excavation: What is a fossil word?

A **fossil word** is a word that primarily appears in the context of phrases or idioms. It typically comes attached to other words. The phrase survives even when the word itself becomes antiquated and rarely appears on its own.

Think about the phrase "to and fro." "Fro" was a preposition and adverb meaning "away" or "backwards." It almost never appears on its own, but "to and fro" remains in wide use.

Another example is the word **"bated"** in the phrase "bated breath." It's a shortened past participle form of the word "abate" (to reduce), but that form is not typically used in English unless it's attached to the word "breath."

The word **"figment"** *can* be used independently to describe something invented, but it most often appears in the phrase "figment of your imagination."

The word **"inclement"** is rarely used outside of the phrase "inclement weather," from the Latin *in-* "not" + *clementem* "mild, placid."

Sometimes fossil words are only fossilized in certain usages. For example, the word **"dint"** is the predecessor to the word "dent," which remains in use as a word for a small indentation or defect. You can have a "dint" in your armor, and "dints" appear in the tops of coconuts. But dint is fossilized in the phrase "by dint of," which means the same thing as the phrase "by means of." Both usages have the same origin: A dint (or, in Old English, *dynt*) was a blow dealt in a battle, so in the context of the phrase "by dint of" it suggests the force by which a blow or other action is carried out. So, you might receive a dint in your armor by dint of fighting in a battle. The later word "dent" is from the same etymological source as "dint," but "dent" became the preferred spelling in the 15th century due to influence from the Latin-derived word "indent."

Caboodle is fossilized in the phrase "kit and caboodle," which is predated by similar terms such as "kid and cargo" and "kit and boodle." A boodle is a collection and can also be found in the phrase "the whole boodle." It's thought to be from the Dutch term *boedel*, meaning "property." Kit, meanwhile, is a term for a collective in several contexts including sports, the military, fishing, and sailing. (It's also, of course, the modern word for any collection of items.) It, too, is probably Dutch in origin, from the term *kitte*, meaning "wooden vessel." Hence "the whole kit and caboodle" implies "the whole ship and its cargo."

Although the word **"bide"** can still be found independently in some English dialects, it's heavily associated with the phrase "bide one's time" in American English. It's related to the words "abide" and "abode," and both are from the Old English *bidan*, meaning "to stay," "to live," or "to remain."

Both **spic** and **span** are fossilized in the phrase "spic and span." A spic is a nail, and span—at least in this context—is a word for a wood chip. The phrase refers to something that's freshly cut by a workman's hands, like a brand-new nail from a smith or perhaps like a fresh cutting from a carpenter. Both of these are Germanic and probably from Old Norse. "Span new" is recorded as a variation on "brand new" in the 1600s.

Turpitude rarely appears outside of the phrase "moral turpitude." This word is from the Latin *turpis*, meaning "vile," "foul" or "ugly." So moral turpitude is utter depravity and vileness.

Lam is rare outside of the phrase "on the lam," and its origin is a bit mysterious. In the Elizabethan era, it was both a verb meaning "to beat" and a noun meaning "heavy blow," so "on the lam," which was originally American crime slang, might imply the same thing as the term "beat it" does when it comes to running away. It's also thought to be related to the word "lambast," sometimes spelled "lambaste." This word combines that "lam" verb, meaning to "beat," with a 17th-century sense of the verb "baste," which comes from Old Norse and also means to thrash someone.

"The whole shebang" is another etymological mystery. We do know that Walt Whitman used the word **"shebang"** as a word for a shelter in his 1882 prose work *Specimen Days*:

> Besides the hospitals, I also go occasionally on long tours through the camps, talking with the men, &c. Sometimes at night among the groups around the fires, in their shebang enclosures of bushes.[8]

It may also be related to various words for taverns; in Irish, Scottish, and South African dialects, a speakeasy or illicit tavern might be called a "shebeen."

The **lo** in "lo and behold" is a generic Old English exclamation. It's probably an imperative of the word "look" or, in Old English, *loken*. But you might also use it as a greeting, or if you're surprised, or if you need to express joy or grief or call attention to something, as in "Lo!".

Another fossil word is **ado**. Nowadays, it's most often found in the phrases "without further ado" and "much ado about nothing," which survived thanks to the name of the Shakespearean comedy.

But did you know that the word "ado" is a contraction—and an infinitive?

As you probably know from your grade-school grammar lessons, an infinitive is the base form of a verb, the form it takes when it's not conjugated.

In English, we pair unconjugated verbs with the word "to" to create the infinitive. An infinitive phrase is something like "to walk," "to go," "to speak," or "to do." The word "to" usually acts as a preposition, but in infinitive phrases, it acts as what we call a particle. This usage of the word "to" came around in Middle English as an adaptation of the word "to" in the Old English dative case.

---

[8] Walt Whitman, *Specimen Days & Collect* (Mineola, NY: Dover Publications, 1995).

But English also has some influence from Old Norse due to the Vikings.

For an example of why this matters with the word "ado," let's take a look at Norwegian, which is a modern Nordic language. Norwegian infinitives are generally introduced by the particle *å*, which is cognate with the English word "at."

So, if Middle English had had *more* influence from Old Norse, our modern infinitive particle could very well have ended up being "at" rather than "to." So instead of "to speak" or "to walk," we could have ended up having "at speak" and "at walk" as infinitives.

And that's exactly what's happening with the word "ado," which is a contraction of "at" and "do."

So why does "ado" mean a commotion or a big deal?

Well, you know how sometimes when there's a lot of drama or commotion, or someone throws a big event, we sometimes say that it's "a big to-do" or "a whole to-do"? Using this infinitive like this literally suggests that there is a lot to do, a lot happening, or a lot that has to be done.

In the phrase "a big to-do," the infinitive phrase "to-do" is cosplaying as a noun.

"Ado" functions the same way, but it uses that Norse-influenced infinitive structure, with "at" in place of "to," and then it's contracted to "ado."

Ado is the older word, first recorded in Norse-influenced areas of northern England, and "to-do" arose later in the 16th century, taking over in a lot of contexts.

Related: The phenomenon of fossil words is akin to lexical **skeuomorphism**. Skeuomorphism (Greek *skeuos* "container or tool" + *morphḗ* "shape") occurs when a newer piece of technology uses iconography or elements from an older piece of technology to communicate what it does, like when your phone camera makes a shutter sound, when a word processing app uses a pen as its logo, or when a light bulb is shaped like a flame.

The bard hath spoken: Unexpectedly Shakespearean words

It's commonly said that Shakespeare invented more than 1,700 words. While it's true that his plays are the first documented appearance of many words, in most cases he did not just pluck them out of thin air (though it's worth noting that he is credited with coining the phrase "into thin air").

The majority are alterations or remixes of preexisting words. He added prefixes and suffixes, changed the part of speech, combined words, and shifted definitions.

For example, his works (along with those of fellow playwright Christopher Marlowe) contain the first known uses of **gloomy**, but the Scottish *gloom*, meaning "a sullen or displeased look," already existed. We get **hint** from *Othello* (ca. 1606–7), but it's predated by Middle English verb *hinten*, "to tell, inform," or literally "to seize upon something," and the noun form *hent*. The first known use of the verb **impede** is in English is in *Macbeth* (ca. 1606–7), though it is a back-formation of "impediment," which dates back to the 1400s.

You'll often see it said that Shakespeare was the first to use the word **"bedroom."** But in *A Midsummer Night's Dream* (ca. 1595–6), it means "room in a bed," not "a room containing a bed": "Then by your side no bed-room me deny." In any case, we have one record of *bedd roome* (meaning "a room containing a bed") dating back to around the 1570s, before Shakespeare penned his plays. And he uses the more common word "bedchamber" frequently across his works.

And whether other lost works contained these words before dear William penned them, or other people had previously spoken them and he was just the first to write them down, we simply don't know.

Now, this is not to downplay Shakespeare's contributions to the English language. The Bard is a titan of linguistic and literary history, and the fact that his works gave us many words we still use today—even if he just wrote down what he heard people saying at the time—is nothing to sniff at. Here are a few more words that you might not have expected to have begun their lives in the mouths of Globe-trotting actors of Shakespeare's day:

Unfriending someone is much older than social media. The word "unfriended" appears in both *Twelfth Night* (ca. 1601–2; 3.3.10) and *King Lear* (ca. 1605–6; 1.1.232).

The word **"swagger"** first appeared in Shakespeare's *A Midsummer Night's Dream*. Puck asks, "What hempen home-spuns have we swaggering here, / So near the cradle of the fairy queen?" (3.1.66–7). It's probably a variation on the Middle English verb *swag* meaning "to sway."

Shakespeare is credited with the first recorded instance of the phrase **"one fell swoop"** in *Macbeth* (4.3.219). Although it's a word that dates back to Old English, as a word for brown-green-gold eyes, **hazel** is first recorded in *Romeo and Juliet* (ca. 1595–6). It was considered a reddish-brown color then, like the shell of a hazelnut. That's why it's a joke poking fun at Benvolio's penchant for taking offense in Mercutio's line "Thou wilt quarrel with a man for / cracking nuts, having no other reason but because thou / hast hazel eyes" (3.1.18–20).

The noun **"excitement"** is first attested in *Hamlet* (ca. 1599–1601; 4.4.58), in which the titular character describes "excitements" of his reason and his blood—not that his blood and reason are having a good time, but that they are roused and racing.

The word **"lackluster"** first appears in *As You Like It* (1599; 2.7.22). It's a combination of the Germanic lack and luster, meaning "shine," from the Latin *lustrare* meaning "to brighten." Shakespeare really liked making compound words with "lack," including **lack-love**, **lack-beard**, and **lack-brain**.

Dwindle first appeared in *Henry IV, Part 1* (ca. 1596–7). It is a diminutive form of the Middle English *dwinen*, meaning "to waste away" or "to fade." Falstaff asks: "Bardolph, am I not fallen away vilely since this last / action? do I not bate? do I not dwindle?" (3.3.2).

Originally a word for a spinning top, one of the earlier appearances of **"whirligig"** as a figurative term is in *Twelfth Night* (5.1.396). It would later be applied to someone fickle and then to a species of beetle that whirls about when alarmed. *Twelfth Night* also seems to have been influential in inspiring the word **"hobnob,"** though in the original context—"Hob, nob is his word" (3.4.227)—it means "hit or miss." It is perhaps related to other phrases such as "hab nab" and "hab or nab," meaning "have or not have." It implies that the result is up in the air: It might work out, or it might not; Sir Andrew might or might not live up to his word. From there, its sense was extended to mean "alternating," especially alternating who was buying rounds of drinks or taking turns toasting, which then gave it the sense it has today: socializing pleasantly.

Archvillain is first found in *Measure for Measure* (1604; 5.1.65). It's related to archangel and archbishop, but not arch as in a curve or architectural feature. It is related to architect, which has nothing to do with building arches but is related to the various -archies (from Greek *arkhos* "leader, chief, ruler") of the world like monarchy, oligarchy, and anarchy. So an architect is a head builder or the person in charge of a build in the way that a monarch is a singular head of state—or an archvillain is a principal villain. (Presumably one could argue that an arch *arch* is an arch that it is primary among arches, like the Arc de Triomphe de l'Étoile or the St. Louis Gateway Arch.)

Zany is first found in *Love's Labour's Lost* (ca. 1594–5; 5.7.507). It's a variation on the Italian nickname Zanni (for Gianni or Giovanni), which was also a common word for a clown or a person who behaves like one.

2

Words Across Time

Old, Middle, Modern

If you've ever read an untranslated edition of *Beowulf*, whose written record dates back to between 975 and 1025 CE but composed as early as around 700, you may have found it nearly unintelligible. That's because Old English, the Germanic language of the Anglo-Saxons in which it is written, is markedly different from the one we currently speak. While it shares some words with Modern English and formed the basis for many of our present-day grammatical rules, the Venn diagram between the language we speak now and the language people spoke 1000 years ago doesn't show enough overlap to make it easy for your average modern-day reader to understand.

The heyday of Old English spanned from 450 CE until the Battle of Hastings in 1066, when William II, Duke of Normandy, began the Norman Conquest. Thereafter, the Norman ruling class flooded Old English with Latin-derived French words.

This process of linguistic colonialism and blending created Middle English, which many people first encounter when they read Geoffrey Chaucer's *The Canterbury Tales* (ca. 1400). It was spoken from around 1150 to around 1500, and it's far more recognizable than Old English—though if "Whan that Aprille with his shoures soote" and so forth made your head spin in school, you'll know how different it remains.

Middle English also introduced some linguistic power dynamics that persist even today, with Latin-derived words often perceived as "fancier" or more sophisticated than Germanic-derived words. For instance, "pretty" is a Germanic-derived word that has existed since Old English (though its meaning and spelling have shifted), while the Latinate term "beautiful" was introduced from French following the Norman invasion. Similarly, the Old English-derived word "house" (Old English *hus*) implies a humbler structure than the Old French-/Latin-derived "mansion," despite the Old French *mansion* (modern French *maison*) meaning the same thing as "house" does today. The most commonly cited evidence of this disparity comes from the world of food. Words such as pig, cow, and chicken are Germanic in origin, while the names of the food they become—pork, beef, and poultry—are Latin-derived, via French, because animals were raised by the Anglo-Saxons who worked the land and served at the tables of the French ruling class. Even today, we understand "cuisine" (a French word) to be fancier than "food" or a "meal" (both Germanic words).

Due to the whirlwind of globalization, power shifts, and modernization, Middle English evolved into Modern English, the version of the English language spoken from roughly the 1500s onward. So, Shakespeare and Marlowe wrote in Modern or Early Modern English.

Today, about 60 percent of English words are derived from Latin, with about half of those coming via Old French and the other half coming directly from Latin. Roughly 25 percent of English words come from Germanic languages such as Old English and Old Norse. Even though more than half its vocabulary is Romance in origin, English is still considered a Germanic language due to its grammar and structure. The remaining words in English are from Greek (5–6 percent) and a miscellany of other languages.

As English grows and changes in response to increasing globalization, these percentages will continue to shift and we may see even more language families influencing our everyday vocabulary.

English words from other families

Another way to look at this is to say that the vast majority of Modern English words arrived via Indo-European languages such as Old English, Latin, Old French, Old Norse, Greek, Dutch, German, Celtic, Spanish, Italian, and even Sanskrit. The last of these, which belongs to a subbranch of the Indo-European language family called Indo-Aryan, is closely related to Bengali, Gujarati, Hindi, Punjabi, and many other South Asian languages today.

Sanskrit gave us words such as **avatar** (Sanskrit *avatāra*), meaning "descent"—originally referring to the incarnations of Hindu deities. Similarly, **juggernaut** comes from Hindu religious traditions, from Odia *Jagannātha*—literally "lord of the world"—a reference to the massive chariots used during the Ratha Yatra festival; in English, it's now a term for an unstoppable force.[1] The word **"jungle"** entered English through Hindi from the Sanskrit *jaṅgala*), counterintuitively meaning "arid" or "wasteland."[2] The meaning of the term in Hindi shifted over time to mean any sort of land that is uncultivated and unpopulated by humans, whether desert or dense forest.

---

[1] William Jones, *A Grammar of the Persian Language* (London: Printed by W. and J. Richardson, 1771), 107, s.v. "juggernaut."

[2] Henry Yule and Arthur Coke Burnell, *Hobson-Jobson: A Glossary of Colloquial Anglo-Indian Words and Phrases* (London: John Murray, 1886), 439, s.v. "jungle."

We've also adopted vocabulary from languages that belong to families other than the Indo-European, including Arabic, Hebrew, and Yiddish (Afro-Asiatic languages); African languages (such as the Niger–Congo language family), Chinese languages (such as the Sino-Tibetan language family), and a vast range of indigenous languages in the Americas (which fall into many language families, including the Algonquian, not to be confused with the Algonquin people)—among many others.

Words from Arabic

Arabic has been a rich source of vocabulary for English, thanks to centuries of trade, conquest, and intellectual exchange. Many Arabic words in English reflect the science, technology, and cultural practices that spread from the Middle East and the broader Islamic world to Europe and beyond.

The words "alcove," "algorithm," "algebra," "almanac," "albacore," "alfalfa," and "albatross" begin with *al-* because they are all at least partially derived from or inspired by Arabic. *Al-* is the English spelling of the Arabic definite article—in other words, that's how you say "the" in Arabic.

Algebra is an Arabic-derived word that first appears in a 9th-century treatise on mathematics. The original Arabic word means a "reunion of broken parts." As a result, in 15th- and 16th-century English, "algebra" was also used as a word for the process of setting broken bones. **Algorithm**, meanwhile, is named after the 8th–9th-century Persian mathematician Al-Khwarizmi, altered on the assumption that it was related to the Greek *arithmos* "number."

The word **"albacore,"** as in the tuna, came to English via Portuguese but is originally from the Arabic *al baqara* "milk cow," because of the fish species' potential to reach a massive size. (However, it is worth noting that the albacore is still the smallest of the bluefin tuna species.) The word "tuna" moved in a different direction, from the Latin *thunnus* to the Arabic *tun*, then to Spanish *atun* and the English *tunny*, later *tuna*.

Albatross went through a couple stages of alteration. It's ultimately probably from the Arabic *al-ghattas* "sea eagle," but it was introduced to English via Spanish and Portuguese, where the Arabic word became *alcatraz*, a word that was used to describe pelicans and other seabirds. (Birds roosted on the island that is now home to the prison Alcatraz.) The name of the white seabird in *The Ancient Mariner* was altered through a folk-etymology association with the Latin *alba* "white."

Sometimes the Arabic definite article can change spelling when it goes from one language to another. That's the case with the word **"hazard."** It's also thought to be from Arabic *az-zahr* or *al-zahr*, meaning "the die," and it was originally the name of a chance-based game played with dice. It was this sense of risk that led to the English meaning of the word "hazard."

In a different alteration, **elixir**—originally a word for a philosopher's stone, said to transmute base metals into gold—came to Medieval Latin, and then English, from the Arabic name for the stone, *al-iksir*. That may, in turn, be from the Greek *xerion*, a type of powder used to dry wounds, which may have contributed to its later use as a catchall for dubious medicinal substances that can supposedly cure pretty much anything.

Other words from Arabic lack the definite article entirely. **Zenith**, the word we give to the point in the sky directly above us, traveled via a game of etymological telephone from the Arabic *samt* (*ar-ras*), meaning "the way (over the head)" through the Latin *senit*, then *cenit*, into Old French as *cenith* (now *zénith*) and then into English.

Many goods that traveled from the Middle East to Europe and Britain simply kept their names, such as **cotton** (Arabic *quṭn*, probably ancient Egyptian in origin), coffee (Arabic *qahwa*), and saffron (Arabic *za'farān*).

Sugar and **candy** might have reached English via Arabic (*sukkar* and *qandi*), but their sweetness is rooted in Sanskrit, *śarkarā* and *khaṇḍa*. "Candy" traveled through Persian as *quand*, a word for cane sugar, then the Arabic *qandi*, which would become part of the Old French phrase *çucre candi* "sugar candy," before entering English in the 13th century. In English, it referred specifically to crystallized sugar. Sugar itself was also introduced to Britain from the Middle East by returnees from the Crusades two centuries earlier. England developed quite the sweet tooth, enthusiastically snapping up Portuguese-imported sugar—as treacle, brown sugar, and refined white sugar, depending on the price point—from colonized Brazil in the 1500s. Queen Elizabeth I attended banquets bedecked with elaborate sugar sculptures. By the 1700s, the construction of domestic sugar refineries had made England one of the largest industrial producers of sugary goods in the world, from a cube of sugar for a cup of tea to the elaborate confections now seen on every episode of *Bake Off*.

The word **"tabby"** came to refer to cats in the 1690s due to their fur pattern, which resembles a striped silk taffeta also called tabby, which came (via French) from the name of the Baghdad neighborhood Attabiy, where rich silks were made. Until the 1770s, it was uncommon to hear the English word "tabby" used on its own to refer to a feline, with most people using the full phrase "tabby cat." Evidently the word "tabby" was also used to refer to female cats in particular due to an association with the woman's name Tabitha during the name's peak popularity between 1718 and 1754.

A few Native American word origins

Many names for animals native to the Americas come from the indigenous words for them, like **caribou**, from the Míkmaq *qalipu*, or "snow-shoveler." In Europe, the same species is called a reindeer. Chipmunks get their name from the Odawa word *jidmoonh*.

Moose—a creature that in Europe is called the European or Eurasian elk, not to be confused with the North American elk or wapiti (from Shawnee, literally "white rump")—came to English from the Abenaki word *moz*.

Raccoon is from the Algonquian *arahkunem*, meaning "he scratches with the hands," which was first clumsily adopted by English colonists including John Smith, with spelling that varied wildly. ("Trash panda" is from the internet, circa … 2016?)

Muskrat is a folk etymology-inspired interpretation of the Massachusett-language name for the animal, *musquash*. **Skunk** is also a borrowing from Massachusett, though Europeans also called this animal a polecat, comparing it to the weasel that also emits an unpleasant odor.

The word **opossum** is from the Powhatan *opassum*, meaning "white, dog-like animal." Strictly speaking, the North American marsupials are called opossums, while "possum" refers to an Australian marsupial. However, in practice, both are often called possums.

Words for food originating in this part of the world were also brought into English (sometimes via French and Spanish, usually depending on which Europeans communicated with indigenous people about their food first), including **pecans** from the Illinois-language word *pakani*, and **persimmons** from the Powhatan word *pasimenan* "dried fruit." **Squash** and **succotash** are also loosely borrowed from Narragansett.

It's perhaps no surprise that **moccasin**, **tomahawk**, and **totem** are also Native American borrowings. But you may be surprised at some of the other words that are derived from the indigenous languages of North America. For instance, despite the fact that it looks very Latin, the word **caucus** is likely from an Algonquian word for an adviser or for counsel in general. **Toboggan** is also borrowed from Mi'kmaq.

Venturing poleward from the U.S. and Canada, we have English words that are taken from the Eskaleut language family, concentrated primarily in the northernmost parts of North America, including the Yupik, Inuit, and Aleut languages. These languages gave us words such as **igloo**, **kayak**, **malamute**, and **husky**.

Farther to the south, many words we use today are derived from words in the Nahuatl and Quechan language families, though some stopped off in Spanish for a while before making their way into English. Nahuatl-derived words include **cacao** (*cacahuatl*), **chocolate** (*xocolātl*), **coyote** (coyōtl), and **ocelot** (*ōcēlōtl*). **Tequila** is named after a place in Mexico, which gets its name from the Nahuatl *téquitl*, a compound of *téquitl* "work" and *tlan* "place."

Words from Quecha include animal names such as **chinchilla**, **condor** (*kuntur*), **llama**, and **puma**; foods such as **jerky** (*ch'arki* "dried flesh") and **quinoa** (*kinua*); and names for psychoactive substances like **ayahuasca** (*aya* "corpse" + *waska* "rope") and **cocaine** (*kuka* or *coca*, the name of the plant it's made from).

From the Arawakan languages of South America and the Caribbean we have words such as **barbecue** (Haitian *barbakoa*, a word for a framework of sticks on which meat could be roasted), **hammock** (from a Taíno word introduced to English via the Spanish *hamaca*), **hurricane** (Taíno *hurakán)*, and **tobacco** (Taíno *tabaco*).

From this region we also borrowed **potato**, from the Haitian *batata*, originally a word for "sweet potato." (English white potatoes were introduced from the Americas later and were initially called "bastard potatoes" or "Virginia potatoes.")

The Tupi–Guarani languages of South America give us food words like **acai**, **cashew**, **cayenne**, and **tapioca**, and animal words like **capybara**, **cougar**, **jaguar**, **piranha**, **alpaca**, **macaw**, and **toucan**.

African words in English

African languages have influenced English in many ways, from vocabulary to dialects originating with people who emigrated or were forcibly relocated by human traffickers and colonizers during the height of the Atlantic slave trade. In the Americas, African American Vernacular English (AAVE) and Gullah have been particularly influenced by a variety of African languages.

Many English words are derived from languages in the Bantu language family, such as Swahili and Zulu, as well as the larger Niger–Congo language family to which Bantu belongs. Other English words come to us from ancient Egyptian.

There are more than 600 Bantu languages, so it's probably no surprise that they've given us so many words. We have **goober** (Kikongo and Kimbundu *nguba*)—a word for a peanut that later became the name for a brand of chocolate-covered peanuts—**gumbo** (Mbundu *ngombo* "okra," while **okra** itself is from the Igbo language spoken in Nigeria), **mamba** (Swahili *mamba*), **jenga** (Swahili *kujenga*, "to build"), **jumbo** (Swahili *jambo* "hello" or Kongo *nzamba* "elephant," initially a popular elephant name in English before it was extended to refer to any large thing), *safari* (an Arabic-derived Swahili word meaning "travel"), **tango** (Ibibio *tamgu*), and **chimpanzee** (Kivili *ci-mpenzi*).

From Wolof—a Niger–Congo language that heavily influenced Gullah—we have the words **banana**, **chigger** (*jiga* "insect"), **jive** (*jev*), and **juke(box)** (*dzug*). Additional words from other Niger–Congo language families include **banjo** (Mandinka *bangoe*), **yam** (Fula *nyami*), **vodou** or **voodoo** (from a word perhaps in Fon such as *vodu* "spirit, deity god"), and **zombie** (Kikongo *zumbi* "fetish" and *djumbi* "ghost").

Afrikaans—a West Germanic language that is heavily influenced by Dutch as well as German and the Khoisan languages of Southern Africa—notably contributed the word **apartheid** ("separateness") to the global vernacular.

Words from Hebrew and Yiddish

Jewish communities in anglophone countries have introduced a selection of Hebrew-derived Yiddish terms into Modern English parlance. Some of these have stuck around because of their capacity to capture complex concepts for which English has few (or no) alternatives. Others are beloved for their wryness and their slang application—like the classic **schmuck**, which is from the Yiddish *shmok* "penis," thought to originally be from the Old Polish *smok*, a word for a snake or a dragon.

Maven, an expert or connoisseur, was first introduced in English in 1965 from the Yiddish *meyvn*. Its Hebrew origin is *mebhin*, literally "one who understands." **Glitz** and glitzy are Yiddish for "glitter/glittery," first appearing in English in 1966. The origin of the Yiddish is the German *glitzern* "sparkle." The similar term **"glitch,"** which was used in radio jargon from the 1940s and 1950s, is likely from the Yiddish *glitsh*, meaning "a slip," originally from the German verb *glitschen* "to slide."

On the slang or colloquial front, **tush**, as in buttocks, is a 1962 abbreviation of *tochus*, which is from the Yiddish *tokhes*. Its Hebrew origin is *tahat*, meaning "beneath." When people call heroin **"smack"** (originally ca. 1942), that's from the Yiddish *schmeck*, meaning both "a drug" and "a sniff." **Schmooze** appeared in English in 1897 from the Yiddish *shmuesn*, meaning "to chat." Its Hebrew origin is *shemu'oth*, meaning "news, rumors." **"Drag"** in the sense of "drag queen" or "to dress in drag" might come from the Yiddish *trogn*, meaning "to wear." (It may alternatively reference voluminous skirts that "drag" on the ground.)

And then, of course, **bagel**, which was originally spelled *beigel* when it first appeared in English in 1912, is from the Yiddish *beygl*. It's Old German origin is *boug*, meaning "ring or bracelet." (Factlet: in Old English, an Anglo-Saxon lord was called a *beaggifa*, or "ring-giver," and this concept would become the inspiration for J. R. R. Tolkien's primary antagonist, Sauron, also a lord and a "ring-giver.") The PIE root **bheug-* means "to bend."

Wandering words

Ever heard of a **wanderwort**? No, it's not a wart run rampant, but a worldly word—quite literally a wandering word. Wanderworts (dubbed thusly in German) are loanwords that have cognates and iterations across many different languages, especially unrelated ones from very distant countries and cultures. The things whose names become wanderworts also tend to do a bit of globetrotting themselves. For example, words for tea, sugar, orange, copper, silver, mint, honey, and wine are much the same in many languages and have wide-ranging global siblings because the words themselves have spread as the goods they refer to have been traded across the world.

Fresh hot words

Lexicographers and linguists estimate that there are more than 1 million English words, maybe even 1.25 million. And new words arrive, arise, and thrive in English all the time. On average, 14.7 new words are born each day. That's one new word every 98 minutes. That's 5,400 words per year. Although not all of them stick around in common enough use to be recorded in official sources, there are still between 800 and 1,000 words that get added to English dictionaries every year.

This process is only accelerating: Word coinage has exploded in the past four decades by virtue of the fact that we can communicate with the entire world virtually instantaneously. And it's not just words. Whole new systems for communicating emotional nuance have come into being, like ironic capitalization, scare quotes, Unicode, glitch text, and initialisms. "LOL," for example, is first recorded in the 1980s by the first people to venture into the wilds of the internet; it was added to the *Oxford English Dictionary* in 2011.

These are a few other words and acronyms that have been added to English dictionaries in recent years. These words are real; they have meaning; they have power. And people like you made that happen.

adorkable
antiwork
copypasta
deadass
doomscrolling
folx
grundle
FTW
GOAT
goblincore
grimdark
hangry
hopepunk
janky
nearlywed
neopronoun
petfluencer
photobomb
ragefarming
shadowban
sharenting
shithousery
shrinkflation
simp
sus
word salad
yeet

3

Logic and Illogic

Why English Makes More—and Less—Sense Than You Think

English is illogical, we say. It's inconsistent, we say. It makes no sense, we say.

But is that right?

I'm here to say that there's far more consistency to be found than you might have realized—if you look in the right places.

English does still tend to slap all kinds of new bits on top of its venerable Germanic foundation, and the result makes for an elaborate tower of synonyms and creative spelling conventions. But since we're all so used to marveling at its oddities, there's a certain satisfaction in finding pieces that make a bit of sense after all.

What follows are just a few surprisingly sensible things that you never stopped to notice about the English language—and the stories of how a few of its quirks came to be.

B silent!

Do you know why there is a silent *b* in the words **"debt"** and **"doubt"**? It's terribly petty.

In Middle English, neither of these words contained a *b*. Debt was spelled *dette*, and doubt was spelled *douten*. Both of these words entered English around the 13th century, from the Old French *dette* and *doter*, which also did not contain the letter *b*. These words are ultimately Latin-derived, which will be important in a moment.

During the Hundred Years' War between England and France (1337–1453), the two nations understandably weren't on the same page. Just a couple of centuries prior, oodles of Latin-derived French words had been crammed into the previously Germanic English language by the Normans, creating Middle English. But thanks to anti-French sentiment during the war, English writers decided they should make English look less French, goddammit—but, er, also keep all the words English had got from French because they were quite useful.

So, what to do?

Take French words like *dette* and *douten*, and look at the Latin words they came from: *debitum* and *dubitare*. Aha! We've found the *b*'s. But because the more French pronunciation of these words was already a fixture, the words were Latinized in spelling, but the *b* remained silent. (The silence of the *b* may also be a result of English phonotactics, or pronunciation standards; pronouncing *b* and *t* concurrently in a single-syllable word is uncomfortable to an English speaker.)

This also happened with other French borrowings that were made to look more Latin around the same time—but many of these changes, unlike these fugitive *b*'s, did impact pronunciation.

For example: **Adventure** and **judge** originally did not contain a *d* in English. The *d* was added based on their Latin predecessors:

> Adventure (French/Middle English *aventure*) added a *d* from the Latin *advenire*.
> Judge (French/Middle English *juge*) added a *d* from Latin *iudex*.

There are others, too. Saliva was originally *salive* in Middle English, just like in French, but it was shifted to the Latin *saliva*. Some adjectives that now end in the Latinized suffix *-ive*, like the word "adoptive," were first recorded with the French ending *-if* in Middle English before they, too, got the axe.

Granted, these spellings remained relatively unstandardized until the 16th and 17th centuries. At that point, the Hundred Years' War was somewhat passé, but the changes had stuck. Meanwhile, the Latinization of words had become commonplace in academic and scientific contexts in which sounding Classical and cultured was the preferred modus operandi—another major contributing factor in the evolution of these words.

Lying brides and lexical gaps

We have the noun "bride," and we have the corresponding adjective form "bridal." And we have the noun "groom" and the adjective form … "groomal"?

We do not have the adjective form "groomal." Why not?

Well, because the adjective "bridal" has been *lying* about being an adjective for 800 years. It looks for all intents and purposes as if it is the Old English-derived word "bride" (*bryd*) with the Latin and French-derived adjective-forming ending *-al* on it. Just like the words "magical," "functional"—or "logical," which this word isn't.

The truth? "Bridal" doesn't have that suffix on it. It doesn't have any suffix at all. Well, it sort of does because it functions that way now. But it didn't originally. Instead, it was a noun—and a compound word. Before the 1200s, a "bridal" was a wedding feast. You might, as a wedding guest, attend a bridal, an event that got its name from the Old English *brydealo* or *byrd ealu*, a word/phrase for a marriage feast that literally means "bride ale."

That's right, the word "bridal" literally means "bride-ale." An event to celebrate a bride by drinking to her health and happiness … with ale. This same structure also appears in other Middle English words for celebrations like a scythe-ale, a party for people who worked in the fields with scythes (*sithes*) after they brought in the harvest.

In Middle English, when French- and Latin-derived words flooded in courtesy of the Normans, along with that *-al* ending, people heard and saw the compound noun "bridal" and very understandably thought, "Gee, that looks a lot like an adjective"—so it became one.

To make it even more complicated: the adjective-forming version of this ending does actually get tacked on to Old English words sometimes, like in the word "tidal" (Middle English *tide* "time," "season," "recurring interval" + Latin-derived suffix *-al*) which is what we call a hybrid word because its elements are from two different language families.

So, one could argue that "bridal" eventually might have become an adjective with that ending regardless of whether its compound noun form stuck around or not. But all the evidence points to this *not* being a hybrid word but simply a misunderstanding of the part of speech in the original compound word.

Okay, but this still doesn't explain why the word "groomal" doesn't exist. Is it just because there were no groom ales in the 1100s?

Well, the word "groom" had a bit of an identity crisis, too.

As you may know, the original word for a groom was "bridegroom." The "groom" element here is from the Old English *guma*, meaning "human" or "man," particularly as opposed to a god, and in Middle English it got its *r* from the unrelated Middle English word *grome* "groom," as in a young man or young male servant, and eventually specifically a servant who takes care of horses. "Groom" didn't become a verb for caring for an animal until the early 1800s, likely building on the association with horse-wrangling, and it was extended to refer to people's personal tidiness only in the mid-1800s.

"Groom" by itself wasn't associated with weddings until around the 1600s, and before that it was always the compound word "bridegroom." You had a bride, who by default at that time was feminine—a woman getting married—and a bridegroom, literally the "bride-man."

When it comes to "groomal," though, what we've done is identified a lexical gap. A **lexical gap** or **accidental gap** occurs when it seems like a word should exist because grammar rules allow for it and one or more words that mirror or correspond to it are in use, but it just doesn't.

One reason that *some* lexical gaps exist is because using certain word elements together could create an awkward hybrid word.

A **hybrid word** is when a word is made up of components from two different language families. In particularly pedantic circles, hybrid words are considered bad form. However, there are *loads* of hybrid words in English that we don't typically consider to be a problem. For instance:

Claustrophobia: Latin *claustrum* "confined place" + Greek *phobia* "fear"
Genocide: Greek *genos* "race, kind" + Latin *-cidere* "kill"
Metadata: Greek *meta* "beyond, about" + Latin *datum* "(thing) given" (see: meta)

There are also hybrids that combine Germanic words with Latin and Greek endings and roots, like **harpist** (Germanic + Greek), **intertwine** (Latin + Old Norse), and **forefront** (Germanic + Latin).

But sometimes a Greek- or Latin-derived ending doesn't sound quite right for an Old English-derived word. For instance, the words "darkness" and "happiness" sound right and correct, but suppose you used a Latin-derived ending instead and said "darkity" or "happity." Sounds a little... dorkity.

But why? Both the Germanic ending *-ness* and the Latin ending *-ity* create nouns from adjectives. Latin-derived words with that Latin ending include **"authenticity"** and **"creativity."** And there are even hybrid words that use these endings, too, like **"effectiveness"** and **"oddity."** But some word pieces just don't sound right when you combine them.

Adding the Latin-derived *-al* ending onto the Germanic word "groom" to make it "groomal" sits a little weirdly in the mouth. But we still have to fill that lexical gap. Of all adjective-forming endings, which do you think is best? Are you part of the "groomic" party? Did you hear his mother is throwing him a "groomulous" shower?

Curiosities of collocation

Collocation is when we collectively decide that words sound right together, to the extent that many people combine them frequently across different contexts. Collocations are almost like idioms in their frequency, but without the metaphorical and logical leaps in meaning.

Many are found with simple verb phrases involving words such as do, go, come, get, make, take, have, keep, have, set, catch, break, pay, feel, and save. These verbs have all been in English for a very long time, many as far back as Old English, and they have had lots of time to take on many meanings—and make friends with other words.

Here are just a few examples of words that have a strong collocation, or are likely to be found together:

break records
catch sight
come prepared
do time
feel free
find a replacement
go astray
keep in touch
have sympathy
make a difference
pay respects
save lives
take a seat
turn on a light

This is not to say that these phrases are glued together: One could just as easily "eat a pill" or "gulp a pill," but more people use the collocated phrase "take a pill."

Strong collocations also occur with **phrasal verbs**, which take on new meaning when combined with prepositions and adverbs. That's the case with phrases such as "get over," "let down," "calm down," or "come around."

This phenomenon is by no means limited to phrases that begin with verbs. Some of the most entertaining examples of collocation are expressions that involve rarer and more complex words that still somehow seem to belong together. They come in lots of different flavors:

- **Verb + noun**, as we've seen above, but also in phrases such as "commit a crime" or "lend credence."
- **Noun + verb**, as in "engines roared" or "snow fell."
- **Verb + prepositional phrase**, as in "filled with awe" or "drifted (off) to sleep."
- **Adjective (or participle) + noun**, as in "deep sleep" or "rich history."
- **Noun (sometimes acting as a modifier) + noun**, as in "business model" or "surge of anger."
- **Adverb + verb**, and vice versa, as in "seriously doubt," "whispered softly," or "vaguely remember."
- **Adverb + adjective (or participle)**, as in "well made" or "fully aware."

A few more to feed your curiosity:

bitter disappointment	happily married	tug gently
blissfully unaware	heap of trouble	woefully ignorant
burst into tears	heavy rain	woefully ill-prepared
conspiracy theory	pang of guilt	world of hurt
deeply regret	round of applause	
excruciating pain	sleepless night	

Just like the other collocated verb phrases we looked at, none of these is set in stone. But they've become so commonplace that they're difficult to avoid. Try coming up with different versions of a few and see how they sound to you. "Explode into tears" is less common and might evoke a different mental image than "burst into tears." And "awfully ill-prepared" isn't found as frequently as "woefully ill-prepared" despite meaning more or less the same thing.

The word "collocation" is from the Latin *collocare*, meaning "to place together" or "to set in place," and an early English variation of this word, the 15th-century term *collocacioun*, was a word for a ligament in the body, presumably because it keeps our bones aligned and set in place.

Why this happens is pretty simple. These phrases work. They make sense, they sound good—and so they've become habitual, like a tune or a joke or a pun that everyone knows. We humans are comfortable with habit. We see these words together in songs, poems, films, or novels—or even in legal, scientific, or medical contexts—and they become cozily affixed to one another in our everyday speech. That's why these terms seem normal and predictable to native English speakers—but, for those who learn English as a second language, it may not be clear why these words team up so frequently.

The flipside of this is that if you want to draw attention to something you're saying—if you want your phrasing to be memorable, jarring, or humorous—try breaking the normal patterns of collocation and see what happens.

Are earls early? What do counts count?

The words "early" and "earl" (the noble title and the name) are not related. It's easy to tell if you have a look at Old English.

In Old English, "early" was *ærlice*. The first part (*ær*) is the Old English equivalent of the word "ere," meaning "before," which you may recognize from Shakespeare and poetry and whatnot. The second part (*lice*) is the Old English equivalent of the *-ly* suffix that we use in Modern English.

So, this Old English word *ærlice* (air-lee-kuh) literally means "beforely."

As for the title earl or *eorl*, it meant "brave man, warrior, leader or chief." Earl is cognate with the Old Norse title *jarl*. After the Norman French invaded, earl became the English equivalent of the title count, or *conte* in French. Count is from the Latin word *comitem*, which was a Roman title for a provincial governor but literally means an attendant or "one who goes with."

The title of count both is and isn't related to the action of counting. A count is not someone who counts, unless you're on *Sesame Street*.

Counting, the action, is spelled the way it is because in Old French, the word was *conter* (in Modern French it's *compter*). The Old French *conter* was also the word for telling a story, literally "summing up" an experience, which is why to "recount a tale" means to tell it again.

The Modern French word *conte* is, perhaps surprisingly, closer to its Latin source, *computare*, which meant "to count," but literally means "to reckon together" and of course is also where we get compute and computer.

Grammatical and glamorous grimoires

Grammar is, quite literally, one of the most glamorous things on Earth. Grammar can be traced all the way back through French and Latin to the Greek phrase *grammatike tekhnē*, meaning the "art of letters."

In Latin and Greek, grammar was a much broader field of study, referring to any type of learning or scholarship but primarily the study of language. When the word made its way into English, grammar first specifically referred to the study of the rules of Latin, and a grammar school was a school for learning Latin. In the 14th century, people who ranked highly enough to access formal education were taught Latin and French because those were the languages of scholarship, religion, and law. "Grammar school" was later extended to refer to any type of schooling.

In 14th-century English and French, *grammar* or *gramary* was also a word for magic, incantations, and the study of the occult, likely because magic words were supposedly in Latin or other esoteric languages. This is also where we get the word **"grimoire"** for a book of spells. (The word "spell" is also used in both regular schools and magical schools, since both the magical and the mundane meanings come from the Old French *espelir*, "to mean," "to explain," "to spell out letters," or "to recite.")

The word "glamour" (and, by extension, "glamor" in American English) is a Scottish variation of *gramary* in the magic sense. In the context of witchcraft, a "glamour" referred to illusion-based magic—and often still does. The term was extended to Hollywood-style glamor because fictionalized character portrayals and reporting around celebrities creates an illusion of luxury and elegance.

Speaking of which, take a look at that ending…

Is it *-or* or *-our*? And is it *-or* or *-er* or *-ar*?

The *u* in the British spellings of words such as colour, armour, humour, honour, and flavour is vestigial from French. It appears in nouns of quality, state, or condition, and not in agent nouns that end with the same sound—but it's a little arbitrary which words take it and which don't.

For example, terror is from the French *terreur* which has the *u*, and British English once included the *u* but it doesn't anymore. The *u* was also "incorrectly" added to a couple of *-or* words that don't have a *u* in French; *errour*, for instance, is sometimes recorded until the 18th century. Same with *tenour* for a brief period in the 14th century.

Meanwhile, the *u* is dropped when adjective endings like *-ous* are added, as in humorous, along with the noun ending *-tion* or *-ation*, or the verb ending *-ize* or *-ise*, like vaporise and vaporisation (both of which take a Latinate *z* in American English instead of a francophone *s* which is more common in British English).

Glamour is one of the few *-or* nouns of quality, state, or condition that often retains the *u* in American English, perhaps due to its association with French fashion. In the 1700s, it was also found with the spelling *glamer*, which is a lot less … well, glamorous.

Note that, to make all this more dizzying, all these spellings have been wildly inconsistent throughout history, with several early Shakespearean folios even varying the spelling of a single word within the same text.

On a similar note, agent noun endings are equally inconsistent. They're all over the place in both British and American English.

When describing professions, some words end in *-er* and some in *-or*. Generally speaking, words that come from Old English and other Germanic languages usually end in *-er* (baker, player, hunter) and words that are from Latin and French usually take *-or* (governor, conductor, impostor).

But, of course, there are dozens of exceptions, because consistency would be too easy.

Take chandler, for example—that's a candle-maker, from the Latin *candelarius*. Or sailor, which was once spelled "sailer," but was Latinized over time, possibly to make it match with the

Latin-derived tailor. And then there are words like deserter, eraser, and laborer, which are Latin-derived but conform to English standards (which are anything but standard in this case).

And then there are words like bursar, which is an Anglo-Latin word that was originally spelled with an *-er* in English but then reverted to the Latin spelling of the base word *bursa* with an *r* tacked on.

There's also the feminine agent noun ending *-ster*, as in spinster. Although this ending is now gender-neutral in words such as gangster and jokester, in Old English (as *-istre*) and Middle English, it was a feminine agent noun ending denoting the professions of women.

Some of these words still appear in profession-based surnames today: A webster was a woman weaver (vs. a male weber); a brewster was a woman brewer; a baxter (literally bake-ster) was a woman baker. These, along with professions such as sewster and, yes, spinster—a woman who spins thread—were all professions thought to be appropriate for women to perform, to the extent that they appear as trade-based surnames today.

How, then, did "spinster" get its modern meaning? Spinning became associated with women who remained unmarried but continued to support themselves, and the term then underwent pejoration due to stigma. Because it would just be *awful* if an independent lady supported herself solo.

What? That. Where? There. When? Then

Isn't it interesting that "that" answers the question "what?" and "there" answers "where?" and "then" answers "when?"

Similar question-and-demonstrative pairs occur in other languages as well, both in Indo-European languages and in non-European languages like Japanese. Granted, these pairs aren't always quite so neat, but you'll find that rhyming question-and-answer word pairs are far from uncommon.

In English, it can be helpful to start with the article "the" as our base word. We can then add information and make it more emphatic by adding a demonstrative ending, an ending that points to an object, concept, or location.

The (Old English *þe*) + [demonstrative endings]
The + *-is* = this (Old English *þis*)
The + *-ese* = these (Old English *þæs*)
The + *-at* = that (Old English *þæt*)
The + *-ose* = those (Old English *þas*)

Each of the demonstrative endings in "this," "these," "that," and "those" provides slightly different information. "This" and "these" point at things that are in front of us or immediately identifiable, and "that" and "those" point at things that are further away.

Next, let's take the word "that," which points at things and concepts, and give it different suffixes (*-ere* and *-en*) that make it point at a location or a time. This gives us the words "there" and "then."

That + location/time suffix:
Location: That + *-ere* (Old English *-r/-er*) = there (Old English *þær*)
Time: That + *-en* (Old English *-nne/-enne*) = then (Old English *þænne*)

So "there" literally means "that place," and "then" literally means "that time."

Just to reiterate, we now know that these endings point at things, places, and times:

-*at* = thing/concept
-*ere* = place
-*en* = time

What, where, and when are interrogatives, or question words.

If we don't know in which direction, time, or place something is, we need an interrogative so that we can ask someone else.

It is a recurring trait of Indo-European languages to have some sort of interrogative root or word-forming element that is used to mean "huh?" This little bit can then be tacked onto other words and word elements to turn them into question words.

The PIE root **kwi-* or **kwo-* is pretty much where this all came from. In Latin and French, as well as in several other languages, this question-forming root became a *qu*. In German it became *w*.

In Modern English, we use the consonant cluster *wh-* for this purpose. In Old English it was *hw-*.

So that's why we have words like who, what, where, when, why, which, whence, whether, wherefore, and many more. "How" is one of these as well, without the metathesis of the Old English *hw-* and its Proto-Germanic root **hwo*, likely because it remained closer to its Old English predecessor, *hu*.

The shift to *wh-* in Modern English happened for a couple of reasons. In Old English, the letter *h* represented a few different sounds, including the ones we associate with the letter *h* today, but also a harder sound, sort of like the *ch* sound in the words "loch" or "blech." Long story short, this sound was difficult to pronounce in French, so after the Normans invaded, the *h* was dropped from the beginning of these words and moved after the *w*.

So, if we want to ask someone else to help us identify a thing, place, or time, we take our demonstrative endings and we add our question-forming prefix, which gives us that "huh?" to get what, where, and when.

wh- (huh?) + -en = point at a time when (OE *hwænn*)
-at = point at a thing what (OE *hwæt*)
-ere = point at a place = where (OE *hwær*)

So really, it's less that the answers to what?, where?, and when? are that, there, and then, and more that the questions to that, there, and then are what?, where?, and when?

What about "at" and "is"? Are they related?

The word "at" has a different PIE root than the ending *-at* that gives us "that." However, it is notable that, even in Old English, the ending *-at* was spelled the same as the Old English equivalent of the word "at," and it is interesting that they both convey directing something toward something else. But while there may have been cross-pollination in meaning, the word "at" is ultimately cognate with the Latin word and directional prefix *ad-*, as in advertise, adjective, and address. To say that they are totally unrelated is an oversimplification, but "that" and "at" are from different roots.

The verb "is" is more distinct: It's a conjugation of "to be" and therefore has entirely different rules, unconnected with the *-is* that we find in "this" at all. One interesting, unrelated thing you might not know about the word "is" is that it is cognate with the word "yes," which is a compound word. It is a combination of the Old English *yea* or *gea* meaning "so (or yes)," and the Old English stem (**es-*) of the verb "is" or "to be." So, the word "yes" literally means "so be it!"

Other *wh-* words

Which is also a compound word. (No, really.) It's clearer to see from its Old English predecessor, *hwi-lic*, that "which" literally means "why-like" or in some cases "who-like."

Why is the instrumental case of the word "what," so it literally means "for what use or purpose." The word "how" was used in almost the exact same way in Old English, but the two diverged in meaning over time.

Whence came whence, hence, and thence?

"Whence" is an example of an anaphoric locative adverb. (Say that ten times fast.) Locative adverbs include words such as indoors, abroad, outside, downhill, sideways, ahead, and many words that end in *-ward*: forward, backward, homeward, wayward, landward, southward.

("Toward" is not a locative adverb because it is a preposition and always has an object. You wouldn't say, "I went toward" without specifying toward what. But you could say "I went forward.")

Basically, a locative adverb tells you something about location or direction. Often they're created using prepositions or parts of prepositions. But the most common locative adverbs are the ones we create using our interrogative and demonstrative pronouns: what, this, and that.

As we've seen, we can add location information to these words by saying "at what place," "at this place," or "at that place." Or, you can just transform these lengthier phrases into the words "where," "here," and "there."

"Where," "here," and "there" are (in many cases) locative adverbs. Because they correspond to pronouns, they're called anaphoric, meaning they stand in for other words just like pronouns do.

There are more words like this that tell you other things about location—we just don't use them very much anymore.

For instance, you can turn "what," "this," and "that" into words that specify whether you're going to or from a place:

> **Whither** means "to what place": Whither has she gone? = To what place has she gone?
> **Hither** means "to this place": She came hither = She came to this place.
> **Thither** means "to that place": She went thither = She went to that place.

Now let's add the sense of "from a place" to these words:

> **Whence** means "from what place." Whence came you? = From what place did you come?
> **Hence** means "from this place." Go hence = Go from this place.
> **Thence** means "from that place." Thence she set forth. = She set forth from that place.

Thus, if you were to say "from whence," a fellow word enthusiast might remind you that the "from" is unnecessary because it is already contained in the word.

This also works with wherefore and therefore.

As anyone who's seen or read *Romeo and Juliet* knows, **wherefore** means "why": "Wherefore art thou Romeo?" doesn't mean "Where are you, Romeo?" but "*Why* are you Romeo (the dude my dad won't let me go out with because you're a Montague)?" And "therefore" is a perfectly acceptable answer to the question.

But why does wherefore mean "why"?

This requires some word math. (I know, I know. But it's not scary, I promise.) There's a formula that is used to create pronominal adverbs, which includes words such as therein, hereabouts, and wherefore.

Very basically, the way these work is that "here," "there," and "where" get transformed into demonstrative pronouns—"this," "that," and "what." Then you attach a preposition to tell the transformed word what to do.

Think about the word **"therein"**:

> **There + a preposition** gives you a word meaning "the preposition + that."
> **There + in = in that.**

You see words like this in legal documentation a lot because their primary function is to prevent lawyers from having to repeat the same things over and over again. (More anaphora!) You say "therein" so you don't have to say "in that document" every time you talk about it.

> **Here + X = X this.**
> Herein = in this ____
> Hereabouts = about/around this _____
> Herewith = with this _____

> **There + X = X that.**
> therein = in that ____
> thereabouts = about/around that ____
> therewith = with that ____

> **Where + X = X what.**
> Wherein = in what ____
> Whereabouts = about/around what ____
> Wherewith = with what ____

So…

> **Where + for(e)** = "for what (reason/purpose)," "toward what (reason/purpose)," or "why."
> **There + for(e)** = "for that (reason/purpose)," "toward that (reason/purpose)," or "because."

Didn't think you'd end up doing math in this book, did you?

Slaughter, daughter, laughter—enough!

For a while in the 13th and 14th centuries, the silent *h* in most English words was pronounced. It sounded like the *ch* in the Scottish word "loch" or the word "blech." So daughter, slaughter, and laughter sounded more like "dochter," "slauchter," and "lochter."

In Old English, this sound was represented by the letter *h*, but *h* also made the softer sound it does today when it came at the beginning of a word. In Middle English, the more guttural *h* sounds started to be spelled "gh."

Over the next century or so, following the Norman invasion, this sound softened and then went entirely silent thanks to French influence because this *ch* sound didn't exist in Latin or heavily Latin-derived Old French.

At the end of words like enough or laugh, the *gh* turned into an *f* sound. Figuring out why is probably more art than science, but our best guess is that making it completely silent may have felt inadequate. (Enough was also pronounced and spelled "enow" in some cases, though, just for some added confusion.)

Why didn't the spelling of laugh change? Well, in the words of 19th-century lexicographer Hensleigh Wedgwood, "If laugh were written as it is pronounced, *laaff*, there would be nothing in the word itself to put us in mind of the thing signified."[1] So, again, more art than science.

In Old English, spellings were not standardized, but the word "laugh" was meant to be imitative, to reflect the actual sound of laughing. Some of the spellings that were used, hilariously, included *hlæhhan*, *hliehhan*, and *hlihhan*. Try reading those out loud for a good laugh.

---

[1] Hensleigh Wedgwood, *A Dictionary of English Etymology* (London: Trübner, 1859).

Literal pedantry: Is the juice worth the figurative squeeze?

If someone uses the term "literally" figuratively, pedants are often quick to correct them. But people have been using this word "to indicate [that] what follows must be taken in the strongest admissible sense" since the 17th century.[2] "Literally" has been used in place of an emphatic "figuratively" for hundreds of years.

Also, even when we use the word "literally" correctly, we are still not using the most literal meaning of the word "literally."

That is, unless you are talking about actual letters (Latin *litera/littera* "letter, alphabetic sign"), the word "literally" is itself figurative.

The definition of literally is "taking words in their most straightforward, usual, or most basic sense without metaphor or allegory."

But literal's literal meaning is "related to letters of the alphabet." Its truest, most basic, most etymological sense doesn't relate to definitions or meaning at all. It's just letters—symbols on a page.

So even when we say things like "according to the literal definition" we're being figurative because you mean "according to the definition's strictest interpretation," not its actual alphabetical letters.

All of that aside, people who are particular about the distinction between "literally" and "figuratively" might do well to consider the works of literary legends like Twain, Dickens, Alcott, and Fitzgerald, who got away with using "literally" emphatically and figuratively without it damaging their authorial reputations:

[2] *Oxford English Dictionary*, s.v. "literally," www.oed.com/dictionary/literally_adv?tab=meaning_and_use. Accessed March 8, 2025.

- After duping his friends into whitewashing a fence, Tom Sawyer found himself "literally rolling in wealth," even though he didn't do any rolling. The "wealth" also consisted of, a kite, a key, a one-eyed kitten, and other objects of uncertain value.[3]
- In *Nicholas Nickleby*, the unpleasant schoolmaster Wackford Squeers "literally feasted his eyes" upon a bedraggled Smike, yet Smike remained undevoured.[4]
- Louisa May Alcott had it both ways, writing "The land literally flowed with milk and honey on such occasions" while also using "literal" to mean "taken at face value" in *Little Women*.[5]
- Jay Gatsby "literally glowed," but the remainder of the sentence reveals that he was not physically shining; it was his "new well-being [that] radiated from him."[6]

Jane Austen is more precise about such things but alludes to the pedantry attached to both terms in more than one text, including *Emma*:

> half an hour stolen afterwards to go over the same ground again with him, literally and figuratively, was quite necessary to reinstate her in a proper share of the happiness of the evening before.[7]

[3] Mark Twain, *The Adventures of Tom Sawyer* (Hartford, CT: American Publishing Co., 1881), 31.

[4] Charles Dickens, *Nicholas Nickleby* (London: Dent, 1975), 153.

[5] Louisa May Alcott, *Little Women* (London: Macmillan, 1926), 291.

[6] F. Scott Fitzgerald, *The Great Gatsby* (Ware, Herts: Wordsworth Editions, 1999), 57.

[7] Jane Austen, *Emma* (London: John Murray, 1816), 257.

Despite all this—dare I say fun?—with the word literally, not everyone approved, just as they don't today. In his 1926 *Dictionary of Modern English Usage*, lexicographer Henry Watson Fowler maligned the emphatic use of "literally":

> We have come to such a pass with this emphasizer that where the truth would require us to insert with a strong expression "not l., of course, but in a manner of speaking", we do not hesitate to insert the word that we ought to be at pains to repudiate; … Such false coin makes honest traffic in words impossible.[8]

There is value in embracing the dictionary definition of "literally" for precision in some instances. But there's also little harm or even confusion in saying "my dog is literally a queen" or that she is "literally a bitch." And if anyone insists that the former is wrong and the latter is right, remind them that the dog is in fact not—by the most pedantic standards—literally a bitch either since there is no bitchiness inherent in the alphabet.

[8] H. W. Fowler, *A Dictionary of Modern English Usage* (Oxford: Oxford University Press, 1926).

4
Too Good to Be True
Debunking Etymology Myths

Etymology has always been subject to a great deal of conjecture and guesswork. Even today, entertaining myths about the origins of words run rampant, especially across digital spaces.

Stories, assumptions, and even jokes about word origins often take hold in our collective imagination as if they are fact.

For instance, there's an interesting impulse to claim that words (especially swear words but also terms such as "news" and "posh") are acronyms, even though acronyms only rarely existed prior to the mid-1800s, and for a few reasons: Spelling was inconsistent, for one thing—but, to a greater extent, acronyms simply hadn't been popularized in the contexts that use them most: science, technology, manufacturing, marketing, government, nonprofits, and so on.

So, let's put on our debunking goggles, disassemble those supposed acronyms, figure out whether sophomore actually means "wise fool," and learn about the terms "boy" and "girl."

While we're on the subject, the "bunk" in the term **"debunk"** is short for "bunkum," meaning—just like "bunk" does today—"nonsense." "Bunkum" is a misspelling of North Carolina's Buncombe County. In 1820, North Carolina representative Felix Walker gave a long, boring, nonsensical speech to the U.S. Congress that he addressed to his home county. In most cases, the prefix *de-* means "down" or "away from," and here it implies "removing the bunk(um)" from a false claim, as popularized by its use in the 1923 novel *Bunk* by William E. Woodward.[1]

Myth: "Slang" is short for "shortened language"

A common etymology myth has it that the word "slang" is short for "shortened language." While that's believable, there's no historical record to indicate that this was ever true.

It also doesn't fully make sense. First, slang terms aren't necessarily shorter than the words they replace. Take, for instance, Cockney rhyming slang: The term "raspberry" is slang for "fart" via the rhyming phrase "raspberry tart."

Also, some slang terms crop up on their own. The short-lived term "cheugy," supposedly coined by student Gaby Rasson in 2013, refers to people, especially millennials, who are accused of being "slightly off trend" because they sport supposedly passé fashion or decorative accessories like "live, laugh, love" signs. This word is clearly slang, and yet it's not shortening any preexisting word.

So, what is slang, really? For a colloquialism to qualify as slang, it has to be informal and specific to a particular group.

The word "slang" was popularized in English during the mid-18th century and first referred to the speech of tramps and thieves.

It's likely that it comes from the verb *slanger*, a Northern English word meaning "to linger" or "to go slowly," perhaps in reference to the wandering ways of vagabonds. *Slanger* is related to Nordic words meaning "to sling" or "to hang loose." It may

[1] William E. Woodward, *Bunk* (London: Harper & Brothers, 1923).

also be related to an older Nordic phrase *slengja kjeften*, which literally meant "to sling the jaw," but also carried the implication "to abuse with words."

The delightful word "slangwhanger" also appeared in 19th-century American English and was used to mean "one who uses abusive slang" or "a ranting partisan." Tragically, slangwhanger is now largely obsolete and in urgent need of a revival.

Etymology myths about "boy" and "girl"

Myth: Until the late 15th century, the word "girl" referred to a child of either sex. Male babies were called "knave girls" and female babies were called "gay girls."

This claim has a grain of truth to it—but it's mostly incorrect. At best, it's a vast oversimplification of what truly happened with these words.

The part about girl referring to a child of any sex was true—but only briefly, starting in the early 1300s, around the time the word (spelled *gyrle*) first came into existence. The root of girl is unknown, though the *-l* or the original ending *-le* implies that it was a diminutive.

But the word "boy" also dates to the same period—even slightly before girl—and is recorded referring to a male child. And even during the short period when *gyrle* was used as a word for any young child, it was primarily used for female children. "Gay" was not specifically a word collocated to "girl," although, because it meant happy, it was often applied to happy children of any gender.

The most common usage of "boy" was as a word for a young male servant or commoner. And for the most part it wasn't used kindly. It was often a name used for men belonging to the lower classes, to imply servitude—much as it has been used by people of a higher social status to demean men of lower classes or different races in historical contexts. Similarly, the French term *garçon* has increasingly fallen out of use as a word for a waiter because it, too, implies an imbalance of power between the customer and the server. The word "boy" may be related to Greek words for "yoke" or "collar"; other evidence points to a relation between "boy" and "babe."

In Old English, the most common word for a young boy was *cnihtcild*, or "knightchild." "Knight" didn't refer to our idea of a warrior or noble in shining armor until at least the 1100s but simply meant a young man or male attendant or servant. *Cnafacild*, or "knave child," was also a word for a boy, or—you guessed it—a male servant.

An ungendered word for child was *bearn*, which is still used today with various spellings in some dialects, notably the Northern English and Scottish "bairn."

Sophomore

Myth: "Sophomore" means "wise fool."

If you're a sophomore in high school or college, you may have heard it said that the word "sophomore" is derived from the Greek words *sophos* meaning "wise" and *moros* meaning "foolish." Which would make you, sophomore, a wise fool.

It's apt and entertaining, but it's not entirely true. The truth behind the word is even more interesting.

The first half of sophomore is ultimately derived from *sophos*, meaning "wise," but the second half is sadly not from *moros*, meaning "fool." And the first half is more closely tied to the concept of sophism than general wisdom.

Sophism was an ancient Greek school of thought that predated philosophers like Socrates but continued into his time and beyond. Sophists were traveling intellectuals or teachers known for their skill at oratory, rhetoric, and persuasive arguments.

In the late 1600s, at universities like Oxford and Cambridge, second- and third-year students were taught the arts of rhetoric, reasoning, and debate. They were called "sophisters" after the Sophists for their focus on these areas of study. Add some French influence to "sophister," and you get *sophumer*, which evolved into the Modern English word "sophomore." So, you might say that, rather than being a "wise fool," a sophomore is a trained debater or arguer—a master-debater, if you will.

This skillset hasn't always been seen in the most favorable light, even long before the word "sophomore" came around. Plato, for example, was less than fond of sophists, especially because of the high prices they often charged for their skills and knowledge. They came to be thought of as greedy, power-hungry faction who used ambiguous arguments and logical fallacies to deceive people. In Greek, *sophisma* was as much a word for a deceptive trick as it was for a clever use of words, and, in Old French, the related word *sophime* described a fallacy. As a result, you might not be flattered to be called a sophist today. It refers to someone who argues in bad faith or uses logical fallacies.

Perhaps predictably, the words "sophomore" and "sophist" are related to the word "sophisticated." Being sophisticated wasn't initially considered to be a good thing, either. It meant "mixed with a foreign substance" or "impure," like the mixed messaging and convoluted logic of a sophist. Similarly, to "sophisticate" something was to make it impure or mix it with something, and "sophistication" was literally the use of sophistry: muddling up a discussion or debate with a fallacious argument intended to mislead.

"Sophisticated" didn't take on its positive connotation—"worldly" or "pleasantly discriminating"—until the 1800s. These new shades of meaning likely came from the idea that sophists were travelers known for their high-minded and discriminating approach to debate.

False acronyms

An acronym is an initialism that is pronounced as a word, such as NASA, SCUBA, or laser.

The word "acronym" was coined in the 1940s, using the Greek elements *akros* meaning "at the end" or "at the top" and *onyma* "name." Thus, an acronym is a name formed by the "top" or first letters of two or more words.

Although terms such as CIA or FBI are often labeled acronyms, they are technically initialisms because each letter is pronounced as a letter. (We don't automatically say See-A or Fibby—or at least I don't.)

For a variety of reasons, including changing conventions around naming institutions and inconsistencies in spelling, acronyms were rare until the latter half of the 19th century.

Therefore, as a rule, if someone claims that a common word that has been around since before the 1850s—or even before the turn of the 20th century—is an acronym, it's probably a myth. Here are some examples.

Posh

True: thieves' cant or Romany slang for coin
False: "port outward, starboard home"

The word "posh" is most likely adopted from thieves' cant or a Romany slang word for "money" or "coin."

However, some have speculated that it meant "port outward, starboard home" because, if you traveled to India from Europe on a Peninsular and Oriental Steam Navigation Company (P&O) ship in the 1800s, the portside cabins remained out of the sun and were therefore considered fancier—and vice versa on the way back. The *Oxford English Dictionary* and most other sources consider this theory to be incorrect due to lack of evidence.

Tag (game)

> **True:** from a Scottish or Middle English word for "touch" or "tap"
> **False:** "touch-and-go"

"Tag," which is a very old word, became the name of the children's game in the 1730s. The word itself is thought to be a variation on the Scottish word *tig*, meaning "touch" or "tap," or simply the Middle English *tek* or *tik* of the same meaning. Tag has also long been a word for things that poke and prickle, which maybe led people to think of whichever kid is "it" in the game.

News(paper)

> **True:** 14th-century term for "new things," from an earlier French sense of *nouvelles*
> **False:** for news—"notable events, weather, and sports" or "north east west south"; for newspaper—"north, east, west, south, past and present event report"

The English word "news" (or *newes*) is first attested in the 14th century. It literally means accounts of "new things," derived from Medieval Latin *nova* via French *nouvelles*.

The French and Latin terms were used the same way as the English term "news" is today. "Paper" also came to English in the 14th century: Greek *papyros* → Latin *papyrus* → Old French *papier* → English *paper*.

The first recorded instance of the term "newspaper" in English was with the spelling "newes paper" in the 1660s, probably referring to the *Oxford Gazette*, which eventually became the *London Gazette*.

Tip

> **True:** slang variation of "tap," implying money changing hands
> **False:** "to insure promptitude"

The word "tip," as in the money you'd leave for a server in a restaurant, was first used in the 1600s as thieves' slang to describe money changing hands.

This didn't stop Frederick William Hackwood from claiming that it means "to insure promptitude" in his 1909 book *Inns, Ales and Drinking Customs of Old England*. He backed this up by saying that "TIP" was inscribed on tip boxes in old coaching inns. This sounds logical, and there may have been boxes that said TIP on them, but it definitely wasn't an acronym—probably just a place to put a gratuity. This sense of "tip" is considered to be a specialized variation of the word "tap," suggesting to lightly toss something to another person.

Sir

> **True:** variant of "sire"
> **False:** "slave I remain"

"Sir" as a title for a knight is first recorded in the 1200s or 1300s and was originally a variation of the word "sire," which denoted knighthood before it was a term of respect for a king. It has always been a term of high rank that comes from a root meaning "senior" or "old."

A common myth is that it's an acronym of "slave I remain" because knights pledged fealty to kings. This theory doesn't hold up because the word "sir" is recorded in English some three centuries before "remain."

Golf

True: from a Germanic term meaning "club" or "stick" for swinging
False: "gentlemen only, ladies forbidden"

It has been posited that "golf" is an acronym of "gentlemen only, ladies forbidden," though this claim was likely made in jest—and within the past 50 years at most.

The Scottish game, meanwhile, dates to at least the 14th century, and the Scottish word and its predecessors (such as *gouf*) date back to the mid-15th century, with older variations found in Middle Dutch and Old Norse. Its various Germanic forms imbue it with meanings such as "stick" or "club," or even "mace" or "bell's clapper"—all alluding to the swing-and-hit nature of the game. The gender-exclusionary false origin may stem from implications first recorded in the 19th century that a woman married to a male golf aficionado may find herself a "widow" to the sport.

SOS

True: recognizable Morse code
False: "Save Our Ship" or "Save Our Souls"

Because it looks and sounds like an initialism, it's logical to want to ascribe words to SOS, but, alas, it doesn't stand for anything other than the letters themselves and the dots and dashes that are used to transmit them in Morse code.

S.O.S. is a universal distress call, so it isn't specific to the English language. It was selected by the International Radio Telegraphic Convention in 1906 because the Morse code for these letters is tough to mistake for anything else. S.O.S. is three dots, then three dashes, then three dots, or: • • • - - - • • •

The fact that it often implies a ship or souls in need of saving certainly made it easy for English speakers looking for words to correspond to it.

An earlier standard radio distress call was CQD, which also, contrary to popular belief, was not intended to be short for "Come Quickly, Distress." Rather, CQ was a general call to ships and land stations, not one that was meant to summon swift help. The D, however, was added to symbolize and correspond to "distress," so it has been treated as a retroactive initialism (though still not an acronym because, after all, it doesn't spell a word).

Some acronymic words

Never fear, though, here are a few, perhaps unexpected, acronyms and abbreviations that really did become everyday words:

- **Jeep:** This brand name emerged from the American military slang term "GP," a "general purpose" car. The style of vehicle was originally intended by Army developers to be a "light reconnaissance and command car."
- **adidas:** Although some have (incorrectly) speculated that the brand name adidas stands for "All Day I Dream About Sport," it's actually a contraction of founder Adolf "Adi" Dassler's name (see: eponyms). People tend to downplay that today, though, due to Dassler's Nazi sympathies.
- **Pakistan:** This country name was created by a group of Muslim students at the University of Cambridge in the 1930s, combining the names of the regions Punjab, Afghan Province, and Kashmir, which were meant to form the new country.

The *pak* element also echoes an Iranian word for "pure," and -*stan* means "country" or literally a place that "stands" or is established.

Is it a backronym?

The term "backronym" has two or three meanings, depending on the source.

It can refer to mythical acronyms like the ones we've already discussed, or it can refer to an acronym that is deliberately reverse-engineered from a term already in use.

The **Apple Lisa**, for example, was a model of Apple computer. Although Apple officially stated that LISA was an acronym for Local Integrated Software Architecture, many believe that the acronym was reverse-engineered—that is, that it was a backronym—and that the computer was named after Steve Jobs' daughter Lisa, with no acronym originally intended.

The term **"CARE package"** is arguably both a traditional acronym and a backronym. It was first used in 1945 to describe aid packages sent to Europe after World War II by charities working under the umbrella of the program Cooperative for American Remittances to Europe. The name of the program was later changed to "Cooperative for Assistance and Relief Everywhere" so that it could include aid going to places other than Europe—but also so that it could retain the acronym. This made it a backronym because it was reverse-engineered to fit the earlier term.

The *OED* entry for "backronym" states that it can be "an acronym deliberately formed from a phrase whose initial letters spell out a particular word or words … to create a memorable name." The same entry cites the United States Geological

Survey's Biodiversity Information Serving Our Nation species mapping system—that is, BISON—as a backronym engineered to fit the word "bison," an apt connection for a program designed to track and protect species including the American bison.

By that logic, the "CARE" in "CARE package" is a double backronym, simply because it is meant to draw upon the apt word "care."

This sense of backronym can also be applied to fictional organizations such as SPECTRE, the Special Executive for Counterintelligence, Terrorism, Revenge, and Extortion of James Bond franchise fame, or S.P.E.W., the Society for the Promotion of Elfish Welfare seen in the Harry Potter books.

What about OK, Okay, and O.K.?

The word and abbreviation "OK" most likely came about as a result of… well, nerds being silly. (Not that anyone reading or writing this book can judge.) Although several other theories have arisen, the predominant theory revolves around the fact that, in the 1830s, collegiate jokesters in Boston and New York came up with a series of slang abbreviations based on deliberately misspelled words:

k.g. was short for "kno go" (no go)
n.c. was short for "nuff ced" (enough said)
k.y. was short for "know yuse" (no use)
o.k. was short for "oll korrect" (all correct)

The following is from the *Boston Morning Post* in 1839. Editor Charles Gordon Greene uses the abbreviation "o.k." to poke fun at a factual error in *The Providence Journal.*

> We said not a word about our deputation passing "through the city" of Providence.—We said our brethren were going to New

> York in the Richmond, and they did go, as per Post of Thursday. The "Chairman of the Committee on Charity Lecture Bells," is one of the deputation, and perhaps if he should return to Boston, via Providence, he of the Journal, and his train-band, would have his "contribution box," et ceteras, o.k.—all correct—and cause the corks to fly, like sparks, upward.

The reason OK stuck around while the other abbreviations didn't is thanks to the 1840 presidential election, when William Henry Harrison ran against Martin Van Buren. William Henry Harrison was known as "the hero of Tippecanoe," and his running mate was John Tyler, so the campaign used the song "Tippecanoe and Tyler Too" to hype them up. Van Buren was born in Kinderhook, New York, and was known as "Old Kinderhook," which was abbreviated to OK. His supporters formed "OK Clubs" and played up the dual meaning of OK as "all correct," to say that they chose the correct candidate. These campaign efforts popularized it in widespread usage.

But apparently, by 1919, many people had forgotten the original meaning and origin of OK, because Woodrow Wilson spelled it "okeh," assuming that it was a Choctaw word meaning "it is so." There is no evidence that this is true, and the abbreviation predates the "okeh" spelling in English by quite a bit.

Nevertheless, Wilson's spelling probably contributed to the popularity of another, more phonetically accessible spelling: okay.

As for the capitalization, the original variation was lowercase o.k.

In the *Associated Press Stylebook* and many other editorial style guides, it's OK without periods because that's standard for any initialism.

So, depending on your stylistic allegiances, you can probably go with o.k., O.K., OK, or okay without anybody going AWOL or saying FML.

5

Folk Etymology

When Assumptions Change Words and Meaning

We use the term "folk etymology" to describe the (many!) instances when misspellings, misunderstandings, and mistranslations have influenced the modern spellings and meanings of words, or, less often, when unsubstantiated and often fanciful etymological explanations of word origins are applied to words retroactively.

Take **"outrage,"** for example. Its original source is the Vulgar Latin *ultraticum*, meaning "excess," which evolved into the Old French *oltrage*, which was misunderstood as *out* + *rage*, first in French and then in English.

Or take **"mongoose,"** an animal entirely unrelated to the goose. The animal's name in the Indian language Marathi is *muṅgū*, or *muṅgisa* in Telugu. This was adopted into English as "mongoose," simply because English-speaking travelers to India thought the second syllable of the word sounded like the name of the animal they already knew. (It might also have helped that mongooses are long in the body, sort of like a goose's neck, and have a pointed face.)

The word **"hangnail"** originally had nothing to do with the word "hang" or even the "fingernail" sense of the word "nail." Rather, it's from the Middle English *agnail* or *angnail*, a word for the sort of corn that might develop on your foot.

The literal meaning was "painful spike" from the Proto-Germanic *ang- "painful, hard" (related through its PIE root to words such as "anger," "anxious," "anguish," and "angst") plus the Old English *nægl*, meaning, not the sort of nail you find on your fingers and toes, but rather an iron nail or spike. The logic here seems to have been that having a corn in your foot feels rather like standing on a spike. However, the two types of "nail" are ultimately related because the PIE root of "nail" actually *did* mean "fingernail" or "claw," so iron nails get their name from a root meaning "fingernail," but hangnails get their name from iron nails. (Yes, it's dizzying.) Over time, the affliction known as an *angnail* came to refer to what we know as hangnails, and the likes of corns and bunions got their own words.

A **pickaxe** was called a *picas* or *pikeis* in Middle English, and the word is ultimately derived from the Latin *picus*, meaning "woodpecker." Although a pickaxe often has an axelike blade on one end, and it does "pick" at things, the word "axe" was not originally involved in the name of the tool, and it's thought to be an understandable misinterpretation of the second syllable of the Middle English term.

Penthouse was spelled *pendis* or *pendize* in the 1300s, and at that time it was a word for a sloped segment of roof that extends outward from the side of a building. It's from the Latin *appendere*, meaning "to hang," and related to words like "appendage" and "appendix." The earlier words were misunderstood as a compound of "pent," here meaning "slope," and "house." Jesus' birthplace is sometimes described as a "penthouse" in Middle English. Later, the name was given to a roofed area or small structure on the roof of another building, which then led to its association with luxury top-floor apartments in skyscrapers.

The word **"gingerbread"** originally involved no "bread" at all. In Middle English, preserved ginger was called *gingerbrar*, or in Old French *gingerbrat*, both from the Medieval Latin *gingimbratus* "gingered." In the mid-14th century, this same preserved ginger (which was not a baked good) was called *gingerbrede*, meaning "ginger bread," despite not containing anything we'd call bread today. In Old English, the typical word for a loaf was *hlaf*, while Old English *bread* meant "bit, crumb, morsel." It seems that people heard the *-brar* and *-brat* portions of the Middle English and Old French words as this kind of Old English "bread," and took it to refer to little bits of preserved ginger. The resulting term "gingerbread" wasn't applied to bakery items until the 15th century.

Wormwood, the herb known for its use in spirits such as absinthe and vermouth, is from the Old English *wermod*, which is unrelated to the words "worm" and "wood." Although its precise meaning is unknown, one theory is that *wermod* comes from *wer* meaning "man" and *mod* meaning "courage." Its modern name may have been inspired by its use as an insect deterrent—that is, a plant (wood) that repels larvae and insects (worm)—as seen in *The Book of St. Albans*, which describes it as "a medecyne for an hawke that hath mites."

In Middle English, **island** was spelled *yland*. The root of the first part of the word means "water," so island literally means "water-land" or "land on water." It does not share a root with the word isle, which is from Old French and ultimately from the Latin *insula*. But people understandably assumed, based on pronunciation and the overlap in meaning, that *yland* and *isle* were related, and so they essentially became a portmanteau in the form of "island."

Sovereign comes from the Vulgar Latin *superanus*, which means "chief" or "principal" and is not related to *anus*, meaning both "ring" and "butthole," but is the source of the Italian word *soprano*. *Superanus* evolved into the Old French *soverain*, with its English spelling adjusted by association with "reign," which has nothing to do with its true etymology.

Comrades in camaraderie

So, you know this word: **comrade**.

But if you type "comradery" into your phone or computer, you'll find that your spellcheck thinks it isn't a word.

And that's because it's spelled **"camaraderie."**

Granted, more dictionaries have started accepting "comradery" as correct—because that's understandably how many people spell it, and as we've already learned many times in this very book, words change with usage.

But that's pretty recent. The 1982 edition of the *OED*, for instance, gives only "camaraderie" as the correct spelling.

So why is this? Why is "comrade" spelled one way, but "camaraderie" another? They are, after all, from the exact same roots.

As you probably have guessed, our friend folk etymology had something to do with it.

Camaraderie was directly borrowed into English from French and has remained unaltered for most of its history. The original French spelling of "comrade" was *camarade*.

Comrade shifted to the *com-* spelling in English because of the false assumption that the first syllable (*cam-*) was actually the Latin prefix *com-*, meaning "together." The idea was that comrade was related to companion, literally "someone you have or break bread with" (Latin *com-* "with, together" + *panis* "bread), and combat, literally "fighting together" (Latin *com-* + *battuere* "beat, fight").

But camaraderie and comrade (*camarade*) don't actually contain this prefix. In fact, they are more closely related to "camera," which in Latin literally means "a vaulted room or chamber." So, camaraderie does imply togetherness, but in the more figurative sense of someone you share a chamber with.

Feminine male? Iron male? No, "female" is a word all her own

What if I told you that the word "female" is not related to the word "male"?

The word "female" has its origin in the Latin word for woman, *femina*. The diminutive of *femina* is *femella*, which means "young female" or "girl." The Latin word was adopted into Old French as *femelle* and then adopted directly into Middle English with the same spelling.

In the late 14th century, the spelling changed because people thought it was a variation on the word "male."

But it's not.

The word "male" comes from the Latin word *masculus* and so is totally unrelated to the word *femina*.

When *masculus* entered Old French, it became *masle*. And when Old French words become Modern French, they tend to drop the *s* in certain circumstances and convert it into a circumflex accent. So *masle* became *mâle*, which is where the English spelling came from.

The Latin word for woman, *femina*, comes from a PIE root that literally means "she who suckles." That's certainly accurate for many people and other mammals that have birthed children. This root connects it to words like fetus, fawn, felicity, affiliation, and fellatio.

But it doesn't share a root with the Latin words for man (*vir*) or male (*masculum*).

Masculum is an adjective form of *mas*, a word for a male of any species. *Vir* was a word for a male human and comes from the PIE root **wi-ro-* meaning "man," which is also the root of words like virile, virtuoso, virtue, and werewolf (literally "man-wolf").

Miniature mayhem

What is "mini" short for?

You could speculate that it's short for "minuscule" or "minimum."

If that were the case, it would be related to "minus" and "minor," which are direct adoptions from Latin, in which *minus* and *minor* mean "small" or "less."

But, ultimately, mini is short for "miniature."

A mini dog breed, a miniskirt, the Mini car—even, in a way, Minnie Mouse: these are all "miniature" things. Indeed, the first small thing to be called "mini" was likely a "mini camera," a commercial shortening of "miniature camera."

But here's the curious part: Miniature isn't etymologically related to minuscule, minimum, minus, or minor (though minister *is*[1]).

Indeed, miniature, and thus mini, have nothing to do with size, but with color. Miniature is from the unrelated Latin *miniare*, meaning "to paint red," from *minium*, the name of a lead-based red paint used to illuminate medieval manuscripts. A "miniature" was originally a word for a manuscript illumination—an illustration within the text of the manuscript—especially (but not exclusively) one pigmented with *minium*.

The meaning of "miniature" evolved because:

One, the paintings in illuminated manuscripts were generally quite small;

Two, a broader range of available pigments reduced the reliance on *minium* in illuminations, and thus,

Three, the reduced synonymy between *minium* and illuminations, combined with the similar sound of "minimum"

---

[1] In addition to its Modern English meaning, "minister" is a Latin word for an inferior ranking person, a servant, or a priest's assistant. The word extended into English with the implication of a servant of the people—as in a prime minister or administrator—or a servant of the Church.

and "minuscule," shifted the definition and assumed origin of "miniature" to what we have today.

One critical stepping stone that solidified the modern definition was the *portrait miniature*, a portrait style popularized in the 16th century that drew upon similar techniques to manuscript miniatures—but didn't necessarily make use of *minium*. These portraits were also very small, so that people could give them to family members or, even better, prospective dates.

Delicious delight

Ever thought about the fact that the word "delight" looks like it should mean "to turn off" or to "remove a light"? Why doesn't it mean that—and why is it a word for elation and joy?

Delight is a sneaky word because etymologically, it has nothing to do with light at all. Once again, folk etymology shenanigans are at play.

You probably know that the Latin-derived prefix *de-* usually means "off," "down," or "away from" and tends to turn words into their opposites—evolve becomes devolve; ascend becomes descend; increase becomes decrease.

But in the case of "delight," that prefix is an intensifier. Aha, you say, so it *de* + light, meaning more light!

Sorry, no. The word "delight" is actually more closely related to "delicious" and "delectable." Both are from the Latin word *lacere*, "to lure, entice," rather than the Old English *light*, and when you add the intensifier prefix *de-*, you get something so tempting that it lures or entices you away from whatever else you're doing.

The Latin became the Old French *delitier*, meaning "to please greatly" or "to charm." The noun form of *delitier* was adopted into Middle English as *delit*, which then became *delite*. For about four hundred years, *delite* stuck around as the primary spelling. Only in the 1600s did the spelling of words such as "light" and "flight" lead us to the modern spelling "delight," perhaps because of its associations with levity.

So, curiously enough, when cheesy brands use the spelling "delite" in their advertising, they're being more authentic to the word's origin than those of us who spell it "correctly."

Why "shamefaced" is faceless

Much like "bald-faced lie" and its successor, "bold-faced lie," (see: eggcorns) the word "shamefaced" has been updated to reflect a more understandable and even blunt folk-etymological understanding. "Shamefaced" is recorded as early as the 1500s, preceded by "shamefast" and its Old English predecessor, *scamfæst*. Like its spelling, its meaning has shifted. Originally, "shame" was less a word for a pang of guilt and more a word for modesty, while the meaning of "fast" was more like that of "fastener" or "to hold fast." Thus, to say that someone was *shamefast* or, later, shamefaced was not to say that their guilt showed on their face, but that they were steadfast (there's that sense of "fast" again) in their sense of modesty. So, if you encounter this word in something written centuries ago, you may find it meaning "modest" or "bashful" rather than "guilty," as it's more likely to mean today.

Root exploration: Metamology

The way we use the word "meta" today is partially based on an error of interpretation.

When you stick the Greek-derived prefix *meta-* onto another word, it often means "beyond" or "transcending." But *meta* did not mean "beyond" in Greek. It could mean "in the midst of," "by means of," "in pursuit of," "between," "after," or "behind." But not usually "beyond." You might say that "after" is pretty close to "beyond," and you'd be right, but they don't mean precisely the same thing, and here's why that's important.

Between the 3rd and 1st centuries BCE, Greek scholars arranged Aristotle's works into collections.

One is called *The Physics*, and it addresses physics and natural sciences.

Another one covers a range of abstract topics including the essence of Being and immaterial existence. This collection is called *The Metaphysics*, or, in Latin, *Metaphysica*. This title inspired the name of the whole field of metaphysics.

"Metaphysics" comes from the Greek name given to the collection: *Ta meta ta physika*. Because the collection dealt with abstract topics, this Greek term was understood by Latin scholars to mean the science of what is "beyond the physical."

But that's not what it actually meant. The Greek *ta meta ta physika* literally just means "that which comes after *The Physics*." The collection's title wasn't referring to its contents but its sequence. In the Greek title, *meta* meant "after," not "beyond." See why that's an important distinction?

This misinterpretation of the Greek title infused the word-forming element "meta" with the sense of "beyond, transcending, or dealing with the most fundamental aspects of things." It's this meaning that also appears in words like "metacommunications," "metahistory," "metaverse," and, of course, the standalone adjective "meta"—as in "that's so meta." This just goes to show that even the brightest disciplines can end up running with folk etymology.

Some words, like "metamorphosis," use one of the other, actual Greek definitions of *meta*: "between" or "in the midst of." This sense also evolved to mean "change." So metamorphosis is the process of "changing shape," but literally the state of being "between shapes" (see: metaphor).

6

Systems of the Wordatorium

Etymological Phenomena You Might Not Have Noticed

Welcome to the wordatorium!

Late 1800s and early 1900s, *-(t)orium* began to be haphazardly affixed to lots of words to create business names. These words use the Latin *-orium* suffix, similar to that seen in words such as "auditorium," "planetarium," "sanatorium" (from Latin *sanare* "to heal"), and "emporium" (from Greek *emporion* "trading place, market," and *emporos* "merchant").

As a result, you ended up with words like:

barberatorium, **bobatorium**, or **shavatorium:** a barber shop
beautorium: a place where one could go to get a license as a hairdresser or beautician
healthatorium: a place where one could go for physical education (one was started by Bernarr Macfadden, the early bodybuilder and purveyor of health theories)
lubritorium: a place where automobiles are greased
motortorium: a car dealership
pantorium, **pantatorium**, or **suitatorium:** a men's tailor shop
pastorium: a parsonage.

printorium: a printing shop
restatorium or **restorium:** an inn or bed-and-breakfast.

And more disturbingly…

infantorium: a sideshow where premature babies were displayed in incubators for visiting spectators
odditorium: a sideshow.

All the above are documented in H. L. Mencken's 1919 reference book *The American Language: An Inquiry into the Development of English in the United States*, but can also be found in business listings and newspapers of the time.[1]

For the remainder of this chapter, we'll take a wander through our own wordatorium—a place to showcase the oddities of English. We'll examine the ways words repeat, flip, blend, jumble, and zig when they ought to zag—and maybe discover why we say things like zigzag in the first place.

Autological and heterological words

An autological word describes itself, while a heterological word does not describe itself.

Words such as "multisyllabic" and "pronounceable" are autological because they represent the qualities they describe. "Written" and "documented" are autological when they're respectively written but not when they're spoken. The word "sesquipedalian" describes long words but literally means "a foot and a half long" (*sesqui-* "half as much again" + *ped* "foot"). It first appeared in the *Ars Poetica* by Roman lyric poet Horace

[1] Henry L. Mencken, *The American Language: An Inquiry into the Development of English in the United States*, 4th ed. (New York: Alfred A. Knopf, 1936).

as an illustrative example of a long word—and therefore it is autological: It's a long word that describes long words.[2]

Most words, however, are heterological in that they do not describe themselves. Some are comically heterological. "Monosyllabic" is not a monosyllabic word. "Hyphenated" is not hyphenated. And long is short.

The word "heterological" also creates the so-called Grelling–Nelson paradox: If "heterological" is a heterological word, that would mean it does not describe itself and is therefore not heterological; if "heterological" is an autological word, it describes itself and is therefore not heterological either.

Contrarian contronyms

Contronyms—also known as antagonyms or auto-antonyms—are words that double as their own opposites or have mutually contradictory definitions. The term "contronym" was coined by Joseph T. Shipley in the 1960s. The phenomenon that creates contronyms can be called **enantionymy**, from Greek *enantio-*, "opposite." For example, consider **"shelled,"** as in nuts. A bag of "shelled" pistachios at the store likely has no shells, but a pistachio with the shell on could also be called "shelled."

Enantionymy happens for a few reasons. Foremost among them is the fact that English is both a poetic and endlessly diverse assemblage of beautiful modes of expression *and* a monstrous, shambling, chaotic, evil Frankenlanguage. To put it another way: Some contronyms are homonyms that come from two different etymological sources but are spelled the same.

Take the word **"cleave."** It can mean to split or divide something, as with a "cleaver," or it can mean to cling to

[2] Horace, *Ars Poetica* (London: Macmillan, 1960).

something—for example "cleave to one's ideals." They're both from Old English, but they have two different roots.

The sticky kind of cleaving in Old English was *clifian* or *cleofian*, "to adhere," from the PIE root **gloi-* "to stick," which also shares a root with words like "clay."

The splitty kind of cleaving in Old English was *cleofan*, *cleven*, or *cliven*, meaning "to split" or "-to separate," from the PIE root **gleubh-* "to tear apart," sharing a root with words like "clever," which first referred to skill with the hands rather than of the mind (see: clever).

But sometimes contronyms are not from different sources. The verb **"to dust"** can mean to sprinkle dust onto something or to brush dust off of something. This happened largely because "dust" was a noun first, and as a verb it came to refer to the many things you can do with dust.

The original, Middle English meaning of dust as a verb was "to rise in the air as dust," and these other meanings appeared about three hundred years later. Using dust as a word for applying dust makes a bit more sense; by that logic, to remove dust would be to undust or dedust. But the sense of "getting rid of dust" was already in wide use by then because the item you use to get rid of dust is called a "duster," so one "dusts" with a duster.

The word **"fast"** has meant both "swift" and "firmly attached" (or, as a verb, firm in one's commitment to abstaining from food) since Old English, because its primary meaning was originally "vigorously or strongly." Thus, one could be running vigorously (swift movement) or stuck vigorously (held fast) to something. Fast running might also involve sticking close to whatever you're chasing.

Sanction can mean "to grant permission" or "to prohibit," and in both cases it's because the word "sanction" means "to make valid" or "binding by law," ultimately from the Latin *sanctionem* "act of decreeing" (Latin *sancire* "to decree").

Sometimes regional colloquialisms can cause contronyms to emerge. For example, to **table an idea** in British English typically means to put it up for debate, while in the U.S., it usually means to set aside for later.

Some words are contronyms of their older meanings, which have since become apocryphal. **Awful** originally described something that fills you with awe or respect—and until the 1800s, it was primarily a good thing. Thus, one can have an awful time, or an awfully good time.

To describe something as **"artificial"** (Latin *artificium* "a work of art") was also a good thing until the 16th century. Up to that point, it referred to things that were not natural in the sense that they were artisinally crafted by human hands.

Other examples of contronyms:

apology: "an admission of error" or "a formal defense"
bound: "run" or "securely tied"
hold up: "support" or "hinder"
original: "new, innovative" or "an unchanged first"
left: "departed" or "remaining"

Burning (in)flammability and irrespective regardlessness

Nothing quite sets word nerds boiling like the fact that **flammable** and **inflammable** mean the same thing. They both refer to a substance or object that is susceptible to catching fire, leaving us to fill the lexical gap of its opposite with slightly more awkward alternatives such as "nonflammable" or just "not flammable."

Inflammable is older than flammable: Much like today, when it was first recorded in English in the 1600s, it meant "able to be inflamed or set alight."

However, the *in-* prefix understandably caused some confusion because it can mean either "not" (as in "incredulous" or "inept") or "in" or "into" (as in "investigate" and "inquisitive"). These senses are ultimately from different PIE roots.

"Flammable" arose in the 1800s as a clarification of the earlier word, especially in industrial settings where the difference can mean life or death. Due to the importance of this phrasing in these contexts, "flammable" became the preferred phrasing.

A similarly controversial term is **irregardless**, which is often considered to be incorrect due to its redundancy. After all, **regardless** means the same thing. However, "irregardless" has been in use since the 1870s and is found in all major dictionaries as a synonym for "regardless." It's likely been absorbed into common parlance as a conflation of "regardless" and "irrespective"—but reduncancy notwithstanding, it is and has been a word for quite some time.

The potatoes and meat of metathesis

This term, which is made of the Greek components *meta* "change" and *tithenai* "to place, to set"—therefore "a changing of places"—refers to the swapping of letters in a word as written or pronounced.

For instance, speakers of some English dialects pronounce the word "ask" like *aks.* Many people say *comftorble* instead of "comfortable." And just consider the way almost everyone pronounces "Wednesday."

In some cases, words have changed spellings by way of metathesis. The Old English equivalent of the word "bird," for example, was *bridd*, though the more common word for a bird was *fugol*, which is related to "fowl."

The word **"trouble"** is from the Old French *trubler*, but the Old French is a metathesis of the earlier spelling *turbler*. "Fright" is the result of a metathesis that occurred in Old English when *fyrhtu*, or "fear," metathesized into *fryhto*. A "Sheltie" dog's name (and a "Shelty pony," sometimes) is a metathesis of a "Shetland" sheepdog.

Thrill is a metathesis of the Middle English *thirlen*, meaning "to pierce," aptly calling to mind both a pang of fear and the resulting screech it might draw from you.

Sometimes, instead of letters changing places, entire syllables do. The word **"rag-tag"** is first recorded as "tag-rag," notably in this line from Shakespeare's *Julius Caesar*: "If the tag-rag people did not clap him and hiss him" (1.1.68–9).

This phenomenon happens in many world languages, and for varying reasons—but often because the new way of writing or saying a given word simply feels more, shall we say "comftorble," rolling off the tongue.

Polysemy

Polysemy is when a word has several different, yet ultimately related, meanings. It's from the Greek elements *poly* "many" and *sema* "sign."

Unlike homonyms (such as "bear," as in the animal or the act of carrying) and homophones (such as "heel" and "heal"), which are from different sources and sound the same and sometimes share a spelling through pure coincidence, polysemy describes two or more meanings of the same word, from the same source.

Helping verbs and passive auxiliary verbs are the likeliest candidates for polysemy. For example, "get" serves different purposes in each of these phrases:

get (acquire) a beer
get (increasingly feel) nervous
get (understand) a concept
get (become) pregnant

This also happens frequently with swear words because their casual nature—not to mention their shock value—makes them easy candidates for interjections and emphatic modifiers. For example, on the milder side, "damn" can be used to mean pretty much anything, from good to bad, and can serve as several different parts of speech.

Prepositions are also notorious for polysemic behavior—and that's true for English, too. For instance, "for" has at various points in English history meant (among others) "before, during, instead of, amid, in sight of, because of, in place of, as far as, in favor of, in front of, forward, and in"; "on" has had meanings including "about," "concerning," "on top of, in, into, in contact with, on top of, regarding, upon, and in operation"; and "to" has had meanings including but by no means limited to "toward, for the purpose of, furthermore, until, at, as far as, as long as, upward, and concerning."

That's one reason prepositions can be tough for people whose first language isn't English (and vice versa when English speakers are learning prepositions in other languages): It can be tough to remember which preposition makes the most sense in idiomatic or collocated phrases like "at last," "in advance," "out of reach," "for instance," "by chance," "at once," or "on behalf of." And then there are the ones that feel like inconsistencies, such as "in the car" vs. "on a bus."

Beknowing a befuddling prefix

The persistent polysemy of prepositions is one of the reasons that it's a bit hard to pin down exactly what the prefix *be-* in words like **begrudge**, **bespectacled**, and **bejeweled** means.

Simply put, it means a lot of things. This Old English prefix is not related to the verb "be," but it is related to the preposition "by," and it does a *lot* of work.

Its most common meaning is "around" or "on all sides," like in the words **"bejewel,"** meaning "to cover with jewels," **"bespatter,"** meaning "to spatter on all sides," and **"besiege,"** meaning to surround a place in the hopes of capturing it. This is also the sense we see in **bewildered** which means to figuratively be lost in a mental wilderness.

But the prefix *be-* can also do a lot of other things. It can be privative, which means it removes or deprives you of something, as in the word **"behead."**

It can be causative as in the word **"befuddle."** Fuddle was a 16th-century verb meaning "to get drunk," so to befuddle originally meant to cause someone to be confused by getting them drunk.

The *be-* prefix is also sometimes used for effect or intensification, like in the word **"bedraggle."** Draggle is a 16th-century word that means "to make something wet and muddy," and bedraggle means more or less the same thing, but even more so: extra wet, extra muddy.

The word **"besmirch"** is an interesting case. Without its prefix, to smirch means "to make something dirty or discolored." With besmirch, then, that *be-* is again acting as an intensifier, so the word means to make something especially filthy. Smirch is recorded as early as the 14th century, and before that we had the Middle English variation *smorchen*. Before that, its origin is a mystery. It's thought to be from the Old French *esmorcher*, which means "to torture"—from a root meaning "to bite." It's not clear how we got from biting and torturing to smearing or dirtying, but the Old French term may have also meant "to befoul" or "to stain." Perhaps the act of torture morally besmirches the torturer (or the clothing and body of the torturee), or perhaps it was conflated with the English word "smear" and took on some of its meaning.

Be- can also create transitive verbs, as in **bewail**, which means "to loudly complain about something." The prefix turns wail from an intransitive verb—one that doesn't need an object—to a transitive verb, which does need an object. So, I can just wail, or I can bewail an unfortunate circumstance.

This is also what's happening in the word **"begrudge"**: Grudge was first a verb—originally *grutch*, or the Middle English *grucchen*—and it meant "to grumble or murmur in complaint." So, if to "grudge" is to grumble, then the transitive form in "I begrudge you your success" means that your success causes me to grumble.

Be- is also privative in the word **"bemused,"** which means "puzzled" or "confused." The base word here is "muse" in the sense of musing on or pondering something, so to be amused literally means that something is holding your attention because it's interesting to you, causing you to muse on it, and to be bemused is literally to have your ability to muse or think about a subject taken away by confusion.

Be- words were immensely popular in the 15th and 16th centuries. Some especially charming ones that don't get nearly enough modern airtime:

bethwack: "thrash soundly"
betongue: "verbally thrash someone"
befool: "make a fool of"
beshrew: "deprave, pervert, or corrupt"

Kadigans and placeholder names

Words like **thingamajig**, **whatsit**, and **doohickey** are called "placeholder names" or "kadigans."

The origin of kadigan isn't clear. Some suggest it could somehow be related to the generic word "gin," as in a "cotton gin." This kind of gin is not related to the drink; it's a shortening of the word "engine." But it may be related to the Irish or Welsh name Cadigan, suggesting that it might refer to someone who was once well known for using kadigans frequently.

If this is actually the origin of the word "kadigan," it would make kadigan itself a kadigan. That's because placeholder names don't have to be nonsense words like **thingamabob**. The generic names **John Doe** and **Jane Doe** are also examples of kadigans because they take the place of actual names. The tech brand Apple uses **Johnny** and **Jane Appleseed** as kadigans in its products.

You could also consider a recurring fictional brand to be a kadigan. The company **Acme**, for instance, shows up in classic Warner Bros. cartoons, much to the dismay of Wile E. Coyote. Acme means "the highest point" in Greek and is a plausible company name, albeit an ironic one given the constant failure of its products. (There are many real companies called Acme, but the cartoon Acme is not named after a specific one.)

Another example is the fictional cigarette brand Morley, which is based on Marlboro, and appears in *The Twilight Zone*, *Friends*, and *Seinfeld*.

The generic Latin *lorem ipsum* text used in publishing and graphic design is also an example of a kadigan. It is a nonsense corruption of a first-century BCE text by the Roman statesman Cicero.[3]

---

[3] Marcus Tullius Cicero, *De Officiis*, trans. Walter Miller (Cambridge, MA: Harvard University Press, 1913).

Kadigans can also be numbers: **"Umpteen"** stands in for any annoyingly large number, as in the phrase "for the umpteenth time."

There are also geographical kadigans: People use the word **"podunk"** to mean a town in the middle of nowhere. It comes from the name of the Native American Podunk people, who lived in a marshy, remote area of Connecticut that is near what is now Hartford. In their language, Podunk means "where you sink in mire." It became a kadigan thanks to an 1846 humor column called "Letters from Podunk" in the *Daily National Pilot*, which was published in Buffalo, New York. Writers like Mark Twain picked it up and further popularized it.

A similar example of a geographical kadigan is **"the boondocks"** or, in short, "the boonies" as a word for a rural area. It's from the Tagalog word *bundok*, meaning "mountain," which American soldiers borrowed while stationed in the Philippines as a word meaning "a wild, remote place." Today, boondocking remains a word for camping in the wilderness outside of a designated campground, and during World War II, boondockers was a word for field boots.

Unpaired words

We often say we are **overwhelmed** or **underwhelmed**, but did you know that you can, in fact, be just "whelmed"? Etymologically speaking at least.

Overwhelmed and **underwhelmed** are examples of **unpaired words**, or words that look like they should exist without their prefixes or suffixes—but don't, or at least very rarely do.

The root word here is, of course, *whelm*, which comes from the Old English *hwielfan*, originally meaning to "cover over," "overthrow," or "submerge completely," as in a ship in rough water.

That means that whelm once meant the same thing as overwhelm does now, and "over" was simply a repetitive intensifier.

So, if you are whelmed, you probably feel like you are being battered like a ship on a stormy sea, but if you're overwhelmed, you probably feel like the waves are even more intense, threatening to swallow you up.

And if you're underwhelmed, you're likely bored because your metaphorical sea just isn't choppy enough.

Similarly, we have **exuberant** but not "uberant." Still, it's a perfectly logical word with the potential for use in English. After all, exuberant is hyperbolic: the Latin *uberare* means "to be fruitful," and the *ex-* in the Latin *exuberare* is an intensifier that gives it the sense of "abundant" and "growing luxuriously."

Many unpaired words are also **orphaned negatives**, because they are not commonly used without negative affixes such as *de-*, *dis-*, or *-less*. Like other unpaired words, they create a **lexical gap** because it seems as though the word without the negative affixes ought to exist.

Here are a few examples of interesting unpaired words and orphaned negatives that imply the existence of related words without affixes—along with some conjecture about what those words would mean if they were in more common use.

Exasperate / Asperate

Exasperate, meaning "to frustrate or annoy someone", entered English in the 16th century directly from the Latin *exasperare*, literally "to roughen" and figuratively reflecting the English sense, with the root *asper* meaning "rough." The *ex-* prefix is an intensifier meaning "thoroughly." Due to the meaning of *asper*, to "asperate" would also mean "to make rough." Note that this word is not related to aspirate, which is from the Latin *aspirare* "to breathe upon" (*ad-* + *spirare* "to breathe") or aspersion, which means "to sprinkle upon" (*ad-* + *spargere* "sprinkle, strew"). Exasperate does, however, have a relative in asperity, meaning "a hardship," implying a literal "rough patch" in life.

Disgust / Gust

The word "disgust" arrived in English in the 16th century from the French *desgoust* (*des-* "opposite of" + *gouster* "taste"), and its Latin root is Latin *gustare* "to taste." So "gust," if it existed in English, would probably also mean "taste."

Improvise / Provise

The word that ultimately inspired improv comedy was drawn from early 19th-century Italian theater, specifically the term *improvisare*, "to sing or speak in the moment or ex tempore"—that is, to perform without preparation. To "provise," then, would be to prepare, which we use in the noun form "provisions"—necessary supplies. The Latin word *provisus*, which forms the heart of this word, means "foreseen."

Ineffable / Effable

Adopted directly from Old French in the 14th century, ineffable describes something that is beyond expression due to its greatness (sadly not because you are unable to give an eff about it). This word's Latin elements make it look like a double negative at first glance: *in-* "not, opposite of" + *effari* "to utter." Something "effable," by that logic, would be something you are able to speak about, as opposed to the speechlessness implied by ineffable.

Nonchalant / Chalant

The verb *chaloir* in French means "to care about" or "to matter to." So, if someone calls you "nonchalant," that suggests that nothing matters to you, or at least that your behavior suggests a lack of interest in what's around you, while calling you "chalant" would (hypothetically) mean you're interested or emotionally invested.

Nonplussed / Plussed

Nonplus is Latin for "no more," suggesting that a person who is nonplussed is in such a state of surprise and confusion that they have "no more" to say or do. To be "plussed," then, would suggest an ability or motivation to take further action.

Reckless / Reck

"Reck," if it were in use, would mean "care" or "consideration." It's originally from Old English *reccan*, "to take care of" or "to be interested in," which lives on today as the word "reckon," but notably not "reck." So, to be reckless is to behave without care or consideration for safety or consequences. This word is a strong example of an orphaned negative because it doesn't have an opposite like "reckful."

Ruthless / Ruth

Ruth is a noun form of the word "rue," which means "to bitterly regret something," as in the phrase "you'll rue the day." A ruthless person doesn't regret their actions, no matter how awful.

While "ruthless" does have an opposite in the word "rueful," and therefore isn't precisely an orphaned negative, "ruth" is not typically found without *-less* in English.

Rue and ruth share a root, but they may have entered English separately—rue being the older word and appearing in Old English; ruth from Old Norse and appearing in the 1200s—and melded together, modeled after the pairing of the adjective "true" with the noun "truth."

As for the name Ruth, it is unrelated. It's a Hebrew name and is thought to be related to the Aramaic *re'th*, a woman who is your "friend" or "companion."

Unwieldy / Wieldy

"Wieldy," or rather *wielde*, is an Old English word meaning "active" or "vigorous" but it didn't stick around. In the 14th century, unwieldy meant "powerless" or "without strength." Someone who lacks strength may be clumsy with a weapon or heavy tool. Hence, by the 16th century, unwieldy had evolved into a word for clumsiness or gracelessness, or—in the sense that persists today—something that is difficult to handle gracefully due to its size.

Wistful / Wist

"Wist" is a largely archaic term meaning "to know," from the Old English verb *witan* of the same meaning. It became associated with bittersweet melancholy or nostalgia through the Middle and Early Modern English term *had-I-wiste* or *haddywyst*, a noun meaning "regret for a rash action," especially in the common turn of phrase "had-I-wiste cometh ever too late," meaning essentially "regret for or knowledge of the rashness of one's actions always comes too late."

Nonce words

What happens if you use a word such as "whelm" or "plussed" in conversation? You'd be using a **nonce word**, also known as an **occasionalism**. (Before your jaw hits the floor, please note that this sort of "nonce" predates the British slang sense of "nonce" by many centuries, and the two are unrelated. And for those who are unaware, this more modern sense of "nonce" is used in British prison slang to refer to a particularly terrible class of sex offender.)

Nonce words and occasionalisms are relatively rare in everyday speech and writing. Often, they're created for a particular situation and are meant to be funny or intentionally esoteric.

If you say you're feeling "whelmed," for instance, the people you're speaking to will likely understand you to be making a humorous reference to the fact that "whelmed" is rarely used without *over-* or *under-* affixed to it.

Nonce is from the Old English phrase *for þan anes* "for the once," which became *for þe naness*, "for a special occasion" in Middle English (see: rebracketing for the shift of the *n*). The Old English *anes* is related to words such as "an," "one," and "none." The *Oxford English Dictionary*'s first editor, James Murray, was the first to use this word to refer to occasionalisms, writing that they were created "for the nonce."

Nonce words have an implied meaning, at least in context. A **nonsense word**, by contrast, is a nonce word without a meaning.

Neologisms, or new words introduced into widespread usage, often start out as nonce words. For instance, rizz, a term referring to "style, charm, or attractiveness" or "the ability to attract a romantic or sexual partner" and ostensibly short for "charisma," was a nonce word introduced by YouTuber Kai Cenat in 2021. Because only he initially used the term, it was a nonce word unique to his content. But rizz soon took off like wildfire across TikTok and beyond, eventually becoming the Oxford Word of the Year in 2023 and the name of an AI-powered dating app—so it is no longer a nonce word or even a neologism, but a widely accepted and recognized term.

Pseudowords are nonsense words that are easy to pronounce and plausibly could be words but aren't in use—even if a meaning can be inferred given the context. They can be truly random, or they can have an inspiration.

Many of the words that Lewis Carroll included in the poem "Jabberwocky" (1871) are (or were) pseudowords; he would—in some cases, much later in letters and comments—explain the meaning and inspiration for many of them, revealing them to be portmanteaus or inventions inspired by similar English words. For instance, "frabjous" is said to be inspired by "fair," "fabulous," and "joyous." Carroll did say, however, that he had no logical explanation for the name of the "vorpal sword" (see: portmanteau).

Pseudowords may also be called **"wug words"** after the Wug Test, which was developed in 1958 by psycholinguist Jean Berko Gleason as a means of testing children's ability to apply the morphological rules of English.[4] Researchers showed children a simple illustration of a nonspecific creature with the phrase "This is a wug." The children were then shown an image showing two of the creatures side by side, with the caption "Now there is another one. There are two of them. There are two ________." Another question in the Wug Test is: "A man who 'zibs' is a ________?"

The test revealed that children were able to complete the sentences using forms such as plurals ("wugs") and agent noun forms ("zibber") even given the unfamiliar pseudowords, suggesting that we internalize many morphological features of the languages we speak at a very young age.

Sniglets are another type of nonce word. These words, named by comedian Rich Hall on the HBO series *Not Necessarily the News* (1983–90), are created when someone makes up an intentionally humorous word for something with no existing word in the dictionary, Sniglets' definitions are part of their humor. They may be puns, portmanteaus, compounds, or imitative words, but their distinguishing feature is the intentional humor that imbues the word and its definition. For instance, Hall lists "doork" as "a person who pushes on a door marked 'pull'" and "lotshock" as "the act of parking your car, walking away, and then watching it roll past you." Barbara Wallraff, author and editor at *The Atlantic*, has

[4] Jean Berko Gleason, "The Child's Learning of English Morphology," *WORD* 14, no. 2–3 (1958): 150–77.

also called them "word fugitives" because they are words that are "wanted" but don't exist.[5]

A **hapax legomenon** (Greek: "said only once") is a word or expression that's found only once—in a book, in an author's lifework, in an entire language. A word can be both a nonce word *and* a hapax legomenon, but a hapax legomenon doesn't need to be a made-up word. For instance, this, right now, is the only time I will ever write the word "koala" in this book, making it a hapax legomenon for our present purposes. I've now written "hapax legomenon" five times, though, so it isn't one.

Pleonasms and tautologies

Pleonasms are linguistic redundancies, which is when you essentially say the same thing twice—like I just did there. The word itself comes from the Greek *pleonasmos* meaning "more than enough."

Terms like "free gift," "tuna fish," and "safe haven" are common pleonasms. In most cases, a gift is free; a tuna is a fish; and "haven" implies safety, so saying the full phrase is redundant.

There are also syntactic pleonasms, which is when grammar rules and common parlance make a word optional. Take the phrase "I know that you will do great." If you drop the "that," the meaning wouldn't change, and including "that" might sound overly formal.

Sometimes it's not entirely clear that a pleonasm is a pleonasm because the redundancy gets lost in translation:

- The "Milky Way galaxy" is a pleonasm because galaxy literally means "milky" (from the Greek phrase *galaxias kyklos*, literally meaning "milky circle").

[5] Barbara Wallraff, "Word Fugitives," *The Atlantic*, July/August 2008.

- If you say, "please RSVP," you're saying "please" twice, once in English and once in French, since RSVP stands for "*Répondez, s'il vous plaît*, or "Please respond."
- Despite the distinction between the words' meanings today, "head chef" is technically redundant because *chef* means "chief, leader, head" in French.
- La Brea means "the tar"—so "the La Brea Tar Pits" literally means "the the tar tar pits."

Geographic features and place names are common pleonasms. The "River Avon" means "River River" because "Avon" comes from a Welsh word for river, and the Connecticut River is similarly pleonastic because "Connecticut" is from a Mohican word meaning "at the long tidal river." The same thing happens in the Sahara Desert (Sahara is a transliteration of the Arabic word for "desert"—thus, the "desert desert") and the Faroe Islands (from the Faroese word *Føroyar*, which already means "sheep island"—thus, the "sheep island islands").

Pleonasms are usually not considered incorrect, either because they're widely used and accepted, or because they can be used intentionally for effect. If I say, "I built this house with my own hands," the word "own" isn't necessary, and is therefore a pleonasm, duplicating the meaning of "my," but it emphasizes my agency in building the house.

Shakespeare is always throwing in pleonasms for effect and to make his verse flow better. One of the most famous ones is the line from *Julius Caesar* that goes "This was the most unkindest cut of all" (3.2.183). "Most unkindest" is both redundant and grammatically incorrect, but it is intentionally done to emphasize just how unkind the metaphorical cut was—and to ensure that the iambs are properly pentametered.

Sometimes pleonasms are also tautologies (Greek *tautologos* "repeating what has been said," from elements *tauto* "the same" + *logos* "speech, saying").

Tautologies aren't just limited to language and rhetoric—there are logical and mathematical tautologies as well. But in the context of language and literature, pleonasm and tautology are used semi-interchangeably.

But, typically, a linguistic redundancy isn't called a tautology unless it seems like a flaw or mistake. As a result, distinguishing a pleonasm from a tautology is pretty subjective because it relies on determining whether the repetition or redundancy is egregious.

For example, phrases like "ATM machine" and "ISBN number" are usually cited as examples of tautologies, while pleonasms are considered to be more acceptable. But, then again, "free gift" is also cited as an example of both a pleonasm and a tautology, so the distinction is murky at best.

It makes one wonder: Would the phrase "pleonastic tautology" be a pleonasm or a tautology, or a pleonastic tautology, or a tautological pleonasm?

Rebracketing

When compound words are broken down into components that don't match up with their etymological sources, it's called "rebracketing."

For instance, because we tend to tack the ending *-copter* on other helicopter-adjacent words like gyrocopter, it's easy to assume that helicopter breaks down into the elements *heli* + *copter*, but it's actually more like *helico* + *pter* because it's made up of the Greek elements *hélix*, meaning "spiral," and *pterón*, meaning "wing."

The "wing" element in helicopter is the same one found in the first part of the word "pterodactyl," which literally means "wing finger." (The silent *p* in pterodactyl wasn't silent in Greek, but is in English due to phonotactics, or rules of pronunciation.

Basically, English doesn't like a *p* and a *t* next to each other at the beginning of a word so we pretend the *p* doesn't exist. But phonotactics do allow us to pronounce both *p* and *t* in the middle of the word "helicopter" because the vowels around it give it a more comfortable syllabic break.)

The same is true when you see a *-doodle* type of dog breed, which is always at least partially modeled after "Labradoodle," a portmanteau of "Labrador" and "poodle": Other types of "doodle" dogs, such as a "goldendoodle" (a golden retriever + a poodle) and "bernadoodle" (a Bernese mountain dog + a poodle) ought to logically be "goldenoodles" and "bernoodles," but thanks to rebracketing, they all take the *d* from "Labrador" rather than simply combining the dog names with "poodle" because "labradoodles" were among the first popular poodle hybrids to be so portmanteau'ed.

Another example. Have you ever heard the word "nickname" and wondered who Nick is? At first glance, you might think, "Well, Nick is short for Nicholas so that's uhh, it. Nick is a nickname—thus, nickname." But it turns out there *is* no Nick. There never was a Nick. Nick doesn't exist. (Sorry, Nick.)

Nickname is from the Middle English phrase *an eke name*, meaning "an additional name." (Note: This *eke* persists in verb form in the phrase "eke out," which means "to stretch one's resources.")

Then we hit the 1400s, when *eke* is on a different journey and shifting in pronunciation from *eh-keh* to *eek*, and instead of "an eke name," people hear "a nekename," which eventually became "a nickname."

This has happened a good deal with the word "an" when it precedes words that begin with vowels:

"An apron" was originally "a napron."
"An adder" was originally "a nadder."
"An auger" was originally "a nauger."
"An umpire" was originally "a numpire."

Contrary to popular belief, "an orange" was never "a norange" in English—but it was rebracketed earlier in its international journey.

The "n" was dropped in Italian (*narancia* became *arancia*) before it ever entered English, which got it from the already n-less Old French *orange* or *orenge*. (See "orange" for more.)

More examples of rebracketing include…

- **hamburg | er → -burger** (e.g. cheeseburger)
- **cybern | etics → cyber-** (e.g. cyberspace), from the Greek kybernetes "steersman"
- **al | coholic → -holic** (e.g. workaholic), from Arabic al-kuhul "kohl"

Retronyms

A retronym is a term that becomes necessary when human advancements require us to clarify that we mean *the old thing* as opposed to *the fancy new thing*. This term was coined by journalist and former National Public Radio president Frank Mankiewicz.[6]

For example, we now often say "acoustic guitar" as opposed to "electric guitar." But before electric guitars, all guitars were acoustic, so no one ever called them that. "Acoustic guitar" is a retronym since it only became necessary once music technology made it necessary to distinguish between the two. Before Sputnik, the word "satellite" used to refer to naturally occurring objects in orbit; now those same naturally occurring objects are called "natural satellites." Other examples: analog

[6] William Safire, "Retronym," *The New York Times*, January 7, 2007.

clocks, cloth diapers, manual transmissions, landline phones, indie bookstores, manual typewriters, snail mail, print books, and plain text.

The same phenomenon can happen to people. If you have a kid and give them the same name that you have, they become Junior or the Second, and you retronymically become Senior or the First.

Reduplication

Before we "zag" into another chapter, let's consider why we pair that syllable with "zig." This phenomenon is called **reduplication**—when a syllable, word, or phrase is either repeated or repeated with a slight alteration.

We reduplicate terms for many expressive reasons. For instance, reduplication can help us express progression and intensification. We might say it's getting "darker and darker" to create a sense of increasing foreboding, or we might say that a planet is a "long, long way" from Earth to stress how mind-bogglingly faraway it is.

We might also use reduplication to clarify something unusual from something more common: "Do you mean a big cat or a cat cat?" would help us clarify whether we're talking about a lion or a house cat.

Apart from these specific use cases, reduplication may simply be fundamental to the human experience. It's everywhere, from "putt-putt" (minigolf) to "aye aye!" to "mama" and "papa," suggesting that our impulse to repeat syllables and sounds may chart back to our earliest days of consciousness.

Reduplication can also involve a bit of rhyming.

Yiddish introduced phrases like "fancy schmancy" into English. Referring to something as "fancy schmancy" suggests a kind of (often gentle) mockery for that which is fancy;

reduplication here gives us a sense of sarcasm or disdain. Humor—whether it's biting or more whimsical—is often the motivation behind reduplication, as in terms like "holy moly" or "razzle dazzle."

You may notice that many ablaut, or letter-changing (German *Ablaut*, literally "off-sound"), reduplications have a common pattern, and here's where we get to words such as zigzag, chit-chat, pitter-patter, and riffraff. In ablaut reduplication—so termed by Jacob Grimm, of Brothers Grimm fame—we tend to place higher vowels ahead of lower vowels when sequencing them. The usual order is *i*, then *a*, then *o*, as in tic-tac-toe, though the *a* word is optional, as shown in terms such as flip-flop and hip-hop. Ablaut reduplication is so ingrained in us that it can even cause us to violate the most typical order of adjectives in English (opinion, size, age, shape, color, origin, material, purpose), creating phrases such as "big bad wolf."

Part 2
Twists and Turns

Surprise and Delight in the Origins of Everyday Words

7

One Word to Another

Words That Went on Journeys of Meaning

Words often begin in one place, at one time, with one meaning, and then veer off in entirely unexpected directions. In this chapter, we'll trace a select few etymologies into the wilderness whence they came and demonstrate the ways in which meaning can bend and evolve across time and space, for even the most ordinary terms.

Read on to untangle the mysteries of "mystery," the brainlessness of "clever," and learn what a "thing" actually is. As we progress, we'll get wild with unexpectedly zoological etymology, examine words that still nod to the history of printing, explore some colorful words, and more.

Hard of head and hardy like a fool

Foolhardy literally means "brave but stupid." Today, hardy often carries connotations of sturdiness and resilience, but in the 13th century it was more commonly used as a synonym for bold, daring or fearless—essentially describing mental and emotional fortitude rather than physical durability. The word "foolhardy," or *folhardi*, describes someone who is foolish in their bravery.

Its Old French predecessor, *hardi*, could also mean "presumptuous," perhaps drawing upon the same notion as the term "hard-headed" for someone stubbornly confident today.

Innuendo, beginning to end-o

The word **"innuendo"** originally had nothing to do with sexual suggestiveness. Rather, it was—and still is—a legal term often found in libel, slander, and defamation cases. It literally means "a nod forward" and points to the defamatory nature of a given statement.

Suppose you're a famous actor who stars in a lot of Spielberg action movies and whose hair is blue. If someone wrote a newspaper article saying "Spielberg's biggest blue-haired action star embezzled $20 million," even if they didn't say your name, people would assume the writer meant you. If you haven't actually embezzled $20 million, you could go to court and argue that this statement defames you, "by innuendo," and damages your reputation. Innuendo was used this way in legal cases as early as the 1400s, often in cases of gossip, which was seen as a form of slander—especially when it was against important people.

The term "innuendo" was also introduced in parenthetical and explanatory clauses, in which case it meant the same thing as the phrase "to wit" or "which is to say."

Why mystery is a closed case

The word **"mystery"** and its cousin **"mystic"** both trace back to Latin and Greek words (*mysterium* and *mustērion*, respectively) for a secret, especially religious rites (mysteries) performed by secret orders. The Greek root *myein* means "to close" or "to shut."

Even in English, "mystery" was first used in a theological context, referring to divine revelations and mystical truths, but it was quickly extended to refer to any sort of secret or hidden thing.

Stories with mysterious circumstances, dark crimes, and surprising twists have, of course, existed for centuries, but the typical mystery genre structure and plot arose in the mid-1800s. At that time, they were typically called detective stories. The term "mystery" didn't become the name of the genre until 1908.

Edgar Allan Poe's 1841 short story "The Murders in the Rue Morgue" is often cited as the first true work of modern detective or mystery fiction in the English language. Poe himself called it a story of **ratiocination**, or reasoning.

One reason that mystery fiction was rare or unusual before the mid-1800s was that most police forces were smaller, and crimes were either solved right away or not at all.

But urbanization and industrialization brought a lot of people together in one place, creating more opportunities for crime, which in time yielded more robust law enforcement—including inspectors and detectives. Their work captured the imagination of the public and led to both true crime and, on the fiction side, modern mysteries and their derivatives.

Sorry, I've got a thing

When you can't make it to some event or you're just plain avoiding it, you might say something like, "Nah, I have a thing?"

Well, in Old English, a "thing" (*þing*) was a word for a formal meeting or council of tribal leaders.

In fact, "thing" didn't become a word for a generic inanimate object until the 1300s.

So, in Old English, if you were, say, telling your friends you couldn't make it to the recitation of *Beowulf* down at the village tavern, saying you have a "thing" to get to instead would carry far more weight than it does today.

Into oblivion

You know, I used to know the origin of the word "oblivion," but I seem to have forgotten it. Oh yeah—it comes from the Latin *oblivio*, meaning "forgetfulness." The root of *oblivio* is debated, but the most commonly accepted theory is that it comes from a base word meaning "smooth," so that when you add the prefix *ob-*, you get the meaning "to smooth over," perhaps suggesting wiping something away. It's that blank smoothness that gives us the sense of "oblivion" as a state of empty nothingness. That's why sending something into oblivion means sending it to a place or reducing it to a state where it will be forgotten by history.

Similarly, in 15th-century English, the adjective "oblivious" was used specifically to describe someone who was extremely forgetful. In the 1800s, the meaning of the word broadened, so that now it doesn't just refer to forgetfulness but also being generally unaware or just sort of spacey.

The word "oblivion" was also often used politically in the 15th and 16th centuries. The phrase "Acts of Oblivion" referred to instances in which the law intentionally overlooked certain crimes or offenses.

In an interesting parallel, the word "amnesty" comes from the Greek word for forgetfulness—*amnestia*—which is also the source of the word "amnesia."

While we're on the subject, the English word "forget" is pretty interesting. The prefix here is a specialized sense of *for-* that means "away," as also found in "forgo," which means "to refrain" or literally go away from something. "Get" in this case is from a sense of the Old English *gietan* meaning "to grasp." So, to forget is to grasp at something that has gone away.

More on the prefix *ob-*

The direction in which this Latin prefix points varies depending on the word:

Obnoxious breaks down into *ob-*, here meaning "toward," + *noxa*, meaning "hurt" or "injury." This word means "annoying" now, but its Latin predecessor was more intense, meaning "injurious" or "hurtful."

Obfuscate breaks down into *ob-*, here meaning "in front of, before" + *fuscare* "to make dark."

Obliterate originally meant "erase, blot out (writing)," from *ob-*, here meaning "against" + *littera* "letter, script."

Oblige is from ob-, here meaning "to" + *ligare* "to bind," so an obligation is a task to which one is figuratively bound.

One you may not know is **obambulation**, from *ob-*, here meaning "about" or "around," + *ambulare*, meaning "to walk"—thus "a walking about." It's related to "amble" and "somnambulist," a word for a sleepwalker.

Chess plays the etymological long game

Every variation of the word "check" comes from the game of chess.

And it has a curious association with the word "matador." Matador means "killer" in Spanish, from *matar* "to kill." While it's most likely ultimately from the Latin *mactare* "to kill," it could be from the Arabic *mata* "he died," which also appears in the phrase *shah mat* "the king died"—the source of the word "checkmate," after some folk etymology adaptations to English spelling.

The phrase *shah mat* came into Arabic from Persian, with a twist. In Persian, *mat* meant "to be astonished" and *mata* meant "to die," but *mat* could also be a declined form of *mata*, meaning "he died." So, in Persian, *shah mat* meant "the king [or the shah] is astonished," or left helpless, or stumped. When *shah mat* came into Arabic, and then into English as "checkmate," that *mat* was mistranslated so that it came to mean "the king died."

Like checkmate, the word "check" comes from the game of chess, which is ancient as heck. The English name of the game was adopted from the Old French *esches*, or "chessmen," plural of *eschec*, the name of the game itself, which came, by way of Latin, from (you guessed it) the Persian *shah*, or "king."

The original name of the game was the Sanskrit *chaturanga*, which referred to the four subdivisions of the army back then: elephants, horses, chariots, and foot soldiers. "Shah mat" was what you said when you won, just like today's "checkmate."

The word *eschequier* was Old French for check in chess, which was adopted in English as exchequer, originally a word for a chessboard. Exchequer, and the word "check" or "cheque," as in the slip of paper you use to move money around, evidently came to be associated with finance and government because, in Norman England, people did their accounting on a cloth divided into squares, like a chessboard. Other uses of "check"—like checking something off a list or asking for the check at a restaurant—also appear to have come from this process because counters were placed in certain squares on the cloth to note that the corresponding items had been counted or verified.

Splendid words for every extraordinary occasion

Splendor (or splendour) is as dazzling a word as its meaning suggests it should be. It's first recorded in English (as *splendoure* or *esplendoure*) in the 15th century, and its gleaming offshoots such as splendorous (or splendrous) were equally popular in the following centuries, most often as words for godly light and glory.

Resplendent is fairly common today, but the *re-* prefix is an intensifier of the earlier *splendent* or *splendaunt*, which meant more or less the same thing as splendid.

Splendid, meanwhile, was once marginally more splendrous. It was first recorded as "splendidious" around the same time as "splendor" first appeared, with the more complex spelling persisting for many years thereafter. For example, in a series of poems starring popular biblical figures, the Elizabethan poet Michael Drayton describes Moses descending from Mount Sinai with "His browes encircled with splendidious rayes."

This overabundance of meanings and spellings is due to the fact that the word shone into English from Old French and directly from Latin. In both languages, *splendor* meant "brilliance" and "brightness" much as it does in English today; both the Latin and Old French words *splendor* are from the Latin *splendere*, meaning "to be bright" or "to shine."

The similarly effusive word **"gorgeous"** is a throatful—literally. It was adopted from Middle French, but its original source is the Old French *gorge* "throat." In the 1500s, and for several centuries after that, a long, slender neck—and, of course, the sparkly things you wore around it—was considered the height of beauty and fashion. The Old French *gorge* is also the source of the English homonyms "gorge," as in to gorge yourself or eat ravenously, and "gorge" as in a crevice or canyon, which is so named because it is a narrow passage, just like the throat.

Fabulous, on the other hand, literally means "like something from a fable." As recently as the 1940s, it was used in the same way we'd use fantastical or mythical today. The most fabulous people at the time, then, would have been the characters in myths and stories, or the people who told fables, like the Greek storyteller Aesop, who was known as a "fabulist." Because things that were fabulous were mythical, the word also held the meaning "made up, unbelievable, or incredible," which eventually led to today's sense of something unbelievably amazing, stunning, or attractive. Of course, the older sense does occasionally shine through today when something described as "fabulous" is especially over-the-top and fantastical.

Electric like amber

The word "electric" comes from the Modern Latin *electricus*, meaning "resembling amber," originally from the Greek word for amber, *ēlektron*. Modern Latin words are those coined for use in sciences, philosophy, law, and the arts well after the Classical era.

The Latin *electricus* was first used by physician and scientist William Gilbert in a text published in the year 1600 on the subject of magnetism. Gilbert used *electricus* to describe the observation that, when you rub amber against some substances like wool or a cat's fur, it sticks to the amber. We now know this is due to static electricity generated by friction, but at the time, amber was believed to be magnetic. Thereafter, other writers such as Francis Bacon used the English word "electric" to describe supposedly (and actually) magnetic materials that attracted other objects. The word "electricity" first appeared in 1646 with much the same meaning. It was thought to be a property, sort of like elasticity: Amber and other materials were "electrics" and had "electricity," meaning that they attracted other objects, just like "elastics" are objects with "elasticity" or the ability to stretch and bend without breaking.

"Electricity" began to take on the sense it has today—referring to electromagnetic energy, current, and energy flow—in the 1700s, culminating in the 1800s with the invention of the light bulb.

How much is a word coinage worth?

We adopted the word "coin," like so many other words, from Old French—and, over the years, subjected it to a variety of exciting letter salad spellings including *coyne*, *coign*, *coigne*, and *quoin*. It's originally from the Latin *cuneus*, meaning "corner" or "wedge," and indeed that was its original meaning in Old French (*coing* "corner, wedge") and in Middle English as well.

But what do coins have to do with corners and wedges?

Coins are made by stamping symbols onto pieces of metal using dies. Nowadays, this is done with machines, but back then you had to do it by hand using a hammer and two dies. The bottom one of these dies was originally shaped like a wedge or functioned similarly to a wedge.

Echoes of this labor-intensive process remain in the idiom "to coin a phrase." When you coin a phrase, you are inventing a new term that then circulates widely—much like minted coins circulating as currency.

This is further proof that an expansive vocabulary represents a literal wealth of words at the tip of your tongue (see: thesaurus).

Kaleidoscopic observations

The word "kaleidoscope" literally means "observer of beautiful things" or "an instrument for seeing beautiful shapes," from the

Greek words *kalos* (beautiful) and *eidos* (shape) plus the Greek and Modern Latin-derived English suffix *-scope* (an instrument for seeing).

The kaleidoscope was invented—and its name coined—by the Scottish scientist and inventor David Brewster in 1815. His invention was wildly popular and sold by the thousands, but before he patented it in 1817, a prototype was shown to opticians in London, who copied it, so Brewster earned almost nothing from his invention.

Still, he hasn't been forgotten. The Brewster Kaleidoscope Society, "a society of artists who design and create kaleidoscopes," still bears his name today.[1]

The clone doesn't fall far from the tree

Clone as a term for producing genetically identical individuals was coined in 1963 by scientist J. B. S. Haldane. It was predated by the horticultural sense of "clon," or clone, the process whereby a new plant is created using cuttings from another. Both are from the Ancient Greek *klōn* "twig."

In botany, "clon" was first used in the 19th century. The final *e* was added in 1903, supposedly to clarify the pronunciation of the long *o* sound.

Botanical cloning is a long-standing practice. It's an important part of the cultivation of the grapes used to make wine; grape vines are propagated from a "mother vine" that has desirable traits.

It's not much of a leap from there to natural/asexual, molecular, cellular, and artificial cloning.

Haldane is credited as the first person to have thought of the genetic basis for the cloning of humans. He thought that human cloning could eventually be used to create superhuman

[1] https://brewstersociety.com

or super-talented individuals. He introduced the word "clone" as a word for genetic duplication, especially of humans, in a 1963 speech entitled "Biological Possibilities for the Human Species in the Next Ten Thousand Years."[2]

Genetic memetics

The word **meme** is modeled after the word "gene" because of the way memes spread and evolve.

It was coined by evolutionary biologist Richard Dawkins in his 1976 book *The Selfish Gene*. While Dawkins focuses on physical evolution and genetics, he also discusses the way ideas are shared and change with time.

Dawkins started with the Greek root *mimos*, which means "imitator" or "actor" and is also the source of words like mime and mimic. He first came up with "mimeme," but wanted a shorter word that sounded more like "gene," so he dropped the first syllable. He also wrote that "meme" could be thought of as being related to the word "memory" (from Latin *memoria*).

Dawkins' new term ultimately gave us the whole field of memetics (a word modeled after genetics), which seeks to explain how ideas propagate. You might associate memes with the internet, but they aren't actually a new thing. They're recurring tropes, clichés, archetypes, and other ideas in lots of different forms that get passed from one person to another.

Even though he wrote his book in the 1970s, the primary example Dawkins gives aligns well with social media. Dawkins writes that the way a hummable tune gets stuck in your head and the heads of countless others in your community makes

[2] J. B. S. Haldane, "Biological Possibilities for the Human Species in the Next Ten Thousand Years," in G. Wolstenholme (ed.), *Man and His Future* (London: J. & A. Churchill, 1963), 337–61.

it a meme—just like the songs on vertical video platforms. And, of course, these sounds get mashed up with other sounds and evolve as they spread, just like genes. So, sounds, dances, and other recurring formats on platforms such as TikTok and Instagram behave just like classic Dawkinsian memes.

Another example Dawkins shares is God, or any god from any religion, which he describes as an ancient meme—a shared character, figure, or idea—that appears many times and with many variations throughout history as people attempt to rationalize the purpose and source of their existence.

For exploring out loud

The word **"explore"** is rather more dramatic than you might expect. It literally means "to cry out." The base word is the Latin *plorare*, meaning "to cry out" or "to weep." It's thought that it was originally a hunters' term, with the idea being that hunters could spread out in a given area and shout or cry out to one another as they were scouting for game.

That means that the word "explore" is related to deplore and deplorable, literally something you yell about or cry out against. It's also related to implore, meaning "to beg" or, literally, "to weep upon."

There's one other theory, that the base word for explore is *pluere*, meaning "to flow"—in which case explore would literally mean "to flow out." I think this theory is nicer, but the evidence for it isn't as strong.

Clever—what a low word!

Did you know that **clever** was once a slangy, casual, and even uncivilized word?

In Samuel Johnson's 1755 *A Dictionary of the English Language*—which was regarded as the most definitive and important English dictionary until the first full publication of the *Oxford English Dictionary* 173 years later, even though it wasn't especially impartial—he describes "clever" as "a low word, scarcely ever used but in burlesque" and one "without a settled meaning."

And it wasn't especially about smarts originally, either. It originally referred to dexterity or nimbleness of the hands—but not the mind—and had several additional senses including "attractive" well into the 18th century.

It's thought to be related to the Old English *clifer* "claw, hand," also implying dexterity, and the Old Norse *kleyfr* "easy to split," which would mean it's related to cleft, cleave, and clove (as of garlic).

Dude, where's my macaroni?

Dude. Have you ever wondered about the origin of the word **"dude"**?

It's first recorded in the late 1800s as a word for a man who is foppish and fastidious, meaning someone who is tidy, fancy, and cultured.

Dudes at this time were reflective of the aesthetic movement of the late 19th century, which championed pure beauty and "art for art's sake."

Many of the men who fell into this stereotype were high-society city dwellers who lived in the American Northeast—that is, they were Yankees.

In fact, the word "dude" is thought to have originally been a shortening of "Yankee Doodle." In the lyrics of the song, which were written to poke fun at Yankee troops during the French and Indian War (1754–63), you'll note that Yankee Doodle is described as a dandy who is a fabulous dancer and wears a dashing feather in his cap. The term "doodle" is thought to be from a Low German word, *Dudeltopf*, meaning "fool" or "simpleton." (This doodle isn't the "doodle" in labradoodle—see: rebracketing.)

Thus, dude wasn't exactly a flattering term in its early years.

Speaking of which, Yankee Doodle "**call[s] it macaroni**" because macaroni was also used as a term for the aesthetic choices of men whose luxurious lifestyles involved wearing the latest styles and enjoying fancy foreign foods—including macaroni. The pre-Revolutionary "Yankee Doodle Dandy," written from a British perspective, poked fun at American soldiers who were supposedly more concerned about their outfits and their snacks than developing their skills on the battlefield.

The macaroni craze crossed the Atlantic as well. A group of fashionable young British fellows in the 1700s, often represented as sporting the enormous macaroni wig, were known as the Macaroni Club, which was famous for reveling and indulging in foreign goods and apparel. Beyond the towering wig, think of fine, Rococo garments in snug sizes and flamboyant colors, dainty footwear, and tassels galore. Many historians consider them to be emblematic of wealthy British queer culture of the era, in part due to their fondness for French aristocratic style, which was considered effeminate by many in both Britain and the Americas.

Due to stigma surrounding these gentlemen's lifestyles at the time, macaroni was also used as a pejorative term along with words such as "fop" and "dandy" for men whose styles blended cultural influences and challenged gender norms.

In a similar vein, **macaronic language** describes expressions that blend languages. The term was coined in the 15th century to describe writing that blended Latin with a "vernacular" language like English.

The word "macaroni" likely came from a popular, late-15th-century satiric poem by Italian poet Tifi Odasi called *Macaronea.* The title paid homage to a type of dumpling or pasta (*maccerone*, which would later inspire the name of the modern-day noodle) that people of the lower classes ate. To wealthy people, this implied a vulgar but humorous blending of a common language (in this case, Italian) with Latin, which was used by the more educated classes, especially in academic, literary, and scientific settings.

Nowadays, the term "macaroni language" refers to almost any blending of language, to the point where most hybrid words can be termed "macaroni words."

Anyway, back to "dude," which emerged in the century following the rise of macaroni style.

In the early 1900s, "dudes" from the northeastern United States started vacationing in the American West—and the resorts where these city slickers went for an "authentic" Western experience were called "dude ranches."

The way we use the term "dude" today—as a word for any guy or even as a gender-neutral term—is thanks to 1960s slang in Black American communities, which then got picked up by students at universities in California and spread from there around the world.

Amelioration and perjoration

When, over time, the usage of a word becomes more socially acceptable or is perceived as less harsh, offensive, or pejorative, this process is called **amelioration**. "Dude," which once had a mildly pejorative edge, is one such word; "nice," addressed later in this chapter, is another. Others include many religious oaths, such as "damn" or taking the name of God or Christ in vain, which are typically seen as milder insults in more secular societies.

When a word is made more pejorative or insulting over time, it's called **pejoration**. This has happened with swear words including "shit," which in its Old and early Middle English forms was simply a word for the act of defecation. It gradually came to be perceived as rude following the influx of Norman French into Old English—likely because of the class dynamics between the French-speaking ruling class and the Anglo-Saxon-speaking lower classes.

Quizzical quizzes

Pop quiz: What do you think the original meaning of the word "quiz" was? If you know the answer, someone from the 1700s might call you a "quiz."

The word "quiz," as in the brief test you take in school, is from the earlier term *quies*, which meant to give a student an oral test or examination. It's thought to be a contraction of the Latin *qui es?* meaning "who are you?"

In the 1800s, *qui es?* was the first question you would be asked in an oral exam in Latin. Over time, *qui es* was shortened to one word and then transformed into quiz.

But this isn't the first recorded sense of the word "quiz." Several decades before that, it emerged as university slang for an "odd person," especially (but not exclusively) someone who is unusually studious.

It's documented as early as 1780 as a word more or less meaning "weirdo," and in 1782 it's found describing those "who take a pleasure in conversing on letters; but they are solitary mortals, and themselves are stigmatized."[3]

In a 1783 edition of *The London Magazine* there's a humorous article poking fun at university culture, and it says that a "quiz" is anyone who "thinks, speaks or acts differently from the rest of the world in general."

> ...to confine myself within the precincts of the university, from whence I believe this amphibious creature originally sprung: I conceive him to be one of those dull, pedantic, spiritless animals, who jog on in the same beaten track, pulled along, as it were, by rules, and frightened, every step he advances, with a continual terror of sconces and impositions. Influenced in his conduct rather through a dread of punishment, than through a real desire of doing what is right.[4]

The passage also suggests that "quiz" is derived from the Latin question *Vir bonus est quis?* ("Who is a good man?"), a rhetorical question famously posed by the Roman poet Horace: "Who is a good man? He who keeps the decrees of the fathers, and both human and divine laws."[5]

So quiz could—at least from some perspectives—have originally meant "a good person who gets teased," like a "goody two shoes."

There's also a song literally called "The Etymology of Quiz," by Charles Dibdin in the mid-1800s. It doesn't actually describe any etymology, but it offers a range of meanings for the word "quiz," saying that anyone odd, comical, strange,

---

[3] Vicesimus Knox, *Essays Moral and Literary* (1783).

[4] *The London Magazine: Or, Gentleman's Monthly Intelligencer*, November 1783.

[5] Horace, Epistle XVI: To Quinctius, in *Satires and Epistles* (London: Penguin, 2005).

unusually hardworking, or droll—including Dibdin himself—might be called a quiz.

The word Quiz is a sort of a kind of a word
That people apply to some being absurd;
One who seems, as 'twere, oddly your fancy to strike,
In a sort of a fashion you somehow don't like;
A mixture of odd, and of queer, and all that,
Which one hates, just, you know, as some folks hate a cat;
A comical, whimsical, strange, droll-that is,
You know what I mean; 'tis—in short, 'tis a quiz!

Saved by the curfew

Curfew is a variation of Old French *cuevrefeu*, literally "cover fire."

Medieval houses tended to be quite flammable, so it was dangerous to leave your fire burning all night. To avoid all kinds of problems, the town would have someone ring a bell—a curfew bell—to let you know that it was time to start getting ready for bed—and put out your fire. During Norman rule in England, a curfew bell was also a signal to stay indoors—to prevent potential uprisings. The curfew bell is still rung in some towns today.

But you wouldn't want to completely extinguish your fire because the warmth was nice and because you'd want to be able to start your fire up again in the morning. You could either bank your hearth, building a barrier of stones or ashes around the embers and hot coals, which would keep the fire from spreading while it continued to smolder—or you could use a device called a curfew, which was a large bell-shaped device that literally covered the fire. Curfews were also called fire covers or fire bells; they were designed to keep your fire safely going so that you wouldn't have to relight it in the morning.

The Old French *cuevre* (Modern French *couvre*) is also found in the word "(hand)kerchief." A kerchief, or *kovechief* in the 14th century, was (and is) a woman's headcloth, and the word literally means a "head-cover." Therefore, a handkerchief—a cloth kept in the pocket and used with the hands for a variety of sanitary purposes—literally means a "hand-head-covering."

The alarming entrepreneur

Did you know that the word **"entrepreneur"** literally means "undertaker?"

The idea is that an entrepreneur is someone who "undertakes" a challenge or a business venture, or an "enterprise"—which literally means "an undertaking."

These words are both made up of the Old French elements *entre*, which in this context means "under," and *prendre*, meaning "to take."

Now if you speak French, you might be, like, "But, Jess, *entre* means 'between,' not 'under.'" And you are completely correct—today. But prepositions are extremely fluid in their usage and meaning throughout history, and in Old French *entre* could mean "between," "among," "during," or even, occasionally, "under." In fact, *entre* comes from the same PIE root as the English word "under," which also meant "between" or "among" in Old English. And both *entre* and *under* are cognate with the Latin prefix *inter-*, which also means "between" or "in the midst of."

Anyway, back to entrepreneur. If it means "undertaker," why do we have both words?

The Latin-derived French word *entrepreneur* was adopted into English around the 1500s, when the word "undertaker" (which is made up of Germanic elements) already existed in English and meant almost the same thing as entrepreneur: a tradesperson, or someone who "undertakes" a task or profession.

So, at the time, an undertaker wasn't a word for a mortician like it is today in the US (or a word for the person who prepares the body for the undertaker, like in the UK). A mortician, in the American sense, was called a "funeral-undertaker." In the 1600s, the original meaning of undertaker shifted to entrepreneur, while the funerary professional kept the name "undertaker." Why? We don't have any strong evidence for this, but it may be fair to speculate that "undertaker" continued to be associated with death because it's similar to words like "underworld"—and, of course, because they literally take bodies underground.

Perfunctory fungi

Something **perfunctory** is done on autopilot, or without much thought, intention, or effort. One might give a new acquaintance a perfunctory handshake without thinking much about it, or one might perfunctorily say, "You, too!" to the box-office attendant when they say, "Enjoy the movie!"

The elements of this word are the Latin *per-* meaning "through" or "forward," and *fungi* meaning "perform," implying something similar to the idiomatic phrase "going through the motions."

The *fungi* in this word is not related to fungus, but is related to words like function, defunct (meaning "not functioning"), and fungible, which was originally a legal term implying the ability for something to be replaced or used in place of another. (Hence, a nonfungible token, or NFT, is a digital identifier that indicates that a file or digital object is unique and authentic.)

Fungus also comes from Latin, but does not share roots—or a mycelium, as the case may be—with these other words. Instead, it is from the Greek *sphongos*, meaning "sponge." (See where the word "sponge" came from?)

"Fungus" often meant, simply, "mushroom" in the 1500s, even though there are many more types of fungi.

Mushroom, meanwhile, has no relation to the words "mush" or "room," and its origin is a mystery. It can be traced back through Anglo-French (*musherun*) and Old French (*meisseron*), and perhaps Late Latin (*mussirionem*)—but beyond that we just don't know. One likely theory is that it is from the French *mousse*, meaning "moss," "froth," or "scum"—the same as the foofy dessert, so named for its texture—which would mean it's from the Latin *mulsa*, meaning "mead," from *mulsus* meaning "mixed with honey," from *mel* meaning "honey." If that's the case, "mushroom" is ultimately related to the English word "mellifluous" (see: mellifluous).

Understanding understanding

What's the deal with the word **"understand"**? Why does comprehending something involve standing under it?

This is a holdover from Old English. As we saw with entrepreneur, under was sometimes used to mean "beneath," just like we use it today, but it was more often used to mean "between or among."

So, the Old English *understandan* didn't mean "to stand under something," but "to stand in the midst of it"—that is, to have an immersive or thorough grasp of a subject.

We use the same sense of under in the phrase "under the circumstances."

Old English had several other compound words using this sense of under:

> ***Undersecan*** was used to mean "examine or to closely investigate," but literally meant "to seek among" things.

Underðencan was used as a word for thinking critically or considering something carefully, and literally meant "to think between" or "think among"—to immerse your mind in a subject.
Underniman referred to receiving something from someone else, but literally meant "to take between" two people.

Root exploration: Memories and mantids

You can probably guess that the word **"memorial"** is related to words like memory and remember, because a memorial helps you remember something important.

It's also pretty easy to guess that the Latin word it comes from, *memoria*, meaning "memory," is also the source of many other words related to memory:

To **commemorate** something is literally "to remember something together."
To **memorize** is to commit something to memory.
A **memo**, which is short for memorandum, is a note that helps you remember something.
And a **memoir** is a book composed of the author's memories.

This Latin word *memoria* comes from a PIE root meaning "to remember."

However, many other English words that pertain to memory come from the Greek *mnasthai* "remember," rather than the Latin *memoria*, which means they come from a distinct PIE root as well. **Mnemonic** is from this Greek source. As you may know, a mnemonic device is a phrase or an acronym that helps you remember more complex concepts. For example, ROY G BIV is a mnemonic device that helps you remember the order of the colors in the rainbow. (Or if you're in the UK, you might remember it by saying something like "Richard Of York Gave Battle In Vain.")

If you add the prefix *a*-, meaning "not" or opposite of," to the Greek *mnasthai*, you get words like **amnesia**, which you might have if you're forgetting things, and **amnesty**, which you get when your past wrongdoings are legally forgotten.

Another word that you might not expect to have a relationship to memory and thinking is **mantis**—yes, like the insect.

The praying mantis and other insects in the order Mantodea get their name from the Greek word *mantis*, meaning "one who divines, a seer, or a prophet," thanks to their wise and mysterious appearance. The word's literal meaning is "one who is inspired by the gods." It originally comes from the Indo-European root **men*-, "to think."

It shares this root with the word **"Muse,"** one of the nine goddesses who presided over art and science and were thought to inspire people with ideas for new creations.

In fact, many words hark back to the **Muses**, including **music** (which literally means "of the Muses") and **museum**. A museum (Ancient Greek *mouseion*) was probably originally a temple to the Muses. Later, museums became places to study, libraries, and halls of knowledge. In Latin *museum* was a word for a library or study, and in English it was a word used for the seat of at Alexandria, in Hellenistic Egypt, before it was extended to refer to any place where artifacts could be displayed and protected.

Other words that share the same root include **mention**, **maniac**, **premonition**, and **reminisce**.

But back to bugs. The scientific name of the praying mantis is *Mantis religiosa*, which, along with the "praying" part of their name, refers to the fact that mantids hold their forelegs in such a way that it looks like they are praying.

Many people mistakenly think these critters are called "preying" mantises, as in predators that prey on other animals, partially thanks to the fact that mantises are excellent ambush hunters with a voracious appetite (see: eggcorns).

Cattywampus kitty corners

The word **"cattywampus"** means crooked, off-kilter, or arranged diagonally.

When it was first used in the U.S. around 1834 it was an adverb (catawampusly) meaning "completely, utterly or avidly."

About ten years later, the noun "catawampus" appeared in Charles Dickens' *Martin Chuzzlewit* (1843), meaning some sort of hobgoblin or other frightening fantastical creature.

Catawampus may have also been influenced by catamount, literally a "cat of the mountain," another word for a cougar. This word overlaps with the word "caterwaul," which means "to cause a ruckus or make a scene," but literally means "to scream or yell like a cat" (*cater* "tomcat" + Middle English *waul* "to yowl").

The first part of cattywampus may hark back to a now-obsolete meaning of the word "cater," "to set or move diagonally."

This is also the source of the term **"catty corner"** or "**kitty corner,"** which describes something positioned diagonally across from something else.

Another possibility could be that the *catty-* of cattywampus is related to the Greek prefix *kata-*, meaning "downward" or "toward," among other things.

The *-wampus* part of cattywampus is etymologically unclear, but may be from the Scottish slang term "wampish," which means "to wriggle or twist about."

Through the 1840s, British authors used cattywampus to approximate (and mock) American slang, particularly colloquialisms from North Carolina. By 1864, though, it had settled on its current sense, "askew or awry," and by 1873, it had acquired the additional meaning "in a diagonal position, on a bias, or crooked."

Brilliant words

Brilliant was adopted directly from French in the 1680s. At that point, it didn't yet refer to mental or intellectual brilliance but simply meant "sparkling" or "shining." Its Latin source means "to shine like beryl." Beryl is a category of crystalline minerals that includes emeralds and aquamarine. Here are a few examples of beryls, with their etymologies, of course:

Emerald is related to and stems from ancient Semitic words for "shine" and "lightning flash."

Aquamarine comes from the Latin phrase for "sea water."

Heliodor literally means "sun-gift" in Greek.

Goshenite gets its name from Goshen, Massachusetts, where it was originally discovered.

Morganite was named after financier J. Pierpont Morgan—of J. P. Morgan Bank fame—by the New York Royal Academy of Sciences, because he donated many precious stones and minerals to the city's American Museum of Natural History.

Red beryl is also called **bixbite** after its discoverer, the mineralogist Maynard Bixby. (It's not to be confused with bixbyite, which he also discovered but is an unrelated manganese iron oxide mineral.)

Vanishing into the void

The most interesting part of the word **"vanish"** is the literal meaning of the Latin word from which it is derived: *evanescere* means "to disappear" or even "to die," but its components are *ex-* "out" and *vanus*, meaning "empty" or "void." Thus, to vanish literally means "to go out into the void." Its journey from Latin into English involved a stop in Old French as *esvanir*. Somewhere between Old French and Modern English, that *e*… well, vanished. Then again, we also have the English verb **"evanesce,"** which means to gradually disappear from sight or memory. It retains more of the Latin spelling and is, of course, the inspiration for the name of a certain moody band.

Disheveled

Why do we say that someone whose appearance is messy or untidy is **disheveled**? Can one be "sheveled"? (See: unpaired words.)

Like many words, we got this one from Old French, but in Old French "descheveler" meant to have a shaven head. The word's literal meaning is to be apart from your hair.

Over time, disheveled came to mean bare headed more generally (that is, to be seen without a hat, wig, bonnet, or veil). So, while the French *cheveler* never made it into English on its own, if it had, to be "sheveled" would likely mean "to have hair" or "to be hatted."

Head coverings were much more common in the Western world until fairly recently. Hats and bonnets excelled (and still do) at keeping your head warm and your face shaded, but they were also a demonstration of fashion, status, or modesty, especially in polite society. In many cases you would take your head covering off indoors, but to not be wearing something on your head while you were outdoors would have made you look unfinished or untidy.

So, it wasn't long before the word "disheveled" went from meaning unhatted to having messy or undone hair—and then the overall sense of messiness was extended to take in your entire outfit, appearance, and vibe.

Midwife: neither mid nor a wife

A **midwife** is called a midwife not because she is a "between-wife," but because she is a woman beside or "with" another woman during childbirth. Both elements carry meanings from Old English that are otherwise obsolete today.

In Old English, *mid* was not just a prefix but an adjective and standalone preposition. Much like today's prefix, as an adjective *mid* meant "in the middle, amid, or intermediate." As a preposition, however, it meant "with," cognate with the German *mit*.

In the word "midwife," we see this prepositional sense.

The *-wife* part of midwife does not denote marital status, but instead reflects the Old English *wif*, which was a word for any woman, regardless of whether she was married

Bare your midriff—but not in Old English

Some of you may have been told at one point or another that you couldn't wear a certain shirt to school or work because it didn't cover your **midriff**. Variations on this word have spent their lifetime hopping—er, cropping?—in and out of English.

Simply put, *riff* is from the Old English *hrif*, meaning "belly." It's unrelated to the word "riff" in music, which is either short for refrain or for the 18th-century word "riffle," which basically meant a big ripple—the movement of choppy water. So "midriff" literally means "middle belly," and in Old English it was often used as a word for your diaphragm.

Diaphragm is from the Greek *diaphragma*, a word for a partition or barrier (*dia* "across" + *phrassein* "to fence or hedge in"), because, in mammals, the diaphragm divides the ribcage from the lower abdomen. (That "barrier" sense is also why there is a contraceptive device called a diaphragm.) Diaphragm replaced midriff as the preferred anatomical term after Old English gave way to Middle English.

After the word "diaphragm" took over, the word "midriff" faded out of usage almost completely. By the 1700s, it was quite rare, except in the idiomatic phrase "tickle your midriff." If a joke tickled your midriff, that meant it made you laugh.

In the 1940s, the fashion industry revived the midriff, with a twist. Instead of being a part of your body, the midriff was now the part of a shirt that covered your middle. The reason this word was resurrected, especially in women's fashion, was that clothing manufacturers and advertisers were trying to avoid using the word "belly," which, just like today, was used to refer to bigger middles. (There's an etymological basis for this as well, since the word "belly" is from the PIE root **bhelgh-* "to swell.")

Midriff finally came around to today's meaning in the 1960s and 70s, when crop tops surged in popularity (not just for women but also for men)—and the people who wore them were told not to by people from older generations.

Serendipitous storytelling

The word "serendipity" was coined in 1754 by Horace Walpole, a famed and highly fashionable English writer and antiquarian who was a pioneer in the Gothic Revival. The word was inspired by an English translation of the Persian tale "The Three

Princes of Serendip," which is about three princes who make unexpected discoveries and stumble upon happy coincidences during their almost detective-like adventures, which show them solving problems through deductive reasoning. *Serendip* is the Old Persian name for Sri Lanka, originally from Sanskrit *Simhaladvipa*, meaning "Dwelling-Place-of-Lions Island."

The English version of the story Walpole read was a translation of a French version, which was in turn a translation of a Venetian version by Michele Tramezzino, called "Peregrinaggio di tre giovani figliuoli del re di Serendippo" (The Adventures of the Three Young Sons of the King of Serendippo). Voltaire also adapted the story in his 1747 novella *Zadig; or, The Book of Fate*, which influenced modern detective diction and even elements of the scientific method itself.

The distressing history of nostalgia

Nostalgia has a surprisingly tragic origin.

In 1688, Swiss medical student Johannes Hofer wrote his dissertation about a condition that was common to Swiss soldiers and mercenaries who were fighting in other parts of Europe. Hofer documented symptoms such as fatigue, anxiety, heart palpitations, and even fevers, and noted that, when afflicted soldiers went back home, they felt better.

Hofer concluded that their symptoms were caused by being far from home and described their ailment as a pathology that had the potential to be fatal. He called this condition *Heimwehe*, meaning "homesickness" or literally "home-woe." Because medical writing at the time was mostly in Latin, he also coined the word "nostalgia" using Latinized forms of the Ancient Greek words *nostos* and *algos*, "homecoming" and "grief" respectively.

While homesickness was certainly a factor, these soldiers were probably also suffering from other psychological maladies brought about by their experiences of war. (It's worth noting that Hofer thought nostalgia happened when your essential ethers and vital spirits all went to your brain and sucked them out of the rest of your body—but, hey, psychology was more art than science at the time, so any attempt to understand PTSD was groundbreaking for the time.)

Another interesting element of this coinage is that, initially, nostalgia was thought to be peculiar to the Swiss, to the extent that it was also commonly known as "the Swiss disease," or *mal du Suisse.*

But obviously many people who are not Swiss also experience homesickness. By the early 1800s, nostalgia was extended to describe the feelings of sailors, slaves, and prisoners—basically anyone kept away from their home by force or by circumstance. During the American Civil War (1861–5), it was a common medical diagnosis, appearing frequently in medical journals, but still often maligned as a sign of weakness among soldiers.

How did it come to mean what it does today? An 1833 medical journal article said that symptoms of nostalgia arise in people "when they are seized with a longing desire of returning to their home and friends and the scenes of their youth. . . ."

That mention of "scenes of their youth" is a clue as to why nostalgia began to take on the time-based meaning it has today: not just homesickness, but an intense longing for one's past experiences.

It may have been that new shade of meaning that helped bring nostalgia out of medical parlance and into more common use—a process that drastically accelerated when artists began to seize upon it in the early 1900s.

As it appeared more and more often in literature, and as the study of mental health became more nuanced, the word "nostalgia" grew less medical and more romanticized until we arrived at our present usage of this word—namely, that nostalgia is not so much an acute condition so much as it is a universal feeling.

Seafaring words of nautical contortions

I could write a whole book about nautical etymology—and other people have!—but for now we'll stick to some basics.

In most Germanic languages, the word **"sea"** and its predecessors meant "lake," or really any body of water whose edges you could see, including ponds, marshlands, and other pools of water. In Old English, the more common word for a proper sea like the Mediterranean was *haff*. It's thought to literally mean "the rising one," suggesting the impact of the tides, and is likely related to the word "heave."

Many English words are derived from or related to the Greek *naus*, meaning "ship," and *nautes*, meaning "sailor." You can probably guess that the words **"nautical"** and **"navy"** come from this Greek source. Another related word is **"navigate,"** which literally and etymologically means "to set a ship in motion." Indeed, the word **"navicular"** means "boat-shaped."

The word **"nausea"**—the feeling that you're going to vomit—literally means "seasickness" or "ship-sickness." Similarly, the Latin term *ad nauseam* refers to something that has been done or repeated so often that it has become annoying or tiresome. It literally means "to sickness"—or you might say "until barfing."

And the word **"astronaut"** combines *naus* with the Greek word *astro*, or "star," giving it the literal meaning "star-sailor."

The ocean-dwelling cephalopod called a **nautilus** (which is also the name of Captain Nemo's submarine in Jules Verne's 1871 novel *Twenty Thousand Leagues Under the Sea*) gets its name from a poetic form of the Greek for "sailor."

Amazing mazes

To **amaze** literally means "to put someone into a maze," where maze (or **mæs*) was a 13th-century word for "a state of confusion or bewilderment," so to "amaze" someone was to put them into this befuddled state of mind.

The word **"maze"** evolved to refer to labyrinths and puzzles and the like in the late 14th century.

The difference between a maze and a labyrinth depends upon whom you ask. Some people say that a labyrinth is an intricate network of winding pathways that does not have any false branches or dead ends—so, even though it's long and complicated, you can't take a wrong turn or get stuck—while a maze does have these wrong turns and you can get stuck.

But many people throughout history have used the terms interchangeably.

The word **"labyrinth"** might come from a word meaning "narrow passage," but another theory suggests that it comes from a word meaning "the palace of the double-axe." The double axe was a symbol of royal power on the island of Crete, which is the location of a labyrinthine palace—the original Labyrinth—where the mythological minotaur Asterion, or "the starry one," supposedly resided before he was killed by the hero Theseus. And that labyrinth was definitely meant to be a puzzle with blind alleys.

This word's got pizzazz—whatever that is

While some sources including etymonline.com say that **pizzazz** (or pizazz) first appeared in print in a March 1937 issue of *Harper's Bazaar*, it actually appeared earlier, in a 1913 issue of *The Main Sheet*, a humorous publication by the Indoor Yacht Club, albeit with a different meaning than we see today. It is true that today's usage of the word "pizzazz" is likely from the 1920s or 30s, as described in *Bazaar*:

> Pizazz, to quote the editor of the Harvard *Lampoon*, is an indefinable dynamic quality, the *je ne sais quoi* of function; as for instance, adding Scotch puts pizazz into a drink. Certain clothes have it, too.

The word does not appear in any known issues of the *Harvard Lampoon* before 1937, so perhaps the editor in question said the word out loud or in another publication.

The earlier *Main Sheet* column in which pizzazz first appears is a satiric story called "It's All Off with the Rough Stuff" about the fictional Clean Language League of America's campaign against "low-brow lingo." It has a slightly different meaning here, and is used in the phrase "completely on the pizzazz," meaning something (in this case, the song "When I Get You Alone Tonight") done away with or banned by prudes. The whole column is full of slang, idioms, jokes, and low-brow terms that would irritate the League. Some especially wonderful gems include "plum nuts," "flossie," "swimdiggle," and "do the nobby."

The story also lays out which words and phrases are inappropriate for girls to say (including "fudge") and which are inappropriate for boys to say—all while joyfully repeating these very terms in the most tongue-in-cheek way possible:

> [T]hey swore to goodness that "doggone it" was a doggone bad thing to say, and that "gosh darn" was putrid, and that "bully gee" and "I'll be swimdiggled" were expressions that a mucker might use.

It even includes a bleeped-out word that "fathers must not say." Any guesses as to what that was?

Dropping eaves

To **eavesdrop** is literally to stand under the eaves of a house to listen in at a window—but it was originally a noun.

The "eavesdrop" (Old English *yfesdrype*) was the area under the eaves, which kept rainwater from dripping down the sides of a house. This is where one might stand if one were, say, listening in on a conversation at Bag End—or it would if it had eaves, that is.

Naughty and nice aren't naughty or nice

Let's talk about the origins of the words **"naughty"** and **"nice."**

The word "naughty" went from neutral to negative, and "nice" went from "knowing nothing" to "neat and neighborly."

You probably know that naught means "nothing" (Old English *nawiht* "nothing"). So naughty, in a sense, means "nothing-y." In the late 14th century, the word "naughty" was more literal: It meant "needy" and described people who had nothing. The word "naught" was also a word for an evil act, likely based on the idea that an evil person is lacking in morality.

So, today's sense of naughty is closer to this morally bankrupt sense of "naught." But there's likely an element of class bias here as well, based on the stereotype that someone who is needy or has nothing is prone to commit evil deeds.

In fact, the same thing happened with the word **"villain,"** which was originally just a word for a peasant or poor farmer. It evolved to mean "the bad guy" because people started using it as an insult—calling someone a villain was sort of like calling them trashy and low-class, implying that they were a scoundrel.

So, now that we know about naughty, what about "nice?" Turns out "nice" was originally a bit of a naughty word.

To be called "nice" in the 13th century was decidedly not a compliment. It meant you were "foolish or ignorant." It's from the Latin *nescius* "ignorant, unaware," literally "not-knowing," from *ne-* "not" + *scire* "to know."

Interesting side note: This means that the word "nice" is the etymological opposite of the word "science," which comes from the same root and literally means knowledge.

So, to understand how being "nice" became a good thing, let's track how its meaning shifted over time:

1200s: "foolish or ignorant," "timid or faint-hearted"
1300s: "fussy, fastidious"
1400s: "dainty, delicate"
1500s: "precise, careful"
1700s: "agreeable, delightful"
1800s: "kind, thoughtful"

In the 1200s, the "foolish" sense of "nice" shifted to mean "timid or faint-hearted," possibly due to the assumption that people who are easily frightened are overly superstitious or have a weak mind.

"Nice" then evolved to mean "fussy or fastidious." As you might expect, this insult was largely directed at men who were less physically inclined.

But then, in the 1500s, as high society began to put more value on leisurely, genteel qualities, suddenly being "fastidious" was a good thing. So "nice" came to mean precise and careful. It preserved this sense at least until Jane Austen's time (pedants like to use it so now). See the well-known exchange in *Northanger Abbey* (1817), where the mansplainer hero, Henry

Tilney, replies to the heroine Catherine Morland's remark about Ann Radcliffe's famous Gothic novel The *Mysteries of Udolpho* (1794):

> "But now really, do not you think Udolpho the nicest book in the world?"
> "The nicest; – by which I suppose you mean the neatest. That must depend upon the binding."[6]

This sense is also preserved in phrases like "nice and easy," or "nicely done."

If you're precise and careful, you might also be pleasant to be around, so "nice" eventually came to mean "agreeable or delightful," and finally "kind and thoughtful."

So originally, "naughty" and "nice," now basically opposites, were once much closer in meaning. Either way, people found you lacking in morals, money, or intelligence.

[6] Jane Austen, *Northanger Abbey* (Ware, Herts: Wordsworth Editions, 1993), 69.

8

What's in a Name? Eponymous Etymology

What better way to leave our mark upon the world than to name something after ourselves?

If something is named after someone, or another proper noun like a place, that's an eponym, from the Ancient Greek "given as a name" or "named after" (*epi* "upon, [called] after" + *onyma* "name").

For example, **Vanderbilt University** in Nashville, Tennessee, is eponymously named after the American industrialist Cornelius Vanderbilt. **Shrapnel** is named after Lieutenant General Henry Shrapnel (1761–1842), a British army officer and artillery specialist who invented a special kind of exploding shell—which produced, you guessed it, shrapnel.

One of our most common modern words is secretly an eponym: The word **"guy"** is ultimately derived from the name of the infamous Guy Fawkes, one of the conspirators in the 1605 Gunpowder Plot, whose aim was to blow up the Houses of Parliament and assassinate King James I. The plot is now remembered on Guy Fawkes Day, and his infamy (at least according to Protestant royalists) fully embedded "guy" into the English language—but first, in the 1600s and 1700s as a pejorative, meaning a grotesque- or shabby-looking person.

Its derogatory sense has largely faded with popular usage, especially after it made its way into American English in the 1840s, though in British English, a "guy" is still in some cases a word for a straw-stuffed effigy of Fawkes meant for the bonfire. Separation from the historical event ameliorated the term. Prior to "guy," names such as Jack were often used as similar placeholders or generic terms—and we treat names in the same way today in phrases like "average Joe."

Similarly, **pants** are named after a fictional Italian fellow. The word "pants" is a shortened version of the word "pantaloons." Pantaloons has referred to several types of legwear since the 16th century. Originally, it was a word for men's tights or hose. Later, pantaloons referred to men's knee breeches and women's baggy under-trousers, both of which were gathered at the knee or the ankle. This eventually gave us the word "panties" for women's undies, and the British English use of the word "pants" for underpants in general, regardless of gender. In the late 18th century, pantaloons was extended to our modern-day idea of long trousers and later shortened to "pants" as well. The etymological source of the word "pantaloons," and therefore all pants, is Pantaloun (or Pantalone), a recurring comedic character in 16th-century Italian commedia dell'arte who famously wore red rights. Pantalone was a silly, avaricious old man who tended to get into humorous entanglements with women and servants who openly mocked him.

Another eponymous article of clothing is the **fedora**. Even though it's largely associated with men's fashion today, the fedora was first popularized by—and indirectly named after—a woman. If you're a theater aficionado, you've probably heard of Sarah Bernhardt, a French stage actress in the late 1800s and early 1900s. She frequently played the female lead in popular French plays by the likes of Alexandre Dumas and Victor Hugo. And she was one of the first big-name actresses to act in motion pictures. But she was also well known for playing male roles, earning critical acclaim for her performance as Shakespeare's Hamlet in 1899. She was a leading figure in women's rights movements of the day and was one of the first women to publicly wear a pantsuit.

But back to the hat. In the 1880s, Bernhardt wore a hat in this style as she performed the role of the title character in the play *Fédora* by Victorien Sardou, which is about the Russian princess Fédora Romazov. Thanks to the popularity of Bernhardt's performance, the hat was named after the character she played. Thereafter, around the turn of the century, it was adopted as a defining symbol of the women's rights movement. It didn't become a popular men's fashion item until the fashion-forward Prince Edward (the future Edward VIII) started wearing one in 1924.

Sequoia trees are named after **Sequoya**, a Cherokee innovator who developed the Cherokee Syllabary, the first Cherokee writing system. His work not only allowed Cherokee literacy to surge to nearly 100 percent, but also improved relations between the U.S. government and Indigenous groups, and formed the basis for writing systems used in a total of 65 languages in North America, Africa, and Asia. He also became a critical representative for the Cherokee people in a deeply contentious sociopolitical landscape.

This one sounds far too fanciful to be true, but I assure you it is an eponym: **Sideburns** are named after the resplendent and voluminous whiskers of Union Civil War general Ambrose E. Burnside. Starting around the 1870s, they were called "burnsides," but shortly thereafter, the words were transposed. But the transposition of "burnsides" was… er, burned by etymologists, lexicographers, and grammarians of the time. Literary legend Ambrose Bierce included "sideburns" on a blacklist of words to never use in his 1909 book *Write It Right*, instead insisting that "burnsides" is correct:

> *Sideburns for Burnsides.* A form of whiskers named from a noted general of the civil war, Ambrose E. Burnside. It seems to be thought that the word side has something to do with it, and that as an adjective it should come first, according to our idiom.[1]

In addition to being famously pedantic and a fellow Ambrose, Bierce was a Union Civil War veteran so it makes sense that this malapropism would have rankled.

Embedded brands: Proprietary eponyms

Eponyms usually refer to words or phrases derived from people's names—like the **Fahrenheit** scale for temperature, which is named after Gabriel Daniel Fahrenheit—but eponyms can also come from brands.

You probably know that Kleenex® and Band-Aid® are **genericized trademarks**, but you might not know that they're also **proprietary eponyms**, meaning "something named after its ownership." (Proprietary means "owned" or "pertaining to ownership," from the Latin *proprietarius* "owner of property.")

Some proprietary eponyms, like Kleenex and Band-Aid, have been genericized for so long that they are almost fully divorced from their original brand name usage. Here are a few others:

- **Bubble Wrap**® is owned by the Sealed Air Corporation. The stuff was invented by two guys who were attempting to make three-dimensional plastic wallpaper. They failed, but they did make a useful (and entertaining) packing material.

[1] Ambrose Bierce, *Write It Right: A Little Blacklist of Literary Faults* (New York and Washington, D.C.: Neale Publishing, 1909).

- **Moxie®**, used generally from 1930, comes from the brand name of a bitter syrup first marketed as the medicine Moxie Nerve Food in 1876, then sold as a soft drink starting in 1884. (The brand was bought by the Coca-Cola Company in 2018). The brand may be from a Native American Abenaki word for "dark water" that appears in the names of several lakes and rivers in Maine.
- **Ping-Pong®** is currently owned by Escalade Sports (and formerly by Parker Brothers), though it was first trademarked by the British manufacturer J. Jaques & Son Ltd in 1901. The game ping-pong, or table tennis, did exist before that, though, and the term may have been used before the trademark. Same with Breathalyzer, Jacuzzi, Rollerblade, Super Glue, Windbreaker, Zipper, and even TV Dinner.

The word **"soccer"** is a twisted eponym—one named after an association rather than a commercial brand. "Soccer" is short for "association" because, in the 1800s, in British universities, the sport was differentiated from Rugby football by calling it Association football, after the International Football Association Board that governed the sport. It was originally called Assoc, but in British university slang you'd often add *-er* onto a syllable of a word, so rugby became rugger or footer, and "Assoc football" became "soccer." So, despite the British insistence that Americans call "football" by the wrong name, it was the Brits themselves who first gave it that name.

Gasoline is oddly somewhat eponymous and somewhat proprietary. It all has to do with John Cassell, an Englishman who sold refined petroleum for powering lamps. Based on his name, he called it Cazeline. You might think he used the Latin-derived chemical or elemental suffix *-ine*, to make it sound sciency, but nope: He used an Ancient Greek-derived suffix *-elene*, from Ancient Greek *elaia*, "olive."

Cassell even had a fancy ad placed for it: "The Patent Cazeline Oil: safe, economical, and brilliant… possesses all the requisites which have so long been desired as a means of powerful artificial light."

Shortly thereafter, an Irishman named John Boyd began selling counterfeit "cazeline" in his shop. Cassell found out and sent a nastygram insisting he desist. Boyd changed the spelling of his product to begin with a G: Gazeline. American refineries took the name "gazeline" and turned it into "gasoline." Here's where a little bit of chemistry logic does start to come in: *gas-* because it combusts, *-oli-* from the Latin *oleum* meaning "oil" (just like in petroleum), and *-ine* from that Latin elemental ending *-ine/-ene*.

The use of "gasoline" in the States and "petrol" or "petroleum" in most other places pretty much boils down to marketing. "Petroleum" is first recorded in the 1400s, first in reference to crude oil—or literally "rock oil" (Latin *petra* "rock" + *oleum* "oil"). The shorter "petrol" was also used as a word for crude oil as early as the 1580s. "Petroleum" was applied to the refined liquid used in internal combustion engines starting in the late 1850s, and "petrol" was first used to market refined petroleum as a solvent in the 1860s by British wholesalers, and then as a fuel shortly thereafter. Entirely coincidentally, the first British company to use the word "petrol" to describe its products was cofounded by a fellow inaptly named Eugene Carless (see: inaptronyms). British refineries also used "motor spirit" as a generic name for automotive fuel and "aviation spirit" for aviation fuel.

Legendary language: Mythological eponyms

The stories that have shaped our culture have also shaped our language. Words that emerge from mythology and legend are often eponymous in that they are inspired by the names and actions of famous characters. For example, the word **"quixotic,"** which first appeared in the late 18th century, is from Miguel de Cervantes' novel *Don Quixote* (1605 and 1615).

But an outsized proportion of fictionally inspired eponyms emerged from much older texts, especially Greek, Roman, and, to a lesser extent, Norse mythology.

It's of course no secret that **atlases**—books that tell us about our world's geography, and topography—are named after the Greek Titan condemned to hold up the sky until he was transformed into the Atlas Mountains. Feats may be **Herculean**; tasks may be **Sisyphean**; gigantic objects and creatures may be **titanic** like the Titans. And, of course, those who generate wealth may be said to have the **Midas touch**.

A Dictionary of English Folklore describes the distinction between myth, legend, and folktale. **Myths** are:

> stories about divine beings, generally arranged in a coherent system; they are revered as true and sacred; they are endorsed by rulers and priests; and closely linked to religion. Once this link is broken, and the actors in the story are not regarded as gods but as human heroes, giants or fairies, it is no longer a myth but a folktale. Where the central actor is divine but the story is trivial… the result is religious legend, not myth.[2]

Thus, what you might describe as mythology, legend, or folklore is to some degree contextual because whether a story is spiritually or culturally meaningful or not has entirely to do with who is telling and who is hearing the story.

The word **"legend"** literally means "that which is read or collected" and is related to words like legible and lexical.

---

[2] Jacqueline Simpson and Stephen Roud, *A Dictionary of English Folklore* (Oxford: Oxford University Press, 2000), 254.

Many of our most familiar words are eponyms inspired by myth, legend, and folklore (however you define them). Read on to discover the tales lurking in our everyday terminology.

Words of the gods (and their humans)

Tantalize comes from the name of the character Tantalus in Greek myth. There are several versions of his unpleasant story, but in many of them he sacrifices and then cooks his son Pelops as part of a banquet that he serves to the gods. In others, he steals ambrosia and nectar from Olympus after having been invited by Zeus to dine among the gods. Either way, the gods are deeply displeased and condemn him to an afterlife of torture. He stands up to his neck in water with boughs of fruit (often grapes) hanging overhead, but every time he bends to drink the water or stretches up to eat the fruit, they withdraw from his reach—*tantalizing* him for all eternity.

The word **"echo"** (Greek *ēkhō* "reverberating sound") was originally the name of a nymph in Greek mythology. She enraged Hera by serving as a distraction while her husband Zeus was off philandering. In response, Hera cursed Echo to repeat only the last words spoken to her. Unfortunately, her own love life wasn't much better: She fell for Narcissus, source of the word **narcissism**, who was so obsessed with his own beauty that he practically stared his reflection to death—and, in Ovid's account, ultimately resulted in the self-absorbed figure being turned into the narcissus flower. His name's Greek source, *narkê*, means "numbness" or "stupor." It connects narcissism to words like narcotic.

The term **"mentor"** is from the name of the mentor of Odysseus' son—who's named Mentor—in *The Odyssey*. His name is an aptronym (see: aptronym), because it comes from the PIE root **men-* "to think", which links it to words like mental and, more distantly, muse, music, mosaic, and museum. These last four are all more immediately derived from the name of the Muses (Greek *Moûsai*), protectors of the arts and the inspiration behind many creative works (see: museum).

Panic is from the Greek *panikon*, literally "pertaining to Pan." Pan was the god of the wild and also the source of the mysterious sounds out in nature that caused people and animals to, well, panic.

Aphrodisiac, of course, is from the name of Aphrodite, the goddess of love, whose name also forms half of the now outdated and pejorative word **"hermaphrodite."** This word is from the name of Hermaphroditus, son of Hermes and Aphrodite, who is also named after them. This beautiful boy was merged with the naiad Salmacis to become one person with both sexes. The Old English word for this was *wæpenwifestre*—literally, "penis woman."

Brontosauruses are literally "thunder-lizards," from the Ancient Greek *brontē* "thunder." Meanwhile, **brontophobia** is not, as one might expect, the fear of brontosauruses, but of thunder. These words are inspired by the name of the Greek mythological figure Brontes, one of the three Cyclopes who made Zeus his thunderbolt weapon. His brothers were named Steropes (from *steropē* "lightning") and Arges (from *argos* "shining, bright").

Money gets its name from Moneta, one of the Roman goddess Juno's titles, given to her because her temple was on the same hill where money was coined and where precious metals were said to be stored. The name "Moneta" literally means to advise, warn, or admonish, which is somewhat apt given how many tales there are about the power of money to corrupt.

Flora was the Roman goddess of flowers, while **Fauna** was a Roman fertility goddess who was connected to Faunus, god of the forest. Swedish biologist Linnaeus was the first to pair up "flora and fauna" and apply fauna to animal life in his work on taxonomy in the 1700s.

The word **"hermetic"** comes from the name of Hermes Trismegistus, a separate deity from the Hermes we often see in modern adaptations of Greek myth and identified with the Egyptian god Thoth. These gods of science, art, and alchemy were said to have developed a process for making a tube airtight using a secret seal. Hermetic means pertaining to occult science and alchemy but can also mean "airtight" in the phrase "hermetically sealed."

Copious means "plentiful," and Copia was the Roman personification of plenty and abundance. This word is also related to **cornucopia**, horn of plenty, which is in the discourse right now thanks to the Fruit of the Loom® logo.

Aptronyms

Unlike an **eponym**, which is named after a specific person, place, or institution, an **aptronym** is a name that really fits the person who has it.

You see aptronyms often in works of fiction. The allegorical names of Christian, Pliable, Worldly Wiseman, and every other character in John Bunyan's *The Pilgrim's Progress* (1678) are the quintessential literary aptronyms. Charles Dickens' works are stuffed with more creative but still appropriate names: the benevolent Cheeryble brothers in *Nicholas Nickleby*, the jolly Polly Toodle from *Dombey and Son*, the hypocritical and pecking order-obsessed Mrs. Pecksniff from *Martin Chuzzlewit*, and, of course, old Ebenezer Scrooge in *A Christmas Carol* (1843). And for a more recent example, the

Harry Potter universe makes constant use of often Latin-inspired names from Severus and Sirius to Dumbledore and Umbridge.

Famous real-life aptronyms include sprinter Usain Bolt, poet William Wordsworth, psychiatrist Jules Angst (who specialized in anxiety disorders), and Rosalind Brewer, who was an executive at Starbucks and a director at Molson Coors Brewing Company.

You often see people cite Thomas Crapper as the 19th-century inventor of the toilet. He was a sanitary engineer who patented several inventions used in plumbing, so his name is still an aptronym, but his patents do not include an actual toilet, unfortunately.

The word "aptronym" was coined by Franklin P. Adams, an American columnist known for his wit. It works because aptronyms are apt—but also because aptronym is an anagram of patronym, which is a name derived from the name of a father.

The opposite of an aptronym is an inaptronym. That's when your name implies the opposite of who you are or what you do. Two real-world examples: Danielle Outlaw served as Commissioner of the Philadelphia Police Department (2019–23). And for nearly 20 years, a man named Robin Mahfood was president and CEO of the nonprofit Food for the Poor.

9

Hit the Books

The Origins of Literary and Rhetorical Terms

Books, plays, poetry, and other forms of written storytelling are often our earliest introduction to new words—and reading is one of the best ways to expand your vocabulary and encounter creative word usage at any age. In the spirit of appreciation for books and the written word, we'll spend this chapter discovering the stories behind the terms that shaped the way we interact with and learn from literature, the theater, and beyond. We'll start with the ultimate book of words, then dive into some of the terms that help us recognize patterns within our favorite written works.

Today, a **dictionary** contains all the most commonly used words in a language and their meanings. The word "dictionary" is a shortening of the Medieval Latin term *dictionarium liber*, meaning "a book of words," from the Latin *dictio*, originally a term for a saying or expression, but in Late Latin simply a word for—well, a word. The first *dictionarium liber* was a 13th-century book of Latin vocabulary compiled by grammarian Johannes de Garlandia, or John of Garland. The first book to be called a "dictionary" in English is likely *The Dictionary of syr Thomas Eliot knyght* (1538), an exhaustive Latin–English dictionary by scholar Thomas Elyot.

Many early Western dictionaries and word collections compiled Latin words because it was the common language of European ecclesiastical, academic, scientific, and pedagogical institutions (which are, not coincidentally, all Latin-derived words).

The first compilation of English words and definitions that is widely regarded as a dictionary is *A Table Alphabeticall* (1604) by schoolteacher and clergyman Robert Cawdrey. Cawdrey compiled the text for English speakers "Whereby they may the more easilie and better understand many hard English wordes, which they shall heare or read in scriptures, sermons, or elswhere, and also be made able to vse the same aptly themselves."[1]

However, the book that did the most to shape what a dictionary is and can be is probably *A Dictionary of the English Language*, or *Johnson's Dictionary*, written and compiled by Samuel Johnson. Up to this point, dictionaries tended to be limited to "hard" words like those found in Cawdrey's works, and their contents were often haphazardly organized with minimal research. Johnson's dictionary was designed to be much more comprehensive, as it built on a printing and publishing boom that made all sorts of written materials much more widely accessible.

Compiling the dictionary wasn't exactly a swift process: It took almost a decade for Johnson to outline his plan, and several additional years for his publishers to approve it before it was published in 1755. This first edition contained 42,773 words and was prohibitively expensive for the average reader, even when divided into folios.

The entries and etymologies within were also entertainingly selected and wildly editorialized; fortunately, this makes for wonderful reading:

---

[1] Robert Cawdrey, *A Table Alphabeticall, containing and teaching the true writing and vnderstanding of hard vsuall English words, borrowed from the Hebrew, Greeke, Latine, or French&c. … Set forth by R. C. i.e. Robert Cawdrey newly corrected and much inlarged … The 3. Edition* (W. I. for Edmund Weauer, 1617).

Anatiferous, *adjective*: Producing ducks.
Nidorosity, *noun*: Eructation with the taste of undigested roast meat.
Jiggumbob, *noun*: A trinket; a knick-knack; a slight contrivance in machinery.
Slubberdegullion, *noun*: A paltry, dirty, sorry wretch.

Equally entertaining are the entries that make light of the work of lexicographers like Johnson himself:

Dull, *adjective*: Not exhilarating; not delightful: as, to make dictionaries is dull work.
Lexicographer, *noun*: A writer of dictionaries; a harmless drudge, that busies himself in tracing the original, and detailing the signification of words.

What about the dictionary's synonym- and antonym-stuffed sibling, the **thesaurus**?

Beyond its use as a reference book, it's also the most eloquent species of dinosaur.

If only. In truth, and tragically, thesaurus is unrelated to words such as tyrannosaurus, ichthyosaurus, and stegosaurus, as well as dinosaur itself. In all these words, the *-saurus* element comes from the Ancient Greek *sauros*, or "lizard," a naming convention that has stuck around even though we now know that dinosaurs weren't lizards. *Sauros* itself is possibly related to the Ancient Greek *saulos*, "twisting," describing the movement of lizards.

But don't let all this non-dinosaur business disappoint you—because the real origin of the word thesaurus is wonderful in its own right.

The Latin *thesaurus* and the preceding Ancient Greek word, *thesauros*, mean "treasure," a treasury, or a chest where treasure is stored. Even in English in the 1800s, thesaurus was recorded as a word for a storehouse where you'd put your valuables.

But an earlier form of the word, "thesaurarie," dates back to the 16th century as a title used by lexicographers—implying that a dictionary is a "treasure trove" of words. The idea also existed in Latin: a *thesaurus verborum* was a "treasury of words." It's this phrase that was shortened to become today's thesaurus, first as a word for an encyclopedia of any type—a treasure trove of facts or information. In 1852, the meaning of the word narrowed to the one we're familiar with today, thanks to Peter Mark Roget, whose collection of synonyms and semantically linked words, *Roget's Thesaurus*, laid claim the name for his style of reference book.

Let's move on to some of the rhetorical devices one might find both within and beyond the pages of these reference books.

Hyperbole

The word **"hyperbole"** (an obvious or extreme exaggeration) came to English via Latin from the Ancient Greek *hyperbole*, which was used to mean "exaggeration, extravagance" but literally meant "a throwing beyond."

The Greek *hyperbole* is formed of *hyper-* "beyond" + *bole* "a throwing, a casting, the stroke of a missile, bolt, beam." Bole is the nominative stem of *ballein*, "to throw," from the PIE root **gwele-* "to throw, reach," which also influenced words like ballistic, ballet, metabolism, parable, and symbol.

There was also a Greek verb form, *hyperballein*, which meant "to throw over or beyond."

The English pronunciation of hyperbole is directly from the Greek pronunciation of the word (ὑπερβολή). The Greek letter eta (ή) does not correspond directly to any English vowel, so it's usually written as an *e*. When in doubt, just think of the pronunciation of name endings like the *-es* sound in Heracles (Ηρακλής).

Just like simile used to make

Both the words **"simile"** and **"metaphor"** came to English during the Renaissance with the rise of postclassical literary theory and criticism. In literature, a simile compares two things using the words "like" or "as."

The word comes from the Latin *similis*, meaning "like" or "resembling," and is originally from a root meaning "together" or "as one." It is related to words like similar, simultaneous, and ensemble.

In *East of Eden* (1955), John Steinbeck employs simile in the line "Kate inched over her own thoughts like a measuring worm."[2] And in *The Hitchhiker's Guide to the Galaxy*, Douglas Adams writes, "The ships hung in the sky in much the same way that bricks don't."[3]

A metaphor is a direct comparison between two things, without the use of like or as.

The word "metaphor" originally comes from the Greek *metaphora*, meaning "a transfer," or literally "a carrying across," from *meta-* "over, across" + *pherein* "to carry." So, a metaphor "carries" the meaning across from one thing to another—or poetically bridges two objects, ideas, or concepts that audiences might not normally associate with one another—allowing the reader to understand the intended meaning of the words rather than the literal meaning.

In his story "The Call of Cthulhu," H. P. Lovecraft employs a classic metaphor in the line, "We live on a placid island of ignorance in the midst of black seas of infinity."[4] Broader themes

---

[2] John Steinbeck, *East of Eden* (London: Penguin, 2002), 500.

[3] Douglas Adams, *The Hitchhiker's Guide to the Galaxy* (New York: Harmony Books, 1980), 34.

[4] H. P. Lovercraft, *The Call of Cthulhu* (Auckland: Floating Press, 2016), 5.

can also take the form of metaphors, as in Maya Angelou's 1969 autobiography *I Know Why the Caged Bird Sings*, which uses the caged bird as a metaphor for prejudice and racism.

Synonyms and antonyms

Synonyms were originally more strictly words that are similar in sense but not identical in meaning, a notion that persisted several centuries after synonym is first found in English in the late 1400s.

According to Samuel Johnson (filtered through James Boswell in his celebrated biography), only the "negligent" use of words causes perfect synonyms. Otherwise, every word has a distinct meaning:

> Walker: 'Do you think, Sir, that there are any perfect synonimes in any language?'
> Johnson: 'Originally there were not; but by using words negligently, or in poetry, one word comes to be confounded with another.'[5]

Antonym was coined as the, well, antonym (see: autological words) to synonym a few centuries later, after the latter's definition had been relaxed. Predictably, it means "opposite in name." This word emerged in 1867, with the publication of the book C. J. Smith's *Synonyms and Antonyms*; Smith appears to have coined the word himself.

The poetry of onomatopoeia

One of the wonderful things about the etymology of **onomatopoeia** (a word that sounds like what it means, such as

[5] James Boswell, *The Life of Samuel Johnson, LL.D.* (London: Navarre Society Ltd, 1924), 295.

thwack, bam, boing, or thrum) is that it helps you remember how to spell it.

The word is a direct borrow from Latin, and it isn't too far off from its original Greek source.

Let's break it down into its two pieces: *onomato* + *poeia* = Greek *onomatos* "word, name" + *poiein* "compose" (e.g. poetry or music).

The first element, and especially that *-nom-* part, appears as the ending of words like synonym, antonym, pseudonym, and homonym. The second element, *poiein*, is related to the word *poet*—literally someone who is a maker or composer of songs and poems.

One could read onomatopoeia as either a poetic name for something, or a word that makes or composes its own name.

Paradoxically oxymoronic

You are probably familiar with the concept of an **oxymoron**. It's a brief paradox—a term that is made up of words that, without context, contradict one another.

A **paradox** is any ostensibly self-contradictory scenario, statement, or juxtaposition. The word originally meant "an unexpected statement" or one that contradicts one's beliefs or expectations—especially an absurd or fantastical one that manages to be true. It literally means "contrary to opinion" or "contrary to appearances," from the Greek elements *para-* "contrary to" and *doxa*, meaning "opinion" but originally from the verb *dokein* "to appear, seem, think."

Mathematical and logical paradoxes, which were first given the name in the early 1900s but existed prior to that, are those without a clear answer. A popularly cited example is the Ship of Theseus paradox: If every single component of a ship is gradually replaced over time as it is maintained, down to the last nail, is it still the same ship? At what point does it turn into something else, such as a restoration or recreation of the original ship?

Not all paradoxes are oxymorons (which are limited to just a few words), but all oxymorons are paradoxes.

Classic oxymorons include tight slacks, jumbo shrimp, original copy, farewell reception, open secret, passive aggressive, deeply superficial, bittersweet, and barely clothed.

The word "oxymoron" itself is also an oxymoron. It's made up of Greek words meaning "sharp or clever" and "dull or stupid."

J. R. R. Tolkien often said—perhaps with tongue in cheek—that his own name had a similar literal meaning to oxymoron in Low German or Old High German. He suggested that it might have evolved from *toll-kühn* meaning "foolhardy," or literally "stupid-sharp."

There are also phrases that are dependent on context or political point of view to qualify as oxymorons, like "military intelligence" or "business ethics." The comedian George Carlin is famous for his riffs on oxymorons like these.

Oxymorons are also commonly found in literature. Shakespeare loved to use oxymorons to allow characters to express their frustrations with internal conflicts—or just to make fun of each other. His recurring "wise fool" trope is a perfect example (see: sophomore). *Romeo and Juliet* includes a ton of them because the protagonists are self-dramatizing horny teenagers: "Parting is such sweet sorrow" (2.2.186); "Beautiful tyrant! Fiend angelical! / Dove-feather'd raven!" (3.2.78–9). Hamlet says he must "be cruel only to be kind" (3.4.197). And Shakespeare's sonnets include other examples like "tender churl" and "gentle thief."

Actually ironic

The word **irony** comes from the Greek *eironeia*, meaning "assumed ignorance," or the state of concealing your true thoughts or feelings. In the works of Plato, Socrates commonly employed *eironeia*, pretending not to know anything about a subject so the person he was debating would reveal their own ignorance when they tried to explain themselves.

There are three primary types of irony, all of which were employed in classical theatre and literature for humorous or dramatic effect, and none of which appears in Alanis Morissette's eponymous song.

Verbal irony is when the intended meaning of what you're saying is the opposite (or nearly) to the actual words you're speaking. Sarcasm is sometimes verbal irony, like when you say you're *so* excited to pay your mortgage this month. Ironic, oxymoronic similes, which are also often sarcastic, fall into this bucket, too, as when you call something "as clear as mud." But verbal irony doesn't have to be self-aware. If you were to angrily yell that you're not angry, that would be qualify as well.

There's a good deal of overlap between sarcasm and verbal irony, though the latter is broader: It can be when you say the opposite of what you mean. Or it can be when a character in a play says something that the audience understands is untrue, even if the other characters don't get it.

Sarcasm is a type of verbal irony characterized by mockery: You say the opposite of what you mean—but with an eyeroll and a cutting tone. The word "sarcasm" comes from the Greek *sarkazein*, which literally meant "to strip off the flesh," suggesting cutting or biting humor that reveals the intention "beneath the skin," or beneath the literal meaning of the words. You could say, "great weather we're having" during a hurricane with a smile on your face, and that would be verbal irony. It becomes sarcasm when you say something like, "Yeah, thanks—I *love* when a hurricane knocks my house over."

Situational irony hinges on a reversal of expectations. The 1939 movie *The Wizard of Oz* is full of situational irony—Dorothy's three companions already have the qualities they want the Wizard to grant them; the Wizard proves to be a charlatan; and Dorothy has had the ability to go home the entire time. In Shakespeare's tragedy *Macbeth* (1606), we see the witches' prophecy playing out in unexpected ways even as Macbeth and Lady Macbeth attempt to thwart it.

Dramatic irony is a literary technique from Greek tragedy where the audience understands the full implications of what a character is doing and saying, but the character doesn't. For example, in Shakespeare's *Othello* (ca. 1603), the villain, Iago, tells us all about his scheme to bring about Othello's downfall by making it seem like Desdemona has been unfaithful, but Othello does not know about any of that.

How to pack a portmanteau

Coined by Lewis Carroll, author of *Alice's Adventures in Wonderland* (1865), the word **"portmanteau"** is adapted from the French *porte-manteau*, literally "cloak-carrier" (*porter* "to carry" + *manteau* "cloak").[6] Today, the French is a word for a clothes valet or a coat rack, but it's also recorded in the 1500s as a word for a large travel bag for carrying clothes. Humpty Dumpty explains the logic behind the coinage to *Alice's Adventures in Wonderland*'s sequel, *Through the Looking-Glass* (1871): "You see it's like a portmanteau—there are two meanings packed up into one word."

Carroll coined many portmanteaus in his work, especially in the poem "Jabberwocky,"[7] which first appeared in full in *Through the Looking-Glass*, after which Humpty helpfully explains some of the word mashups. Some of the words he

[6] Lewis Carroll, *Alice's Adventures in Wonderland* (London: Macmillan and Co., 1865).

[7] Lewis Carroll, "Jabberwocky," in *Through the Looking-Glass, and What Alice Found There* [1871] (New York: Macmillan, 1872).

coined in the poem are entirely meaningless, but many are portmanteaus. For instance:

> "slithy" = "lithe" + "slimy"
> "frumious" = "fuming" + "furious"

We don't usually use either of those in everyday contexts, but Carroll also coined some that have entered regular use outside of references to the poem, such as **"gallumph,"** a blend of "gallop" and "triumph," and **"chortle,"** a blend of "chuckle" and "snort."

Of course, not all portmanteaus were invented by Lewis Carroll. Some of the others that have entered common usage—to the extent that they are no longer thought of as portmanteaus—include **"splatter,"** originally a blend of the older words "splash" and "spatter," and "stash," an 18th-century mashup of "stow" and "cache."

Another, perhaps unexpected, example is **"electrocute."** It is first recorded in 1889 in reference to executions by electric chair, a morbid combination of "electric" and "execute."

Some portmanteaus are based on names: **"gerrymander,"** for instance, is a blend of the name Elbridge Gerry and "salamander." In 1812, Massachusetts governor Elbridge Gerry (who would later be vice president under James Madison) created a convoluted, salamander- or dragon-shaped voting district intended to capture voters and benefit his party (see: salamander).

Celebrity couple names such as Brangelina, for Brad Pitt and Angelina Jolie, or Bennifer for Ben Affleck and Jennifer Lopez—or Jennifer Garner or Jennifer Lopez again—are common portmanteaus.

More and more portmanteaus are coined every day. Examples from recent decades include **podcast**, a blend of iPod and broadcast, **affluenza**, a blend of affluent and influenza, and **hangry**, a blend of hungry and angry.

Which came first, the protagonist or the antagonist?

As most literary types are well aware, your **protagonist** is the major player, hero(ine), or primary actor in your story—the one around whom the narrative revolves, the person whose journey readers are following. Think of Elizabeth Bennet in Jane Austen's *Pride and Prejudice* (1813) or Jim Hawkins in Robert Louis Stevenson's *Treasure Island* (1883). The word "protagonist" was originally a theatrical term, from the Ancient Greek *protagonistes*, a word for the main actor in a play. It is made up of the words *protos*, meaning "first," and *agonistes*, meaning "actor" or "competitor." Swap *protos* with the prefix *ant-*, meaning "against" or "opposed to," and you get your **antagonist**, or villain—the character acting against your primary actor. *Ant-* is a variation on *anti-*, which you find in words like antibiotic and anticlimactic.

Perhaps unexpectedly, however, antagonist is older than protagonist, at least in English. While antagonist was adopted in the late 1500s as a word meaning "one who contends with another" in any sort of sport or contest—so potentially a real person—a protagonist was always a performer or a fictional player in a story. Similarly, in Greek, *antagonistes* was a word for any sort of rival or competitor, while *protagonistes* was a word for a stage actor. The Greek base word of both, *agon*, meant "a struggle" or "a contest," and also forms the base of the word "agony."

Reaching the climax

The **climax** is the part of the story when the action, emotion, or tension reaches its most intense and dramatic peak. The climax of Flannery O'Connor's story "Good Country People" (1955), for example, is when the salesman Manley Pointer steals Hulga's prosthetic leg. The etymology here makes sense: The word "climax" comes from the Ancient Greek word *klimax*, which literally means "ladder," and we often think about dramatic tension rising or climbing in a story until we get to the climax.

Parts of speeches: Dialogue, monologue, and soliloquy

Dialogue can refer to any sort of conversation in a story, a play, or even in real life. The word is formed of the Greek components *dia*, meaning "across" or "between," and *legein*, meaning "to speak." A **monologue**, then—with the prefix *monos*, or "alone"—implies "speaking alone."

Shakespeare's characters, both comedic and tragic, are famed for their monologues, from Marc Antony's "Friends, Romans, countrymen …" speech in *Julius Caesar* to Hamlet's "To be or not to be …" While both these speeches are monologues, the latter is also a **soliloquy** because Hamlet is not addressing anyone except himself and the audience, while Antony is addressing listeners who exist within the play. The word "soliloquy" means "speaking to oneself," from Latin *solus* "alone" + *loqui* "to speak."

Plotting a plot

Unlike most English literary terms, **plot** is not derived from Greek or Latin. Instead, it comes from the Old English word *plot*, which first meant (and still means) a small piece of land. Its origins beyond that are unknown, but its meaning extended from "small piece of land" to a plan for building or growing on a piece of land, which led to the notion of "mapping" or "charting" something—first land or water in the 1550s, and then, in the 1640s, the storyline of a book.

Tripping over tropes

Tropes are typically associated with fiction and entertainment today, but their predecessors in Latin (*tropus*) and Ancient Greek (*tropos*) were idioms or figures of speech. The Greek word, which emerged in early commentaries on the art of rhetoric, literally means "a turn," giving the word the same sense as the English term "a turn of phrase" has—basically a phrase that is understood to have a meaning outside of its literal sense, a phrase that has "turned" from its literal sense. In rhetoric and literature, this sense of trope is also partially synonymous with cliché or motif. A trope can be an analogy, a metaphor, an allegory, and much more.

In literature, theater, cinema, and television, the idea of a trope has expanded well beyond rhetoric to encompass larger recurring storylines and archetypes that shape genres and our expectations around them. This helps us understand why someone watching a film noir, say, will likely encounter tonal, thematic, and narrative elements that are similar to those found in other films noirs.

The comedy of tragedy

You might be surprised to find that the word **"tragedy"** has a funnier origin than the word **comedy**.

In the Classical Greek theater, comedies had happy endings. The English word "comedy" is from the Greek *komodios*, which was a word for an actor, singer, or poet who performed at festivals and revelries. These performers would put on a *kōmōidia*, an amusing spectacle for everyone to enjoy.

But the word "tragedy" comes from the Greek *tragodia*, which literally meant "goat song."

There are a lot of theories about why this is.

One says that the legendary actor Thespis, for whom thespians are named, earned a goat as a prize for winning an acting competition. But the most likely theory is that goats were associated with the dithyramb, a hymn sung to Dionysus. The dithyramb was the predecessor of tragedy and usually included a chorus made up of people dressed as satyrs.

Satyrs were mythological spirits known for partying hard and having a lot of sex. In early Greek art, they were depicted with horse tails and permanent erections. Stories about satyrs began to overlap with stories about Pan, the goat-legged god of the wilds, and soon satyrs were represented as humans with goat legs. There were also parodies of tragedies called satyr plays, outrageous comedies that often followed tragedies as light relief. So, it's likely that, because of its relationship with dithyrambs and satyrs, tragedy became associated with goats.

10

Imprinted on English

The Origins of Writing, Printing, and Type Terms

The history of words and the history of writing and printing are as intertwined as ampersands. The technology that we use to communicate has influenced the words we use to describe that communication. Although the rules vary widely across countries, industries, and editorial style guides, much of the standardization we ascribe to in English has to do with the technology that has made widespread literacy and education possible.

Even the word **"book"** is named after the material on which the words therein are written or printed. Its Proto-Germanic predecessor, **bokiz*, literally means "beech," likely because some early texts were written on beech bark or beech wood.

But let's look to more recent history for some of the printing and typistry words we use today.

Putting a finer point on it: The origins and impact of punctuation

The word **"punctuation"** is from the Latin *pungere*, meaning "to prick or pierce." It's related to words like pungent, poignant, punch, and pink. This word originally referred to the practice of psalm-pointing. The dots and marks used to notate psalms so that they could be sung or chanted inspired many of the symbols we use to punctuate writing today.

Period (.) comes from the Latin *periodus*, meaning "a period of time." But it could also mean "a complete sentence," suggesting a time span in speech or writing. Over time, a period became the mark that signified when a complete sentence had come to an end. (The sense of a "time span" has stayed with us, too; that's why both eras and menstruation are called "periods.")

Comma (,) is originally from the Greek word *komma*, literally meaning "cut off," although it was also used to mean "a clause in a sentence or a line of poetry." So, a comma indicates a pause or literally "a cutting off" of a phrase that is part of a whole sentence or a line of verse.

The name of an **exclamation mark** or **exclamation point** (!) is pretty self exclamatory—er, self-explanatory—it's a mark that exclaims. It's from the Latin *exclamare*, meaning "to cry out." But what you may not know is that for a time in the mid-1800s, exclamation points were sometimes known as "shriek-marks."

The **question mark (?)** is an evolution of the 8th-century mark called the *punctus interrogativus*, which is described as resembling "a lightning flash, striking from right to left."

The **interrobang** (‽) was proposed by ad agency owner Martin K. Speckter in 1962 as a tool for copywriters to convey a surprised rhetorical question. (Today, the mark tends to suggest a question delivered with surprise and alarm or excitement, rhetorical or otherwise.) Interrobang is a portmanteau of "interrogative," and "bang," which has been printer and programmer jargon for an exclamation point since at least the 1950s.

Sarcastic punctuation

Today, we don't have one specific punctuation mark for irony or sarcasm—though many people find their own ways to express it, such as using alternating capitals and lowercase letters:

> SoOoOo iNtErEsTiNg.

One might also use tildes around a word for ironic emphasis:

> Well, isn't that ~special~

In online spaces, some people end a sentence with **/s** to convey sarcasm. This is meant to echo the structure of XML and HTML tags, implying the closing tag **</sarcasm>**.

Others may italicize select words to emphasize that they are being disingenuous:

> You're *so* clever.

We also use "scare quotes" to convey irony or disdain for certain topics:

> This so-called "word nerd" thinks she knows enough to write a book.

Attempts to express irony and sarcasm in text are nothing new. Here are a few earlier variations and relatives:

Percontation point
In the 1580s, English printer Henry Denham proposed this backwards question mark ⸮ to denote rhetorical questions. It is called a "percontation point" and is visually very similar to the Arabic question mark (؟).

Inverted punctuation
It's common to see inverted exclamation points ¡ and question marks ¿ at the beginning of sentences in Spanish and other related languages. This practice was recommended by the Royal Spanish Academy in 1754 but wasn't fully adopted until

the late 19th century. However, the inverted exclamation point ¡ was actually first proposed in 1668 by English clergyman John Wilkins, who thought it should be used at the end of a sentence to denote irony or sarcasm.

Point d'ironie
In the 19th century, the French poet Alcanter de Brahm proposed the so-called *point d'ironie*, which was designed to be "whiplike," much like verbal irony is.

Dashes and how to use them

A **hyphen** (-), the shortest type of dash, is used to create compound nouns such as "editor-in-chief" and "merry-go-round," as well as adjective phrases such as "keen-minded," "happy-go-lucky," and "topsy-turvy," and number phrases such as "twenty-six" and "forty-two."

The word "hyphen" was adopted from Ancient Greek (*hypo* "under" + *heis* "one"), and means "together" or "in one," or literally "under one"—so the symbol joins two or more words into one concept.

The next longest type of dash is the **en dash** (–). In some style, grammar, and usage guides, an en dash is used in place of the word "through" and can be used to signify things like spans of time or page numbers.

April 23–August 29
pp. 26–143

It can also replace "to" or "and":

the New York–Washington train
the employer–employee relationship

The **em dash**—which is twice as long as an en dash—can be used to enclose a clause within a sentence, especially if the author wants to draw attention to it, rather than using something like parentheses. It can also be used to create a strong break in the flow of a sentence.

"Goodness gracious—etymology is real-life magic!"

In British English, a spaced en dash is typically used in place of an em dash.

But why "en" and "em"?

Ens and ems are units of typographic measurement. An en is usually half the width of an em. An em corresponds to the width of a printing block for the letter *m*, and a lowercase *n* looks like it could be half of a lowercase letter *m*.

In practice, however, this isn't always how the measurement works. Lowercase *n*'s are not always half the width of lowercase *m*'s. And the em *sometimes* corresponds to the width of the *m* block in *some* typefaces, but not always.

A more reliable, but still not airtight, rule, especially in this era of open-source digital fonts, is that the width of an em corresponds to the point size of a font. A point is the smallest unit of typographic measurement, so, for example, in 12-point Times New Roman, an em is 12 points wide, and so is the em dash, while an en dash is 6 points wide.

The secret of the possessive apostrophe

Apostrophes came to English from French. The word **"apostrophe"** is from the Greek *apostrephein* "to turn away," literally suggesting that an omitted letter has been sent away or banished from the word.

It's obvious that a letter has been omitted with contractions such as you're, can't, or hasn't. Did you know, however, that a letter has also been cast out when we use an apostrophe and an *s* to make a possessive word? Why do we use an apostrophe in a phrase like "the queen's crown" if no letters have been omitted?

It turns out a letter *has* been omitted, but few people remember that it was ever there.

In Old English and early Middle English, there were no apostrophes and possession was usually indicated by adding the ending *-es* to the word. For example, if you were talking about a lamb's fleece, the fleece belonging to the lamb, you would make the word "lamb" possessive by adding the ending *-es*. A "knight's sword" would have been styled the "knyghtes sword."

With influence from French printers, who began to use apostrophes in the early 1500s, this *e* was dropped and replaced with an apostrophe, which showed where the letter had been omitted. This presumably provided clarity considering that *-es* was already in use as a plural ending.

Because Old and Middle English were neither standardized nor often written down, the use of the possessive *-es* ending varies a bit, but you can find examples of it in *Beowulf* (*Caines cynne* or "Cain's kin") and in Chaucer's *Canterbury Tales* (*ladyes love-drury* or "ladies' love-drury" and *lambes blood* or "lamb's blood").

Etymologists and historians have speculated that the apostrophe-s and s-apostrophe possessive is meant to be a contraction of "his," with the classic example being that "the king his crown" became "the king's crown" by means of contraction. Apostrophes do occasionally appear in such a contracted context, but inconsistently and infrequently—and this theory is limited in its applications because it fails to explain the many possessives in which "his" would make no sense, and why other possessive pronouns such as "her" or "their" would also follow this model.

And about the ampersand

The symbol we call an **"ampersand"** (&) was originally a Roman shorthand version of the Latin word *et*, meaning "and," with the letters *E* and *T* stylized into a ligature, or a typographic combination of letters. Graffiti including the symbol can still be found around the city of Pompeii.

Ligatures were common in Roman cursive, and some persisted into medieval writing styles including the Carolingian minuscule, the standard calligraphic style of the era in Europe. Another that has persisted, even today, is *æ*.

The English word "ampersand" arose in the mid-1800s and is a contraction of the phrase "and per se and," which means "(the character) '&' by itself is 'and.'" An earlier contraction, recorded in the 1700s, was "ampassy."

The reason for this long name was because the symbol was also used as a part of other shorthand. For example, an early symbol for *et cetera*, which is Latin for "and the others," was an ampersand followed by the letter *c*. So, people had to clarify that the word "ampersand" meant "the ligature symbol for 'and' or 'et'" by itself without anything else attached.

Font foundations

The word **"font,"** as in the style of the letters on your screen and in books, arose in the 1680s as a term used in the printing and movable type industry.

A movable type system uses wood and metal type blocks to stamp the shape of letters onto paper using a letterpress. The first movable type system was developed by the Chinese innovator Bi Sheng around the year 1000 CE. Four hundred years later, give or take, Johannes Gutenberg created the European printing press, enabling the cheap development of books and vastly improving literacy. To make letters for the press, molten metal was cast in molds in a process "typefounding"; the businesses that did this were "foundries." These words come from the Old French *fondre*, meaning "to pour out, or to melt." There are still industrial foundries today that make things like steel beams. Interestingly, *fondre* is also the source of the word "fondue."

The word "font" (or originally "fount") is a nominalization of "found" in the metal-casting sense. Interestingly, it does not share a root with the word "font," as in fountain, or "found," as in "foundation."

Even though they are often used interchangeably today, a font and a typeface are different things if you're working with movable type.

Font describes a full set of metal character blocks, while typeface describes the overall style of the character design. So, you might have a font (or a full set) of one size and weight of the typeface Helvetica, Times New Roman, or Proxima Nova.

The word "type" predates "font" by about 200 years, and means "symbol, emblem," from Latin *typus* "figure, image, form, kind," which in turn is from Ancient Greek *typos* "a blow, dent, impression, mark, effect of a blow; figure in relief, image, statue; anything wrought of metal or stone; general form, character; outline, sketch." So, a typeface is literally the "face" (the symbol or shape on the top) of the metal or wood block that makes the impression on the paper when printing. When we talk about typing, or striking the keys, on a typewriter or computer, we also retain some of the original sense of the Greek *typos* as "a blow."

The beauty of calligraphy

The word **"calligraphy"** entered English in the 1600s as a Latinized variation of the Greek *kaligraphia*. It literally means "beautiful writing."

The first part of the word, *kallos*, means "beauty" in Ancient Greek, and it is also the root of the name of the mythological figure Callisto. She was a nymph who, according to some versions of the myth, followed Artemis. She became pregnant by Zeus, who had disguised himself as Artemis to deceive Callisto into sleeping with her. Because of this, she was expelled from Artemis' retinue and transformed into a bear, either by the huntress goddess herself or by an angry Hera, Zeus' wife. Just as her son Arcas, future king and eponym of Arcadia, was near slaying Callisto in her bear form, Zeus apparently experienced a brief pang of responsibility and saved her by setting her in the stars as Ursa Major.

Kallos is also the source of the first part of the word "callipygian" (*kallos* "beauty" + *pygē* "rump, buttocks"), which means "having beautiful buttocks," and was originally used to describe a famed statue of Aphrodite—or perhaps of a different but still-beautiful woman—commonly known as the *Callipygian Venus*, in which she appears to be looking over her shoulder to look at her shapely backside. At some point between the Hellenistic period, the statue's head went missing, and evidently when it was restored, the angle of the head was accentuated to make it clear that she is admiring her juicy rear.

The second part of "calligraphy" comes from the Greek *graphein*, meaning "to write" or "to draw." This also gave us words like graphite, which is used for writing; cartography, the drawing of charts and maps; photography, literally images "written or drawn with light"; and graffiti, an Italian word that originally described drawings on the walls of Pompeii.

As a word-forming element, this ending (*-graphy*) can also refer to descriptions or records of any kind. This sense appears in words like geography, literally a description of the Earth; biography, literally a description of life; and filmography, literally a record of the films someone has made or appeared in.

Why paragraphs are beside themselves

In medieval writings, you'd mark a break in writing by drawing a little mark in the margin that looked like an embellished version of this symbol: ¶

As a result, **paragraph** literally means "to write beside."

In the 17th century, as printing technology advanced, the word came to refer to actual breaks in the flow of the text on the page, rather than a mark suggesting we should imagine them.

That paragraph symbol, which we still use today, is called a pilcrow. "Pilcrow" is actually a mangled variation of the word "paragraph": In Old French, *pelagraphe* was a variation of the word *paragrafe*, and this variation was misunderstood in English as *pilcraft*, which itself was corrupted to "pilcrow."

Just a tittle bit

The *T* in the phrase "to a T" is most likely short for **tittle**—typically a word for the dot on an *i* or a *j*—which is frankly a terrible thing to abbreviate when we could just be saying the extremely delightful word in full. After all, it has biblical precedent: The King James Version of Matthew 5:18 reads, "For verily I say unto you, till heaven and earth pass, one jot or one tittle, shall in no wise pass from the law, till all be fulfilled."

Just as in this verse, "tittle" is often found paired with "jot," a word originally meaning the least or smallest part of anything and later referring to a short written mark or note, from the Latin and Greek *iota* (ι) the smallest letter of the Greek alphabet.

In this passage, tittle isn't necessarily referring to the *i* and *j* dots, but to any small stroke or mark one might make, including accent marks over vowels. The latter sense is what the King James Bible is drawing on. In Latin, Matthew 5:18 uses the word *apex*, a word for an accent mark over a long vowel; the Latin *apex* is a translation of the Greek *keraia*, a word for accents and diacritical marks in writing. The Greek, in turn, is a translation of the Hebrew *qots*, a "thorn" or "prick"—in this case, one of the marks and extensions that distinguish the letters of the Hebrew alphabet from one another.

The Middle English bibles developed under the direction of John Wycliffe were the first to use "tittle." The translation of *apex* as *tittle* was inspired by the Latin *titulus*, here meaning "heading" or "superscription," but specifically a mark made over a word that has been intentionally shortened to show where letters have been omitted. This sense of the Latin word also inspired the Spanish word *tilde* (~) which looks like a *titulus*.

This mark is found in the *Domesday Book*, which was commissioned by William I, the first Norman king of England, and completed in 1086. It documents the Great Survey of England and Wales, including lands, estates, and counties, as well as the ranks of many of the influential people who owned and occupied them—along with a great deal more documentation of William's new, post-Conquest realm. (The book's name is pronounced "doomsday," using "doom" in the "fate" or "judgment" sense, because, according to 16th-century writer William Lambarde, the survey "spared no man, but judged all men indifferently.")

Many passages in the book are highly abbreviated, with some words such as *longitudine* et *latitudine* (longitude and latitude) abbreviated to "lg" and "lat" with tildes atop the letter pairs.

What the $#%! is a grawlix?

It's commonly understood that a random sequence of typographic symbols and punctuation marks, such as @$%#, is replacing a censored swear word or profanity. A set of symbols like this may be called an obscenicon, or a **grawlix**.

Grawlixes—or would "grawlices" work better?—were introduced in the comics of the early 1900s. In 1901, *The San Francisco Examiner* published a comic strip called "Lady Bountiful is Shocked," in which the titular lady comes upon youngsters trading foul language and insults, including one represented by a series of exclamation points, dashes, an asterisk, and other symbols. She is dismayed to see a smaller child exposed to the profanity and asks, "Are you listening to such language?" The child turns to her with a cheeky grin and says, "Yeh, ain't it great?"

In a 1964 article and then the 1980 book *The Lexicon of Comicana*, the artist Mort Walker introduced the word "grawlix" to a wide readership.[1] However, this word and other comics terms that Walker documents may have actually been coined by author, editor, and columnist Charles D. Rice, who frequently wrote about comics for *This Week* magazine.

"Grawlix" is thought to be imitative of words such as "growl" and perhaps something like "scrawl" with an *-ix* ending possibly meant to echo the spelling "comix" popularized by cartoonists like Robert Crumb.

Many of the other terms documented in Walker's book are similarly vague and fanciful in origin and are certainly meant to be whimsically imitative of the things they describe. Among them, Walker explains that:

> **"Blurgits"** and **"swalloops"** are the curved lines that are drawn beside the limbs of a character who is excitedly or vehemently waving them.
> **"Briffits"** are the clouds that remain behind when a character has swiftly darted away—or absquatulated, if you will.

---

[1] Mort Walker, *The Lexicon of Comicana* (Port Chester, NY: Museum of Cartoon Art, 1980).

"Indotherms" are the wavy lines rising from something hot, steamy, or stinky.
"Plewds" are the droplets of sweat that emerge from a character who is nervous or hard at work.
"Squeans" are the starbursts surrounding the head of a character who has been stunned by a blow.

The typewriter's ongoing legacy

Several modern keyboard terms are based on the mechanics of typewriters.

Many typewriters show **uppercase** (also called "capital" or "majuscule") letters at the top of each typebar, and **lowercase** (or "minuscule"—see: minuscule) letters below. The "-case" terminology comes from traditional type foundries, which typically stored the capital letters in the upper part of a type block storage cases and drawers. However, it makes sense on typewriters as well because the uppercase letters are higher on the type bar than the lowercase letters, and to type a capital letter, one needed to press the **shift** key to literally shift up the carriage—the round part of the typewriter that carries the paper side to side in order to position it for the letters to land in the correct place from left to right—so that the capital letters on the typebars align with the ribbon.

On traditional typewriters, the carriage's leftmost side shifts the left side of the paper to the center of the typewriter, and as one types, the carriage gradually moves to the left until the rightmost side of the paper is positioned in the center. Then, when one hits **return** (which is short for "carriage return") the carriage slides back to its starting position so that the typist can continue typing on the next line. The advent of data entry and coding required the distinction between an **enter** button on modern keyboards, compared to a carriage return, which only takes type to the next line. Today, on most computers, "return" and "enter" have basically the same functionality.

Solidly stereotypical

To print, say, a newspaper or magazine originally required the assembly of type blocks featuring individual letters—that is, movable type. But if you were a printer selling many print runs of a popular book, you might be better off investing in **stereotypes**—a single block cast in one big mold that allowed you to print an entire page worth of text again and again without resetting the type.

The word itself literally means "solid type." In the 1800s, a stereotype was a block of words and images printed and reprinted without change. In 1922, the reporter and political commentator Walter Lippmann wrote *Public Opinion*, in which he applied the word "stereotype" to cultural practices and preconceived notions that become a rigid and repeating facsimile of life.

Cartoonish etymology

In the late 16th century, when it was first used in English—borrowed from the Italian *cartone*—the word **"cartoon"** referred to the heavy paper or pasteboard on which preliminary sketches for artwork were made. (The word "carton," as in the packaging, is related.) While political cartoons and caricatures (literally "an overloading," from Italian *caricare* "to load; exaggerate" and ultimately from the Latin *carrus* or "cart") are much older, "cartoon" was applied to them around 1843, and then to animation around 1916.

Punch, also known as *The London Charivari*, was a weekly British satire and humor magazine founded in 1841 and is credited with popularizing the word "cartoon" in reference to editorial drawings and humorous illustrations.

Animation as we think of it today began either with the invention of the magic lantern by Christiaan Huygens in 1659, or even earlier, with the development of the camera obscura, a type of pinhole camera. It was likely the animation pioneer and newspaper cartoonist Winsor McCay who led people to apply the word "cartoon" to early animated films. His short films *Little Nemo* (1911) and *Gertie the Dinosaur* (1914) employed two different early animation techniques that would come to influence contemporary animation.

The dynamic dingbat

The word **"dingbat"** boasts an incredibly wide range of meanings and applications. In 1838, in its first recorded instance, it referred to an alcoholic drink.

It quickly developed a meaning similar to words such as doohickey, gizmo, and thingamabob, which stand in for items with unknown names (see: kadigan)

Throughout the next century and a half, dingbat came to denote a vast array of other concepts, including—but not limited to—one of a broad range of typographical ornaments (as in the typeface Zapf Dingbats by Hermann Zapf), a muffin, a woman who is neither your sister nor mother, a foolish authority figure, and, in the plural, male genitalia.

While the word took on its current, most common sense of "a foolish person" as early as 1905 in the comic strip *The Dingbat Family* by George Herriman, many people in the U.S. most associate that usage with the 1970s TV show *All in the Family*.

The emoji coincidence

It is wonderfully serendipitous that the word **"emoji"** sounds and looks similar to the Latin-derived English words "emotion" and "emote."

"Emoji" comes from these two Japanese words, meaning picture and character. Neither of them has anything to do with emotions:

Japanese *e* (絵, "picture") + *moji* (文字, "character")

"Emoji" was coined in Japanese in 1999 by Shigetaka Kurita, an employee of NTT DoCoMo.

Meanwhile, the English word **"emoticon"** *is* a portmanteau made up of Latin-derived English words ("emote" + "icon") and it's actually older than the word "emoji" by at least five years. The two words developed completely independently—though, of course, "emoji" likely caught on as the more popular alternative to the English "emoticon" after emojis were added to the iPhone in 2008 in part because it already sounded similar and familiar, albeit by happy coincidence.

11

Animalogical

Critters Hiding in Other Words

In this chapter, we'll take a talk on the wild side and discover just now many animals appear in words that seem to have nothing especially zoological about them at all.

Let's start with **muscle**. What animal do you think is lurking beneath the etymological surface of this word?

Any guesses?

It's actually from the Latin *musculus*, a diminutive of *mus* "mouse," and therefore means "little mouse." The logic here is evidently that the rippling of muscles was thought to resemble mice running and wriggling under the surface of the skin—disturbing, but charming. So, etymologically speaking, if you're mousy, you're also muscular—or, you might say, mighty—and vice versa.

Honorable mention goes to anybody who guessed "lizard." In Middle English, the word *lacertous* (literally "lizardy") was another word for muscular, from Latin *lacertus* "lizard."

Read on to discover more common words with animals lurking under their skins.

Arctic and Antarctic: Of bears and no bears

Arctic is from Ancient Greek *arktos* "bear," because the constellation Ursa Major, "the greater she-bear," also known as the Big Dipper, is always visible in the northern polar sky. **Antarctic**, therefore, literally means "opposite the bear." Serendipitously, polar bears reside at the North Pole but not the South Pole, making the Antarctic the land without bears in more ways than one.

The PIE root at play in the Greek *arktos* is **rkto-*, which is also the root of many languages' words for "bear"—in Latin (*ursus*), Welsh (*arth*), Armenian (*arj*), and more—but not in English. The English "bear," instead, derives the Proto-Germanic root **bero*, literally meaning "the brown one" or "the brown animal." (This is why the word "bear" is also related to the word "beaver.")

Some etymologists think that the English word "bear" was originally euphemistic, used in place of other, more specific (but now lost) words for bears that were derived from **rkto-*. That is, we think maybe that bears were so frightening that rather than speak their actual name, people chose to call them "those brown things" instead. Kennings—metaphorical compound words that meant something else entirely—also offered a method of working around mentioning such a harrowing creature in Old English. The name of the hero Beowulf literally means "bee-wolf," but its practical meaning is "bear"—the idea being that bears are large predators like wolves, and perhaps that they are round and furry like a bee, or like snacking on honey.

Catty caterpillars

The word **"caterpillar"** literally means "shaggy cat," and originally comes from Latin *catta* "cat" + *pilosus* "hairy, shaggy, covered with hair."

The Old English term for them was *cawelworm*, or "coleworm"; *cawel* was a word for cabbage, which caterpillars love to eat.

While that makes more sense than "shaggy cat," Modern English isn't the only language in which the word for caterpillars compares them to other animals. The modern French word for caterpillar, *chenille*, literally means "little dog." In some Italian dialects, the critter is called *gattola*, or "little cat." The Portuguese word for caterpillar, *lagata*, comes from the Latin *lacertus*, meaning "lizard."

Back to English. We have one species called the wooly bear caterpillar (the larval form of the *Pyrrharctia isabella* moth)—and many of the moths and butterflies into which caterpillars transform, like tiger moths, hawkmoths, and swallowtail butterflies, are named after other animals.

Cattle worder

Etymologically speaking, the word **"peculiar"** has nothing to do with strangeness, but everything to do with cows. It's also related to the word **"pecuniary,"** meaning "involving money/wealth."

Both are from the Latin *peculium*, literally "property in cattle."

Peculium was used to describe property in general as well, but—just like they are for the Maasai people today—cattle were considered a mark of wealth and social standing in Roman times because they were used to harvest crops and to transport goods, as well as (obviously) being a rich food source. Owning, purchasing, and breeding cattle was considered an investment in the future, and practices involving cattle were handed down from generation to generation.

This association of "peculiar" with property lingers in the phrase "peculiar to," meaning "belonging solely to." This harkens back to the Latin adjective *peculiaris*, meaning "belonging exclusively to one person," which carried its meaning over into English in the 15th century. From there, in the 16th century, "peculiar" came to mean "distinguished or special," suggesting someone endowed with great wealth (no longer necessarily in cattle) or held in high esteem. This led to what might be considered a more common use of the word today—"unusual, strange, curious"—from the 17th century onward.

But there are cows to be found elsewhere in English words as well. Take **bucolic**. Today, it means "pleasantly pastoral," but it literally means "cow-tending" (Ancient Greek *bous* "cow" + -*kolos* "tending").

What about **vaccine**?

Smallpox ravaged the world for centuries. It was finally defeated by the smallpox vaccine, which was developed by a doctor named Edward Jenner. Jenner inoculated people for smallpox by injecting them with a small amount of the related cowpox virus. Because of this bovine connection, people started using the word "vaccine" for Jenner's treatment, drawing on the Latin *vaccinus*, meaning "from cows."

Horsin' around with the hippocampus

The **hippocampus** is a component of the vertebrate brain located in the medial temporal lobe. As part of the limbic system, it plays a role in controlling emotion, memory, and the nervous system. It is vital for moving information from short-term memory to long-term memory and also helps with spatial navigation, so damage to it (sometimes caused by Alzheimer's or by oxygen deprivation) results in memory loss and disorientation.

The word itself is an English adoption of Late Latin *hippocampus*, from Ancient Greek *hippokampos*, which is comprised of *hippos* "horse" + *kampos* "sea monster." Interestingly, *kampos* is also likely related to Ancient Greek *kampe* "caterpillar," and, of course, the hippopotamus is literally a "river horse," with the second half from Greek *potamos* "river."

In Greek mythology, *hippocampus* often referred specifically to the aquatic equestrian creatures that pulled Poseidon's chariot.

So, what do horse-like sea monsters have to do with brain bits? Well, in Ancient Greek, Latin, and even historically in English, "hippocampus" meant "seahorse," due to the fact that seahorses are tiny adorable horsey-looking sea monsters. *Hippocampus* is also the name of the genus to which all seahorses belong.

In 1587, Julius Caesar Arantius (a.k.a. Giulio Cesare Aranzi), a surgeon and anatomist, discovered the part of the brain in question and compared its appearance to—you guessed it—a hippocampus, or seahorse.

However, Arantius also waffled a bit on whether it looked more like a seahorse or a silkworm. The anatomists who continued his work through the early to mid-1700s continued to debate whether the peculiarly shaped protrusion of the hippocampus ought to be referred to as a silkworm, a dolphin, or a ram's horn. The result of all this is that the scientific term *cornu Ammonis*—meaning "Ammon's horn," harking back to the Egyptian god Ammon (or Amon), who often appeared in the form of a ram—is now used to refer to different parts or "fields" of the hippocampal formation.

Octopuses, octopi, or octopodes?

If you have more than one octopus (congratulations!), are they called **octopuses**, **octopi**, or **octopodes**? Many may find my position frustrating: All three have a reasonable logic (and some illogic) behind them. That is, one could reasonably judge any one of them to be "correct" using precedent from other Latin, Ancient Greek, and English words with similar elements. Here is why.

Octopi would be the plural of octopus if it were Latin-derived with the nominal ending *-us*.

However, octopus is not Latin-derived. It's Greek, and *-us* isn't really an ending at all. Octopus is actually fundamentally a compound word: It's made up of the components *oktō* "eight" + *pous* "foot." Because it is made up of these Greek elements, "octopus" could be pluralized using the plural of *pous*, which is *podes*.

Conclusion: Octopodes is reasonably correct.

However, the word *oktōpous* didn't exist in Ancient Greek. The Greek term for this creature was *polypous* or *polupous* ("many-footed"), which entered Latin as *polypus*, and was then adopted directly into English in the 1400s. "Polypus" has also been used as a word for a cuttlefish or anemone, and inspired the medical term "polyp," which looks rather like one of these sea creatures has attached to your body. Its plural is also murky but is sometimes recorded as polypi. Octopus is a 16th-century Latinization of its Greek elements, standardized in 1758 by Swedish taxonomist Carl Linnaeus.

Therefore, "octopus" could in fact be pluralized with the Latin ending *-i*, as seen in words such as alumni, radii, and, notably, polypi.

In Latin, *octopus* is treated as a second-declension noun, which would not take the *-i* plural ending. But polypus, which has the same Latinized Greek ending, is also treated as a second-declension noun, but as we've already learned it is sometimes pluralized as polypi.

Conclusion: Octopi is also reasonably correct.

However, English does not often use Greek plurals—isopod (a kind of crustacean) is pluralized as isopods, not "isopodes," and it uses the same "foot" element—and English only *sometimes* uses Latin pluralization for words ending in *-us*. We say "campuses" and "viruses," not "campi" and "viri."

Conclusion: Octopuses is also reasonably correct.

All the above also applies to platypodes, platypuses, and platypi, words from the Greek *platypous* "flat-footed" and sharing the same Latinized *-pous* "foot" ending.

Pedigree by the foot

The word **"pedigree"** first showed up in English in the 15th century as a word for the physical documents on which your family tree was recorded.

It's derived from the Old French phrase *pied de gru*, meaning "foot of a crane."

In genealogical charts of the time, descent from one generation to the next was indicated by a small forked symbol—which, you guessed it, looked like a bird's footprint.

On a related note:

- The word "genealogy" itself comes from the Greek *genea*, which means "descent," and comes from a PIE root meaning "to give birth." This is also the root of words like genetics, generation, gender, and indigenous.
- The words "ancestry" and "ancestor" come from the Latin *antecedere*, meaning "to precede," or literally "to go before."

The ever-present pig

Pigs have a habit of turning up in other words. The oddest, perhaps, is **porcelain**, which comes from the Italian word *porcellana*, a word for a cowrie shell; it's probably the similarities between the two materials that caused people to make that leap. But the shell gets its name from the Italian *porcella*, a word for a young female pig, supposedly because of the shell's resemblance to either the curve of a pig's back,[1] or, if you flipped the shell over, the pig's nether regions. The latter sounds far-fetched, but then again, cowrie shells have long been associated with female fertility—perhaps because of their somewhat yonic undersides.

Porpoise literally means "pig-fish," from the Old French *porpais*, which is probably a Romance language adaptation of Germanic words for porpoises and dolphins like the Old Norse *mar-svin*, or "merswine," literally meaning "sea-pig," much like a "mermaid" is a "sea-girl." (The terms "porpoise" and "dolphin" are sometimes used interchangeably, but technically speaking, porpoises lack the dolphin's long "beak" and tend to be smaller and stouter, with spade-shaped teeth and a small triangular dorsal fin. The word "dolphin" is related to the Greek *delphys*, meaning "womb," because dolphins bear live offspring.)

Aardvark is an Afrikaans word literally meaning "earth-pig." There is also an African mammal called an aardwolf, or earth wolf, which is an insectivore and is related to the hyena.

Porcupine comes from the Old French *porc-espin*, literally meaning "spiny pig" or "thorny pig." It's originally from the Latin *porcus* "hog" + *spina* "thorn, spine." "Porcupine" has been subject to all manner of letter-salad spellings and pronunciations, including "porke despyne," "portepyn," "porkpen," "porkenpick," "porpoynt," and "porpentine." (The last of these actually appears in a line from *Hamlet* [1.5.20]: "Like quills upon the fretful porpentine.")

The name of the **bandicoot** (yes, that's a real animal) is first attested in the late 1700s and was originally an English corruption of the Telugu word *pandi-kokku*, meaning "pig-rat."

---

[1] As posited in *The Century Dictionary* (New York: The Century Company, 1897).

It first referred to a few different varieties of Indian and Asian rat known for their destructiveness and (often) large size. It wasn't until 1827 that several species of insectivorous Australian marsupial from the order Peramelemorphia came to be known as bandicoots due to their resemblance to the Indian rats. Since then, bandicoot as a standalone word can refer to either a bandicoot or (informally) a bilby, while several rat species native to Bangladesh, China, India, Indonesia, Laos, Malaysia, Myanmar, Nepal, Sri Lanka, Taiwan, Thailand, and Vietnam are identified as "bandicoot rats." The video game character Crash Bandicoot is an eastern barred bandicoot.

What does that critter's name *really* mean?

Gopher is thought to come from the Louisiana French word *gaufre*, which meant "honeycomb" or "waffle," because gophers' tunnels take the form of an interlocking grid.

Squirrel comes from Ancient Greek *skiouros*, literally meaning "shadow-tailed." It's unclear whether this is because a squirrel's tail moves like a shadow or because squirrels will use their tails to shade themselves from the sun.

Otter comes from a PIE word meaning "water creature." It shares this root with the Ancient Greek *hydra*, one of the monsters fought and slain by Heracles during his famous Twelve Labours. In 17th-century English, sea otters were also sometimes called "sea-apes."

Falcon is ultimately from the Latin *falx* "curved blade, pruning hook, sickle, war-scythe." The Late Latin word for the bird was *falconem*, with the bird thought to be named after the curved blade due to the shape of its talons, beak, or spread wings (or perhaps all three).

Dog: The greatest mystery of English etymology

By now, you've probably gathered that we can trace the roots of most words in English quite a long way back. But there are also some words we know almost nothing about because we can't trace their roots beyond a certain point or determine any related words. **Dog** is one of them.

It remains one of the greatest etymological mysteries in our language. Yes, it existed in Old English; yes, it's probably Germanic or Norse; but it has no known cognates.

We can trace it back to the Old English word *docga* (*dogga*) and the Middle English *dogge*, but it's a late Old English word, and was fairly rare until Middle English. The usual Old English word for dog was *hund*, which later became "hound." In fact, hound was the generic name for any type of dog as recently as the 1300s.

Dog, on the other hand, was more specific and was thought to refer to a dog breed or group of breeds. It's most often recorded referring to big dogs like mastiffs.

In the 1300s, these two flip-flopped a bit. Hound became a word for a category of hunting dog, and dog became the generic name for any domesticated canine. So, to a certain degree, the word "dog" is like a genericized trademark, like Kleenex® or Frisbee®, except with fur.

Barking cynical

Now that this book has gone to the dogs, let's stay a while. The word **"cynic"** comes from the Greek *kynikos*, literally meaning "doglike."

The Cynics were philosophers who followed the teachings of Antisthenes, who was nicknamed "the (Absolute) Dog."

Why they were called "doglike" is a matter of debate. It could have been a reference to their lifestyle. They lived a coarse, ascetic life (like a dog, according to the Greeks) due to Antisthenes' credo that all one needs in life is virtue and strength of spirit, and that "ill repute is a good thing and much the same as pain." Or it might have just been a reference to where they hung out: the Kynosarges, or the "Gray Dog," was a temple of Heracles and gymnasium just outside Athens where Antisthenes taught.

Over the centuries, the term came to refer to disdain or sneering sarcasm in general as an extension of Antisthenes' rejection of pleasure, which he identified as both unnecessary and evil, as were people who pursue it ("I'd rather be mad than feel pleasure" was one of his sayings).

The (word) origins of dog breeds

Dachshunds were bred to chase badgers out of their holes, so their name means "badger hound," from the Old High German *dahs.*

Mastiff is from the Old French *mastin*, meaning "great cur," which is originally from the Latin *mansuetus*, meaning "tame, gentle."

The **corgi**, bred for herding cattle, gets its name from Welsh, in which *corgi* means "dwarf-dog."

The Japanese dog breed called the **shiba inu** is usually translated as "little brushwood dog," referring either to the color of their fur or the landscape in which they were bred to hunt.

Saluki, or *salu-ki*, is an ancient Sumerian word meaning "plunge-earth," perhaps owing to the idea that desert hunters would launch them after prey from the backs of camels to give them a running start.

The **shih tzu**'s name is from the Chinese *shizigou*, literally meaning "lion dog."

Schnauzer literally means "growler," from the German *schnauzen* "to snarl, growl."

First called "Eskimo dogs" in reference to the term once used pejoratively to describe the Indigenous peoples of the Arctic, the word **"husky"** (first spelled "hoskey") is short for *Ehuskemay*, a variant of the word "Eskimo."

Basenji is from the Lingala language of the northeastern Congo: *mowa na basénz* is sometimes translated as "dogs of the villagers."

Mutt was originally an insult for a human (it's short for "muttonhead"). Before it came to mean a mixed-breed dog, it just meant a particularly stupid one. People may have also used the term "Mutton!" to scold dogs for sheep-worrying.

A unicornucopious diversion

Unicorns are called "unicorns" instead of "unihorns," because unicorn is borrowed from Latin, and the Latin word for horn is *cornus*. This means that unicorns are related, through a common PIE root, to words like carrot, cervix, corner, cranium, keratin, rhinoceros, and *Triceratops*.

But the etymology magic doesn't stop there.

Unicorn is also related to the word "cornucopia," which literally means "horn of plenty." (The second half of cornucopia is related to the word "copious.") By that logic, a place from which many unicorns come could be said to be "unicornucopious."

On the other hand, unicorn is not related to the word "corn," as in the grain. That kind of corn is related through its own PIE root to words like kernel, granule, granite, garnet, grenade, and pomegranate.

Given its literal meaning—"one horn"—unicorn could be a great name for one-horned rhinoceros species, such as the greater one-horned rhinoceros or the great Indian rhinoceros. Curiously, it has an indirect connection to rhinoceros. Unicorn is a Latin translation of the Ancient Greek *monoceros*, which means "one-horned," with the same second element (Greek *keras* "horn") also appearing in "rhinoceros," literally "nose-horned." However, the Greek monoceros was a somewhat different mythical creature described by the Roman naturalist Pliny the Elder in his book *Natural History* (77–79 CE). Pliny's unicorn wasn't just a horse with a horn. It had a horse's body, a deer's head, an elephant's feet, a boar's or lion's tail, and one black horn that was two cubits—or about three feet (1 m)—long. It's entirely possible that the animal he described was a real creature such as a rhinoceros or some sort of antelope.

12

Edible Words

Terms You Can Snack On

We humans think about food a lot, and it shows in the words we use.

The words **"company"** and **"companion"** combine the prefix *com-*, meaning "together," with the base word *panis*, or "bread." So, a companion is someone you take bread with or eat your meals with.

Similarly, the word **"mate"** comes from a Proto-Germanic word and literally implies someone you have meat with—with "meat" meaning any kind of food, not just animal products.

It turns out there are a lot of words that have meaty origins.

The swashbuckling pirate type we call a **"buccaneer"** is literally "one who cures or roasts meat on a *boucan*," which was a type of grill used by the Tupi people. The Tupi were native to what is now Brazil; their language blended with European languages during the Golden Age of Pirates.

When you say someone is **"brawny,"** you're literally saying they have a lot of meat on their bones—"brawn" meant "boar's flesh" in Middle English.

Another oddly meaty word is the word **"shambles,"** as in something that is "in a shambles" or messy. Shambles comes from an Old English word for a vendor's table in a market—specifically one who sold meat. Over time, a "shambles" became a word for a slaughterhouse, and then, because slaughterhouses are messy places, it became a word for a mess.

Cooked words

On a food-adjacent front, **"precocious,"** meaning "developing before the usual time," is from the Latin *praecox*, literally "to ripen before," which was originally applied to plants. *Praecox* is made up of *prae-* "before" + *coquere* "to ripen," wherein "ripen" literally means "to cook."

The PIE root of *coquere*, **pekw-*, is also the root of words like cook, culinary, biscuit, concoct, and terracotta.

Apricot ultimately comes from the same Latin construction (*praecoquum* "early-ripening"), but it took a detour through Byzantine Greek (*berikokkia*), Arabic (*al-birquq*), and Catalan (*abercoc*) or Portuguese (*albricoque*) before entering English.

Pumpkin also shares the same PIE root, coming to English via the Ancient Greek word *pepon* "melon," which seems to have implied "cooked by the sun."

Edible words of random assortment

Several satisfying words in English were once names for recipes that entailed, essentially, "an assortment of random things."

The word **"hodgepodge"** has been part of the English language since the 14th century, but at the time it was spelled in all sorts of different ways: *hotchpotch*, *hoggepot*, or *hochepot*. It was a word for a type of stew, especially "one made with goose, spices, wine, and other miscellaneous ingredients." Its literal meaning, given its French sources, is "to shake in a pot."

Here is a recipe for a goose-based hodgepodge stew from the 1390s:

GEES IN HOGGEPOT. XXXI.

> Take Gees and smyte hem on pecys. cast hem in a Pot do þerto half wyne and half water. and do þerto a gode quantite of Oynouns and erbest. Set it ouere the fyre and couere it fast. make a layour of brede and blode an lay it þerwith. do þerto powdour fort and serue it fort.

But hodgepodge also had another meaning before it meant "stew." In the 13th century, one variation of this word (*hochepot*) was an Anglo-French legal term. It referred to the process of combining things or property owned by a group of people into a common "pot," so that it could be redivided equally among them.

Another word like this is **potpourri**, which was borrowed from French in the 1600s. In English today, potpourri can mean a "medley" or collection of things, or it can refer to a heavily scented mix of spices and dried flowers. Originally, however, it was a word for a meat and vegetable stew.

In French, *pot pourri* literally means "rotten pot." It may be derived from the Spanish *olla podrida*, which is the Spanish national soup and also means "rotten pot." None of the ingredients is rotten—they're just cooked for a long time, which means they're very broken down. It's also possible that the name of the soup is a misunderstanding of the phrase *olla poderida*, which sounds similar but means "powerful pot"—perhaps because it's a rich, flavorful, and hearty soup.

The "medley" sense of potpourri probably comes from the soup, and "the spices and flowers" sense is probably further influenced by the supposed "rottenness" of the soup, because the ingredients that make up potpourri are dried and aged.

Another interesting word for your lexical treasure box is **gallimaufry**, which first appeared in English in the mid-1500s and means "a confused jumble or medley of things."

It's from the French *galimafrée*, which was a word for a hash, a dish made of odds and ends. It's thought to be a mashup of the Old French *galer*, meaning "to make merry" + *mafrer*, meaning "to eat a lot."

Salmagundi, a word and dish which first appeared in the 1600s, is composed of "chopped meat, anchovies, eggs, onions, with oil and condiments," and comes from the French *salmigondis*, meaning "seasoned salt meats," with influence from *salemine*, a "hodgepodge of meats or fish cooked in wine." Similarly, *salmi* was recorded as a word for a ragout of game bird meat in the 1700s and 1800s.

Assuming the word "salmagundi" is a combination of both, it draws influence from the Latin *sal* "salt" and *condire* "to season, flavor"—*condire* is also the root of the word "condiment"—but also the Middle English *salomene*, a variation of the hodgepodge dish's name. The Latin *sal* would also connect it to words such as salsa, salad, and salami.

Writer and essayist Washington Irving, who is largely responsible for the use of "salmagundi" as a more general word for an assortment or mishmash of things, created a humorous periodical called *Salmagundi* (subtitled *The Whim-whams and Opinions of Launcelot Langstaff, Esq. & Others*). It was incredibly popular and influential in New York and New England in its day. It's also where the word "Gotham" was introduced as a nickname for New York City, inspired by the 15th-century work *Merrie Tales of the Mad Men of Gotham*, which chronicled the antics of townsfolk in Gotham, in Nottinghamshire, England.

And finally—**chimichurri**. This word comes from the Basque word *tximitxurri*, which is loosely translated as "a mixture of several things in no particular order."

Waffling waffles

The two senses of the word "waffle" have entirely distinct origins. The word "waffle," as in the food, is Germanic in origin, with the earliest variations appearing in Frankish and Middle Dutch, usually with the meaning "cake" or "honeycomb." It's not hard to imagine how these two senses blended into the name of today's treat.

Waffle-like cakes cooked between hot metal plates are far from being a new thing. People ate them in ancient Greece and medieval Europe and many other cultures. Variations on the word "waffle" appeared in 15th-century Belgium, and the English word "waffle" first appeared in English in a 1725 recipe book called *Court Cookery* by royal cook Robert Smith.

Of course, "waffle" can also be a verb. In American English, "waffling" can mean having trouble making up your mind, especially when faced with a choice between two options. There's also the British English phrase "waffling on," which means rambling on and on for a long time without saying anything of value.

These senses derive from the Scottish and Northern English uses of the word "waff," with a frequentive suffix on the end. "Waff" is thought to be a variation of the words "waft" or "wave," which seems to have influenced the indecisive sense of "waffle" today. "Waff" is also sometimes recorded with the meaning "to bark like a dog," which may have led to the "rambling on and on" meaning of "waffling on."

Just fudge it

The word **"fudge,"** sometimes spelled "fadge" as far back as the 1500s, was originally a verb meaning to do something noncommittally or in what you might call a half-assed way in order to make information fit expectations or cover up an error. This meaning gained traction in the 1700s, especially in ships' logbooks. Indeed, the cry of "Fudge!" was not originally a mincing of the saltier F-word, but was a declaration meaning "Lies!" and was most commonly found in accounts of seafarers and their adventures.

A "Captain Fudge" is mentioned in the writings of British naval administrator Samuel Pepys, whose diaries have been widely studied because they provide such rich documentation of the Restoration period in Britain (1660–88). Evidently, Fudge was widely known as "Lying Fudge," and his reputation as "a lying rogue" (per Pepys) may have contributed to changing the spelling of "fadge" to "fudge."[1] The treat "fudge" got its name because, when it was developed in late 19th-century women's colleges, it was a recipe "fudged up" with minimal ingredients and simple preparation, compared to more complicated confections.

The comical avocado

The word **"avocado"** journeyed into English from Nahuatl, an Uto-Aztecan language native to the Nahuatl people of southern Mexico and Central America. In addition to being a word for the fruit, the original word *ahuakatl/āhuacatl* meant "testicle," because avocados were thought to resemble the body part.

Botanically speaking, avocados are berries, and they were cultivated as early as 5000 BCE in Central and South America. Much like tomatoes, they were introduced to Europeans in the 16th century as a result of colonization. (On a related note, "tomato" is also from another Nahuatl word, *toma¯tl*, meaning "fat water," "fat thing," or "swelling fruit.")

[1] Samuel Pepys, *The Diary of Samuel Pepys*, Monday, June 13, 1664. www.pepysdiary.com/diary/1664/06/13/. Accessed March 18, 2025.

Variations on this word (*aguacate*, *ahuacate*) were used in English and other European languages until the late 1600s. After that, as the fruit became more common, English speakers began to settle on the spelling "avogato." This sounds quite close to *abogado*, the Spanish word for "lawyer" or "advocate." This variation may have become the most popular word for the fruit because of persistent mishearing, or it could have been more intentional. Some have suggested that the implied lawyer-testicle association was intentional (and snarky).

In the 1700s in English, another word for an avocado was "alligator pear," and it is also known as "butter fruit" in parts of the world even today.

The Nahuatl word *āhuacatl* can be combined with other words. For instance, *ahuacamolli* means "avocado soup" or "avocado sauce," and that's where we get the word "guacamole."

Apples, apples everywhere

In Indo-European languages, apples appear everywhere in the names of different kinds of fruits and vegetables.

In Old English, the word *aeppla* could refer to any kind of fruit or mean "fruit" in general, and was regularly combined with other words to make the names of other fruits. A **date**, for instance, was a *fingerœppla*, or a "finger apple," and **cucumbers** were called *eorþœppla*, or "earth apples."

Chamomile, as in the plant whose flower is often used as an herbal tea, comes from the Greek *khamaimēlon*, meaning "earth apple" or "apple on the ground." (Those of you who know a bit of French will know that *pomme de terre*, or potato, also literally means "apple of the earth.")

Melon originally comes from the Greek *mēlopepon* "gourd-apple."

Peach was adapted via French from the Latin *malum Persicum*, meaning "Persian apple."

Pomegranate literally means "apple with many seeds," from the Medieval Latin *pomum granatum*.

In the 1500s, **marmalade** was made from the pear-like fruit known as quince. The word "marmalade" comes from the Portuguese word for quince, *marcelo*, which comes from the Latin *melimelum*, meaning "sweet apple."

In Middle English, a **banana** was called an *appel of paradis* ("apple of paradise").

Tomatoes have historically been called "love apples," apparently based on the theory that they had aphrodisiac properties.

What about pineapples?

English is one of the few Indo-European languages that doesn't use a variation of the Guarani word *ananas* to mean "pineapple."

In Middle English, the word "pineapple" was a word for a pinecone, which makes a lot of sense if you think about the way pinecones grow on pine trees, much like apples on apple trees.

During the European colonization of the Caribbean in the 1660s, English and Spanish people encountered these spiky fruits and thought they looked a bit like big pinecones. But while "pineapple" stuck for the fruit, it somewhat illogically failed to stick for pinecones—perhaps because, unlike other apples, they aren't terribly appetizing for anyone who isn't a squirrel.

The same thing happened in Peninsular Spanish, with the word *piña* predominating as the word for pineapples.

But apparently the resemblance between pinecones and pineapples didn't make much of an impression on other languages, including other varieties of Spanish, which adopted the Guarani (Paraguayan) word *ananas*. The plant's official genus name is *Ananas* as well.

Finally, to add yet another layer of identity crisis to the tragic saga of the semantically confused pinecone: In Old English, pinecones were also sometimes called *pinhnytes*, or "pine nuts" (again, not the kind we eat today, just another word for pinecones).

Apples to oranges

Word nerds of the world know that the fruit called an **"orange"** got its name before the color. Persian oranges, which were bitter compared to the oranges we think of now, were introduced into Europe in the 11th century. Their European names came from the Arabic *naranj*, which in turn came from Sanskrit. In French, the Arabic *naranj* became *orange*, which was then adopted into English in the 14th century. The color orange was probably considered a shade of red or yellow at that time, though orange things were sometimes called "citrine" or "saffron."

While some people claim that "orange" was a victim of n-rebracketing (meaning that "a norange" became "an orange"), there was never any such spelling in English. The *n*- had already been dropped when *naranj* came to French as *orange* or *orenge*.

Sweet oranges arrived in Europe about 100 years later; the color was named after the sweet version of the fruit

13

Some Word Over the Rainbow

How Colorful Language Colors Our Perceptions

Speaking of colors, English didn't have a specific, distinct word for the color **"blue"** until about the 1300s. In fact, blue is often one of the last color names to emerge in many languages. In 1969, Brent Berlin and Paul Kay did a study suggesting that languages tend to develop color terminology in a recurring pattern. First, they develop words that convey light and dark, then reddish colors, then greens or blues, and then finally all the nuance needed to fill out the rest of the color spectrum.

To this day, many cultures approach color distinctions differently. For instance, in many languages, the colors we call "blue" and "green" in Modern English are **colexified** (*co*- "together" + Greek *lexikos* "pertaining to words"), which means people use a single word to cover both. At the same time, there are many examples of the complete opposite, where other world languages consider what English speakers regard as shades of blue or green to be completely separate colors. For just a few examples:

- The Tibetan སྔོན་པོ (*sngon po*) refers to both the color of the sky and the color of some types of plants that English speakers would call green.
- The Japanese word 青 (*ao*) is a word for blue things like the sky but is also used as a word for what English

speakers would call a green traffic light and some green vegetation. The Modern Japanese word *midori* is used for most green things now, but the older and colexified *ao* stuck around for some green things.

- In Russian, light blue (голубой) is considered a separate color from dark blue (синий).
- In Korean, 푸르다 (*pureu-da*) can describe a blue sky or a green forest.

Ancient Egyptians used a great deal of blue and green hues in their artwork. The word *wadjet* was used for both, as well as shades in between. The cobra goddess Wadjet was "the Green One."

It can be frustrating, especially for those familiar with graphic design and art, to learn this while being able to point to measurable color values and hex codes that show blues and greens on different parts of the color spectrum. However, the relationship between color values and the terminology we use is not one to one. For instance, English speakers typically consider more vibrant shades of pink such as "Barbie pink" to be distinct colors rather than just "light red." And then you have variations like magenta that are pink, but not light red all, since they skew toward purple. Color awareness also varies from person to person; some people are better at distinguishing between subtle color variations and as a result often use a wider variety of words for colors. What one person calls "teal" might be simply called "blue" or "green" by someone else.

Similarly, color names and groupings don't always cleanly translate between languages, and the range of colors that corresponds to a word that translates to "red" or "yellow" or "blue" in English may include values and shades that we wouldn't use that word for.

With all this in mind, let's get back to English etymology. What did Old English speakers call blue things if the word "blue" didn't exist yet?

Many were described in terms of how light or bright (*leoht*, *bryht*), or how dark or black (*derk*, *sweart*) they were. The words for very dark or black things was *sweart*, which is related to the word "swarthy," and *derk*, the Old English predecessor to the word "dark," though that was mostly used to describe nighttime darkness. The word "black" (*blaec*) existed, but it was associated specifically with the aftermath of burning—like the darkness after a fire goes out, or the color of soot or coal. In fact, **black** actually comes from a root meaning "to burn" or "to flash," the same PIE root that gave us the word "flame."

Some shades of what we now call "blue" were called "yellow" (*geolu*, *geolwe*) in Old English. Etymologically speaking, yellow is hundreds of years older than blue. Its PIE root is **ghel-* "to shine," and it was used to describe pale or light-colored things, including light-colored blue things. Interestingly, the word "blue" shares this same PIE root, as does the word "gold."

The Old English words for **yellow** are recorded referring to actual yellow things, but also things that were light green, gray, white, hazel, orange, and light blue. Indeed, these words carried much of the meaning that we would probably ascribe to the word "blue" today—the color of the daytime sky, water, even blue or light-colored eyes. The fundamental idea was that yellow described lightness in contrast to darkness, so it ended up being the word for things that were paler or brighter than other things.

English ultimately adopted the word "blue" from the French in the 1300s, but even in Old French, *bleu* meant pale, light-colored, or blond in addition to referring to light blues like the color of the sky.

Other color names were similarly broad: Old English did have a word for **green**—*grene*—which specifically described the color of growing plants. This covered many different plant colors, so the sorts of bluish greens found in plants may have fallen into this category as well.

The word for **red** (Old English *rēad*, pronounced like "to read a book") was used to describe many red-adjacent colors including shades of orange, purple, pink, and perhaps some purplish blues.

This sort of approximation is also why we still refer to people according to drastically simplified notions of skin color. I'm pale as can be, but if you saw a paint swatch in my skin tone you would not call it "white"; similarly, while there are some Black people with very dark skin, the vast majority of Black people have skin in various shades of what a color-matching system would identify as brown. In a similar vein, the color yellow has been used to describe a whole range of people. Now, it's considered a racist term for Asian skin tones, but it has in the past been used to describe white people, Indian people, and lighter-skinned Black people as well.

White is from a different root than blue and yellow but also originally meant something like "bright," "radiant," or "clear."

Back to blue. There has been a great deal of speculation about the use of words for blue in Ancient Greek as well as in English—including discourse about whether Ancient Greek had a word for it at all. In short, it did have many words that covered the modern concept of blue but also included other colors. One reason for the confusion is that Homer's *The Iliad* and *The Odyssey* do not contain references to the color blue. He regularly describes the ocean using a term that's often translated into English as "the wine-dark sea" (a translation of *oînops póntos*, literally "wine-faced sea"). The word *kyanós* does appear in Homer, and later in Ancient Greek it is recorded as a word for a blue shade—and it's the source of the English color word **"cyan"**—but scholars believe that Homer used it to mean "dark." Homer also uses the Ancient Greek term *glaukos*, which is usually translated as "gleaming" or "silvery," to refer to the sea. *Glaukos* was also used to describe lighter eye colors including blue, gray, and green—and it is the origin of the word "glaucoma." So here we see the same colexification and blurring: In Greek, too, color words often covered a greater range of hues (including, in the case of these Homeric words, blue shades, even if they weren't words for blue in Homer's works), and in some cases implied lightness or darkness rather than pinpointing a color that would correspond to a Modern English speaker's crayon.

In 12th-century English, **lit** was another word for any color or hue. It's from an Old Norse word for the color of the sky at dawn or dusk—which, of course, could be a lot of colors—or for something dyed or stained; a cognate appears in Old English that meant "brightness" or "beauty." This word isn't related to the past tense of light, as in "I lit a candle," or to the slang term "lit," meaning "very cool." It *is* related to the word "litmus," as in "litmus test," which is a naturally blue dye extracted from certain types of lichen that turns red in acids and turns back to blue when in bases or alkaline substances.

Azure is recorded in the 14th century as a word for a shade of blue specifically made from lapis lazuli. It comes from a rebracketed form of that second element, *lazuli*, which originally came from a place in historical Turkistan where the stone was sourced. "Lapis" just means "stone" so a ruby in Medieval Latin was a *rubinus lapis*, or "red stone."

What about **woad**? Woad is a plant native to Europe with yellow flowers that belongs to the cabbage family. Once dried, powdered, and fermented, its leaves yield an indigo-blue dye that was used as far back as ancient Egypt. As a color name, it's not easy to pin down. The word "woad" literally means "water-like" and was used to mean "the color of glass," variously describing things that are blue, gray, black, or clear. The writings of Julius Caesar say that the Britons dyed their skin with *vitrum*, a word for a type of glass popular in Rome that often had a blue or green tint to it. Because *vitrum* was sometimes translated as "woad," Caesar's writings are often held up as evidence that Celtic people dyed their skin blue with woad. However, there isn't much proof that this is true, or that woad makes an effective dye for skin, or even that blue tattoos and body paint were common among Celtic Britons at all. Woad does, however, make a fair dye for textiles and can yield a range of shades from gray to blue to black—and evidence suggests that Anglo-Saxons may have used it in that way. Concrete evidence of its use in England emerges later in the medieval era, around the 1400s, when woad was a staple dye alongside a yellow dye called "weld" and a red dye called "madder." Woad would be largely replaced by imported indigo in the 16th and 17th centuries.

One color word that has varied very little over time in meaning, though it has changed a bit in spelling, is **gray**, which has basically always meant what it means today. It also features in an interesting bit of folk etymology to do with the word "greyhound," which in Old English was *grighund.* Surprisingly, the *grey* in greyhound didn't refer to the color but to the Anglian word *grig-*, meaning "bitch," as in "female dog." (Hound is simply a Germanic and Old English word for "dog.") Grizzled also meant "gray-colored" or old long before it was associated with grizzly bears, which is why we use it for "grizzled old men." Grizzly meant "partially gray," from the Old French *grisel*, "gray." Grizzly bears might be named after the color because some do have what's called silver-tipped fur, but grizzly might also be a misspelling of the word "grisly," meaning "gory" or "brutal," as in "a grisly crime."

The origin of the word **"purple"** is unknown. It was the name of the snails from which purple dyes were made—murex snails from the family Muricidae. Because this dye was so costly, the color purple was often associated with wealth. The use of the word "purple" in the term "purple prose" (which refers to excessive verbosity or thesaurus abuse) dates to the 18th century, when purple dyes were expensive and rare, and purple garments were uncommon among all but the extremely wealthy. Kings and queens, of course, were very rich, and so it's probably not surprising that, as far back as the 1500s, purple was used to describe royal things and royal people. This is likely why the purple part of "purple prose" means "ostentatious" or "gaudy."

Puce is a brownish purple color, but it literally means "flea-color." It's probably not the flea itself that people were talking about but rather the color of the scab or stain that marked a flea bite. This is also why flea-bitten is a term often used to describe certain spotty patterns on horse and dog coats.

The word **"incarnadine"** refers to a red or pinkish-red color. It's originally from the Latin *carneus* "of flesh" (from *caro* "flesh") and is related to words like carnivore. Macbeth uses it to mean "blood red" in the phrase "the multitudinous seas incarnadine" (2.2.76). It's also related to the name of the carnation flower, which is named for its pink and red shades, the colors of flesh. In the 16th century, incarnadine is also recorded as a word for light pink and pinkish skin tones.

14
Terminological
Sciences and *-ological* Words

From archeology to etymology, demonology to ornithology, the *-ologies* define our disciplines. This ending is from the Greek *legein* "to speak, tell" and the root *logos*, "word, speech." The *o* that often precedes it is a common connector for the purpose of attaching it to other word elements in a more pronounceable and less awkward way.

Words ending in *-logy* are not always fields of study—but they all do pertain to discourse, in one way or another. In some cases, *-logy* refers to methods, systems, and practices, as in pedagogy and ideology, or to treatises and speeches on a subject, as in eulogy and related words like monologue and dialogue.

In the spirit of **philology**—the love (*philo-*) and study of words (*logos*)—let's go through a few curious and interesting *-(o)logies* and their origins. (And while we're on the subject, check out the *Ologies* science podcast with Alie Ward, if you haven't already. It's great.)

Many people confuse **etymology** and **entomology**. This book is about the former—the study of the word origins. Entomology is the study of something else entirely: insects. The Greek root there, *entomon*, means "to cut," referring to the way insects' bodies are divided or segmented into parts such as the head, abdomen, and thorax. Similarly, the word "insect" itself comes from the Latin *secare* meaning "to cut," for much the same reason.

I'm told this joke perhaps twice a week—and, granted, it's a pretty good joke: "People who confuse etymology and entomology bug me in ways I can't put into words."

If you were to combine etymology and entomology into a single super-discipline, you'd end up with something like **etymentomology**, the study of the truest sense of bugs.

But this book is about words, not bugs. Okay, maybe a few bugs. But mostly words—and etymology.

Etymology and entomology are also under no circumstances to be confused with **emetology**, the study of vomiting (from Greek *emein* "to vomit")—outside of word vomit, I guess.

A few other interesting ones:

Arthrology (from the Greek *arthron* "joint") and **dactylology** (from the Greek *daktylos* "finger, toe, date"), both 17th-century terms, refer to the use of the fingers and hands to communicate—basically, sign language.

Autology (from the Greek *autos* "self"; 1833). The favored discipline of the narcissist and the Daoist master, albeit in very different ways, this is the "study of oneself" or "self-knowledge" (see: autological words).

Chaology (from the Greek *khaos* "abyss, vast emptiness"; 1728). Using the 16th-century theological and astronomical sense of the "chaos" that characterized the formless state of the universe before creation, this is the study of how the universe came to be.

Chromatology (from the Greek *khrōma* "color"; 1846) is the science of colors. If you want to know why the sky is blue, why leaves turn red, and why certain shades influence our emotions, ask your friendly neighborhood chromatologist.

Chrysology (from the Greek *khrusos* "gold"; 1842). The science of gold or wealth. This is a fitting discipline for anyone with the Midas touch or at least a fascination with get-rich schemes and with the gleam of precious metals.

Cryptology (from the Greek *kryptos* "hidden, concealed, secret"; 1645) is the study or practice of decoding or encoding information. Not to be confused with **cryptozoology**, which is the study of creatures whose existence remains unsubstantiated outside of legend, such as Bigfoot, chupacabras and the Loch Ness monster. Cryptology is similar to **teratology** (from the Greek *téras* "a marvel, prodigy, monster"), a 17th-century term for the study of monstrosities and abnormalities in nature.

Cynology (from the Greek *kyon* "dog"; 1878) is the natural history of dogs, which is the purview of anyone devoted to the study, psychology, breeding, or behavior of their canine companions.

Emmenology (from the Greek *émmēna* "menses"; 1742) is the study of menstruation. In a similar vein, **tocology** (from the Greek *tókos* "childbirth"; 1828) is an early word for obstetrics and midwifery.

Hoplology (from the Greek *hopla* "arms, armor, tools of war"; 1884) is the science of weapons and armor. It has two interesting and notable relatives: the word "**hoplite**," a class of heavily armored foot soldiers in ancient Greece, and "**panoply**," which usually refers to "a complete span or range of things," but literally means "a whole suit of armor."

Nasology (from the Latin *nasus* "nose"; 1848) is the study of noses as a branch of **physiognomy** (from the Greek *physio-* "nature" + *gnōmōn* "a judge, interpreter"), the practice of discerning someone's character by examining their facial features—reading the book of a person by its cover, so to speak. **Osmology** (from the Greek *osmē* "smell"; 1857) is adjacent to nasology as it is the study of odors.

Nephology or **nephelology** (from the Greek *nephos* "cloud"; 1890) is the scientific study of clouds.

Oneirology (from the Greek *óneiros* "dream"; 1818) is the study of dreams and the interpretation of dreams. The term "oneiromancy" means divination by way of dreams.

Onology (from the Greek *ónos* "ass"; 1670s) is a word for foolish speech. It literally means "the practice of acting like an ass."

Oology (from the Greek *ōión* "egg"; 1830) is the study of eggs, especially birds' eggs. You're supposed to pronounce each of the first two letters of this word as its own syllable ("oh-ology").

Orology (from the Greek *óros* "mountain"; 1870) is the study of mountains. Someone who loves mountains is an orophile. The equivalent for river enthusiasts is **potamology** (from the Greek *potamós* "river," which is completely unrelated, interestingly enough, to the name of the Potomac River, which is thought to be named after a Native American name for a village in what is now Virginia).

Psammology (from the Greek *psammos* "sand"; 1897) is the scientific study of sand—and, presumably, how coarse it is and why it gets everywhere.

Psephology (from the Greek *psephos* "pebble"; 1949) is the study of elections and the statistics used to predict election results. The "pebble" root traces back to the ancient Greek practice of voting with white (yes) and black (no) pebbles—a system that would also inspire the word "blackballing" starting in the 1700s. Consider this your reminder to register to vote.

Pseudology (from the Greek *pseudēs* "false, lying"; 1646) is the practice of lying or making false claims.

Ptochology (from the Greek *ptochos* "beggar"; 1891) is the study of poverty, begging, and unemployment, as well as the systemic factors that lead to economic disparities.

Uranology (from the Greek *ouranos* "heaven, the sky"; 1735) is not the study of the planet Uranus, but rather the study of the stars, the sky, and the heavens in general. Uranology was, for a time, another word for astronomy. Ouranos—or Uranus in Latin—literally means "heaven" or "the sky." The Greek god Ouranos was a personification of the heavens and the father of the Titans. The planet Uranus was identified in the late 1700s and named after the god; before that, it had been mistaken for a star.

Xenology (from the Greek *xenos* "stranger, foreigner"; 1954) is the scientific study of extraterrestrial phenomena, especially **xenobiology**, the study of life from anywhere other than Earth. **Ufology** (fancifully constructed with the initialism UFO for Unidentified Flying Object) isn't just for conspiracy theorists. It examines sightings and reports of unidentified flying objects with a serious eye—whether they're weather balloons, aircraft, or something more out of this world.

Zymology (from the Greek *zúmē* "leaven"; 1753) is the science of fermentation, especially the fermentation of foods and beverages.

15
Out of This Word
Words from Space

We call our galaxy the Milky Way because the stars and other matter that compose it look like milk splashed across the night sky. But did you know that's where the word **"galaxy"** itself comes from, too?

It's originally from the Greek phrase *galaxias kyklos*, meaning "milky circle." Funny enough, that means that lactose, the sugar present in milk, is cognate with galaxy, meaning they share a root.

The word **"planet"** literally means "wandering" and originally comes from the Greek phrase *asteres planetai*, meaning "wandering stars."

The word **"nebula"** was adopted directly from Latin, in which it meant "mist, vapor, or fog."

What about the **cosmos**? The Greek verb *kosmein* meant "to order or arrange," and the noun *kosmos* could mean either "order" or "an arrangement or decoration," especially the decoration on a fancy dress.

The philosopher and mathematician Pythagoras, inventor of the Pythagorean theorem, was the first to use cosmos to refer to the universe, possibly because the stars decorated the sky much like decorations on lavish fabric.

You might think of **chaos** as being the opposite of "order," but in the context of the chaos of space, it means "emptiness."

This word comes from the Greek *khaos*, meaning "abyss" or "that which is vast and empty."

"Chaos" eventually came to mean confusion and disorder because it was linked with the religious idea of the supposedly formless, primeval state of the universe before Creation.

Words from the stars

When you call something a **"disaster,"** you are literally saying that whatever misfortune has occurred was foretold by the stars. The word "disaster" (*dis-* + *aster*) literally means "ill-starred."

The base word, *aster*, is the Greek word for star, which means that "disaster" is related to words like astronomy and astrology (which have swapped in meaning several times), asteroid ("star-shaped"), and asterisk (from the Greek *asteriskos* "little star").

Astronomy and **astrology** have been closely—and confusingly—linked for centuries. Astronomy showed up in English first (in the 12th century) but originally encompassed both the spiritual and the scientific study of celestial bodies.

Astrology showed up in the 14th century but was divided into "natural astrology" (foretelling tides, seasons, eclipses) and "judicial astrology" (foretelling how the stars impacted human affairs).

Astronomy eventually became the more science-focused term in the 17th century as an echo of the classics: in Latin, *astronomia* was more scientific than *astrologia*.

You already know that the root of **"asterisk"** is the Greek *aster*, meaning "star." The ending, though, makes it cute. It's the Greek diminutive suffix *-iskos*. So, an asterisk is a "little star" both in shape and by name.

That *-isk* ending is also cognate with the ending -ish, which acts as a diminutive in words like smallish, blueish, and sixish. It's also a diminutive, in a way, in words that speak to nationality and culture (English, Spanish, Jewish), since the individual described is a smaller extension of the whole culture or nation.

Asteroid more or less means "star-like" or "star-shaped," with the ending from *eîdos*, "form, shape"—the same one we learned about in "factoid" earlier in this book. (This is also why starfish belong to the class Asteroidea.)

Meteoric etymology

Meteor comes from the Greek *metéōron*, literally "a thing high up" in the air. In 15th-century English, meteor could refer to any atmospheric phenomenon visible from the ground. That's why meteorology refers to the study of atmospheric conditions, rather than just shooting stars.

These atmospheric conditions were divided into four categories based on four elements (air, water, light, and fire):

- aerial meteors included tornadoes and other windstorms
- aqueous meteors included water-based atmospheric phenomena such as rain, snow, hail, dew, frost, and clouds
- luminous meteors included auroras, rainbows, and other light-based phenomena
- igneous meteors included fiery-looking phenomena such as lightning and shooting stars.

Around 1590, as astronomy advanced, the word "meteor" began to take on the more specific, fiery, extraterrestrial meaning it has today.

Comet, meanwhile, is from the Greek *komētēs*, meaning "longhaired," in reference to comets' tails. Meteors and comets can both look like streaks of light, but they are different: Comets are made of ice and dust and orbit the Sun, and their tails appear when the Sun vaporizes that ice and dust; meteors are made of rock and metal, and they appear as shooting stars when they burn up in Earth's atmosphere. A meteorite is what remains of a meteor when it hits the ground.

Ring around the zodiac

The word **"zodiac,"** referring to the division of the night sky into segments, each of which contains certain major constellations, originally comes from the Greek phrase *zodiakos kyklos*, literally meaning "circle of little animals."

But, as you may know, one of the zodiac signs is not an animal at all—not even a human or mythological animal, as in the case with Gemini, Sagittarius, and Aquarius.

Libra is represented by a set of scales. Today, there are 12 signs corresponding to the zodiac constellations, but to the Greeks there were only 11. However, Scorpio was considered a "double constellation," with what is now Libra composing its claws.

In Old English, the zodiac was called *twelf tacna*, meaning "the 12 signs." In Middle English, it was sometimes called "the Bestiary" or "Our Ladye's Waye," referring to the path of the moon through the night sky.

People have been watching the stars for centuries, and the concept of **constellations** comes from ancient Mesopotamia. The Greeks adopted the idea around 500 BCE, and Ptolemy recorded 48 official constellations. Today there are 88 constellations that were officially recognized by the International Astronomical Union in 1922. The word "constellation" is from Latin and literally means "stars shining together."

Unearthing Earth

The planet **Earth** gets its name from the Old English *eorþe*, meaning "dirt, soil, or country." It was also occasionally used as a verb meaning "to bury someone."

In Old English, "earth" was also a word for the material human world, but that was more commonly known as *middangeard* (middle-dwelling). That name shows up in *Beowulf* and also much more recently in the Marvel Cinematic Universe. It was also the word "midden-geard" that inspired the name of J. R. R. Tolkien's Middle-earth. In Germanic mythology, which includes Old Norse and Anglo-Saxon legends, Midden-geard, or Midgard, is one of the Nine Worlds and the only one visible to humankind. It is surrounded by an impassable ocean, which is inhabited by the sea serpent Jörmungandr, who is so huge that he encircles the world and grasps his own tail like a massive ouroboros (Ancient Greek "tail devourer").

Just like the Roman Terra and the Greek Gaia, it's thought that Earth may have been personified as a goddess in Germanic mythology.

Earthlings of old

Despite evoking science fiction and interactions with aliens, the word "earthling" dates back to Old English.

You'll notice that we don't use this *-ling* ending when describing the residents or attributes of other planets. There are no "Marslings" or "Venuslings," but there are Martians, Venutians, and so on—at least in stories about these planets. Earth is the only planet in our solar system that commonly goes by its Germanic name. The others are named after Roman gods, and therefore their adjective-forming endings are also Latin-derived. You could, of course, refer to Earth by its Latin name, *Terra*, which would make all of us "Terrans." There are a few science fiction franchises that follow this convention. But most anglophones call their home by its German name, "Earth," and use a Germanic suffix when they refer to themselves as "earthlings."

Interestingly, though, the Old English word *yrþling* ("earthling") did not originally mean "a being from Earth."

To get at its original meaning, let's take a look at its suffix: the *-ling* ending is actually a mashup of two Old English endings, *-le* and *-ing.*

The *-le* ending usually makes a word into a tool or something used for a purpose: A thimble is literally a thumb-tool; a handle is a thing your hand can use; a girdle is used for girding or enclosing your body.

The ending *-ing* can, of course, be used to create different verb tenses and participles (walking, shouting), but when it's attached to the *-le* suffix, it's being used as a diminutive.

So put the *-le* and *-ing* endings together, and you get small things that do things or are defined by certain qualities.

A **hatchling** is a little thing: a bird that just hatched. A **yearling** is a little thing: a young deer that's about a year old. A **sapling** is a little tree: a little thing full of sap.

These words don't directly reference the big thing that they are small versions of. We say hatchling, not "birdling" or "birdlet" or other variations. Rather, these *-ling* words describe small things by invoking their qualities, uses, or behaviors.

But what about **duckling** and **gosling**? That's just like a little duck or a little goose, and they say exactly what animal it is. True—except those words describe behaviors and qualities, too.

Ducks are so named because they duck or dive under the water. So, a duckling is literally a little thing that ducks under the water.

The root of the word "goose" is meant to be imitative of its honking, so a gosling is a little honking thing.

When it comes to people, these endings can also describe lower rank in addition to small size.

Like in the theatre of Shakespeare's day, commoners would watch plays from the floor, standing on the ground, and so they were called **"groundlings."**

A **hireling** is someone who works for hire—that is, a working-class person.

A **shaveling** used to be a mocking term for a friar with a shaved head, a low-level member of the clergy who lived an ascetic lifestyle.

In Old English, there was also the word *frumbierdling*, meaning "young man," literally a man still on his first beard.

So, let's take this back to earthling. It literally means a low-ranking person who works the earth. So, in Old English, an *yrþling* "earthling" was originally a word for a plowman.

This word acquired the meaning it has today in the 1500s, but instead of contrasting earth-dwellers with aliens, it was used to contrast them (us) with deities. So, you had heavenly beings, or gods, and earth-beings, or earthlings.

Its first use in science fiction is thought to be in 1949, in the novel *Red Planet* by Robert A. Heinlein.

16

Temporal Etymology

Behind the Names of the Seasons and Months

Have you ever considered the different types of dates?

The use of the word "date" to refer to the days on your calendar arose in English in the early 14th century, from the Old French *date* of the same meaning, but originally from the Medieval Latin *data*—feminine singular of *datus*, meaning "given," and past participle of *dare*, "to give, grant, offer." (As you might expect, this is also the origin of the English word "data," suggesting "given" numbers or facts.) The original source, the PIE root **do-*, also means "to give," and forms part of the following words (among many others): fedora, Pandora, betray, pardon, anecdote, perdition, and antidote.

Seems an oddly vague origin, eh? It was popularized as a term for "date" thanks to the Romans, who typically closed their letters by writing "given" + the day and month (and often place) the letter was given to the *cursus publicus* (the Roman Empire's state-run courier service). For example, if I were a Roman, I might close a letter with "given at Mantua on the last day of June." Over time, as the most common practice became to "date" a letter with the day of the year, the meaning was refined, and the word *data* became the common term for a specific time.

Date in the sense of a romantic liaison arose surprisingly recently, in 1885, around the time that the meaning of the term broadened to include something like "appointment." By 1902, it was often used to refer to regular and repeated "dating," or "going steady."

The fruitier meaning of date is older—late 13th century—than the calendrical sense of the word, which I find fairly surprising. It does make sense, though, given the origin. Depending on where you are, date can refer to both the individual fruit and the entire tree, although usually that's called a "date palm." In either case, its origin (by way of Latin and French) is the Ancient Greek *dáktulos*, meaning "finger" or "toe" due to its resemblance to a human digit.

Of course, there's far more calendrical etymology to consider beyond this singular word "date."

On the calendar

Today, most of the world uses the Gregorian calendar, named after Pope Gregory XIII (r. 1572–85). It aligns calendars with the position of the sun over the course of the year. Although the names used for the months are derived from both Latin and Greek, their timing is a result of the Roman months blending with those of other calendars. The old Roman calendar, used before 46 BCE, began in March.

In Latin, some months were called "the month of ______." For example, February was called *februarius mensis*, or "the month of purification."

January gets its name from Janus (*Ianuarius* in Latin), the two-faced Roman god of doorways, changes, beginnings, and endings.

February comes from the Latin *februare*, meaning "to purify." This was the last month of the ancient Roman calendar and was a time for renewal. In Old English, the name for the second month of the year was *solmonað*, which supposedly meant "mud month."

The term **"spring"** refers to the springing of plants from the ground, and in its earliest forms, starting in the 14th century, this season was invoked using phrases like "springing times" and "spring of the year." "Spring" could also describe what's happening to a person showing signs of puberty, or to the rising of the sun or the tide, as in the phrases *spring of dai* "sunrise" and *spring of mone* "moonrise." During the 15th century, this season was also sometimes known as *prime-temps*, related to the Modern French *printemps*, which is based on the Latin *tempus primum*, literally "first time, first season." In Old English, the usual term for spring was *lencten*, which would eventually become the word "Lent" in Modern English, but is literally a compound meaning the "lengthening of the days" as the weather warms.

March or **Martius** was the first month of the ancient Roman calendar, which is thought to have been used starting in the 7th or 8th century BCE. Its name refers to the Roman god Mars, whose equivalent in the Greek pantheon was Ares. In Old English, this month was called *hreðmonaþ*, which probably meant something like the "quick month" or the month of nimbleness and activity.

April or **Aprilis** was the second month of the old Roman calendar. Folk etymology influenced the spelling of "April," so that it looked more like the Latin *aperire* "to open" (related to "aperture), but it's probably derived either from the name of an Etruscan version of the Greek goddess Aphrodite, or from a root meaning "the following" or "the next." In Old English, April was called *Eastermonað*.

Easter meant "dawn" and was also the name of a goddess of fertility and spring. It's related to the word "east." Anglo-Saxon Christians started using the word "Easter" for the resurrection holiday around the 6th or 7th century CE.

May or **Maius** was the third month of the ancient Roman calendar, from the Roman Earth goddess Maia, whose name is thought to mean "she who is great." In Old English, May was called *Þrimilcemōnaþ*, literally "three-milking month," or the month in which cows can be milked three times a day.

Summer has remained relatively consistent since the Old English *sumor*, a word that referred to the hottest season of the year and, later, to one's age counted in summers because they were considered the most pleasant.

June's name is from the Latin *Iunius* (*mensis*), the month sacred to Juno, the Roman goddess who oversees women and marriage, and corresponds mostly to the Greek goddess Hera (with some Athena in the mix as well). Her name in Latin may literally mean "the young one," related to words such as "junior" and "juvenile."

July is from the name of Julius Caesar, who was born in the fifth month of the year, originally called *Quintilis*. It was renamed after his death and later shifted to the seventh month.

For similar reasons, **August** is named after Augustus Caesar, Julius' great-nephew. The name itself means "venerable" or "noble," literally "blessed by the augurs," officials who read signs in the behaviors of birds (also the source of the word "inauguration").

It's fitting that we have two words—**autumn** and **fall**—for what is irrefutably the best season of the year. (Fight me.) Until the 16th century, the Old English word for autumn was "harvest" (or *hærfest*), so we had a third one.

The Anglo-Saxons didn't consider **harvest** to be a season unto itself. Instead, they split the year into six months of summer and six months of winter, with harvest being the last period of summer. Harvest was actually the name for that transitional period before it became a word for gathering up crops, which tended to happen during that time.

Fall is also from Old English. The Old English *faellen* not only meant "to drop from a height" but also to fail, decay, or die—hence warriors falling in battle.

Like many words that entered English thanks to the French, **autumn** comes from Latin. Beyond that, it's a bit of an etymological mystery. The Latin *autumnus* either comes from the Latin *auctus*, meaning "increase" (which would likely link *autumnus* to harvesting crops), or it might mean something like "drying-up season."

There was never a single PIE root referring to autumn, unlike the other seasons, so there are several very different European words for it. They mostly have literal meanings like "harvest" (German *Herbst*), "after-year" (Danish *efterår*), "late" (Catalan *tardor*), or even "reddish" (Latvian *rudens*).

September, **October**, and **November** come from the Latin words for seven, eight, and nine because they were the seventh, eighth, and ninth months of the old Roman calendar, which began the year in March. The Julian calendar, which was proposed by Julius Caesar in the year 46 BCE, eventually moved the year back two months, but the names stuck around, nevertheless.

September replaced the Old English word *hærfestmonað*, meaning "harvestmonth." "October" replaced the word *winterfylleð*, which meant "winter full (moon)" because the first full moon of the Anglo-Saxon winter took place in October.

The Old English word for "November" is delightfully witchy—it was *blotmonath*, meaning "blood month," the time when the early Saxons prepared for winter by sacrificing animals, which they then butchered and stored for food.

December continues the numerical theme, meaning "tenth month," from the Latin *decem* "ten"—with these months likely sticking with numerical names because they fell at the end of the year, after the harvest. In Old English, the name of this month was *Gēolmōnað*, meaning "yule month."

Winter, which hasn't changed its name since Old English, may literally mean "the wet season," or "white," depending on its Germanic source.

On the days of the vernal and autumnal equinox—March 20 and September 23—daytime and nighttime are of approximately equal duration all over the planet. So, the word **"equinox"** literally means "equal night" (Latin *aequus* "equal" + *nox* "night").

The **solstices**—usually around June 21 and December 21—are the days when the sun reaches its highest or lowest point in the sky at noon, which means these are also the longest and shortest days of the year. Solstice comes from the Latin *solstitium*, meaning "sun stillness," or the point at which the sun seems to stand still. In early English, the word was "sunstead," using the word "stead" as in steady, steadfast, and homestead.

One last one. The **moon** in "honeymoon" means "month." (Indeed, month literally means "one moon cycle.") A **honeymoon** was originally not a post-wedding trip but the days immediately following the wedding when new spouses bask in a "honeyed" glow of happiness. More cynically, it also suggests that marital bliss lasts *only* a month.

Part 3
Whimsy and Wonder

Humor, Play, and Passion Through Enchanting Etymology

17

When Words (and Their Origins) Get Silly

Sometimes words are just plain quirky. In the 16th century, the term **"quirk"** meant "an artful evasion" or "a twist and a flourish." This twisty sense gave us the adjective "quirky" in the early 1800s, which then shifted the meaning of the noun "quirk" to today's meaning: "an eccentricity or odd quality." Interestingly, and serendipitously, quirky is also thought to be related to the word "queer," which comes from a Germanic root meaning "twist."

Queer was primarily used to mean "strange" or "odd" until the 1920s, when it started describing romantic or sexual interest as well. At first, it was used in a pejorative way, reflecting the original meaning, but since then of course the term has been artfully reclaimed and reframed as the positive gender identity term we know today.

Eccentric, meanwhile, was originally an astronomical term. In geocentric models of the universe, planets whose orbits did not seem to rotate around Earth were called "eccentric," from the Greek *ekkentros*, meaning "out of the center." Like these supposedly uncentered planets, an eccentric person might behave unusually or follow their own social orbits.

The word **"absurd"** has some absurdity—and unfortunately a dash of ableism—baked into its etymology. Its Latin elements are the prefix *ab-*, which means "off" or "away from," and *surdus*, which was an adjective primarily used to describe people who were deaf or nonverbal. So why do these two elements mean "illogical" or "ridiculous" when they're put together?

There are two explanations. In Latin, the full word *absurdus* meant the same thing as the English word does today and was often used to describe silly and improper behavior. At the same time, it was also used to describe a sound or bit of music that was out of tune, discordant. So, one explanation is that "absurd" was meant to imply that something is out of harmony with what is normal, reasonable, or proper, something that was somehow "tone-deaf."

Linguist Michiel de Vaan has a slightly more interesting and almost punny explanation. Because that Latin *surdus* was applied to both "someone who cannot hear" and "someone who is not heard," the term "absurd" could be said to describe things that are literally "unheard of" because they are so illogical and ridiculous.

One additional interesting fact about the Latin word *surdus* is that it's probably from a root meaning "to buzz" or "to whisper," which seems to mimic the symptoms of hearing loss. As a result, it also shares a root with the word "susurration" which refers to whispering sounds and often appears in the context of wind wafting through leaves and the oscillation of birds' wings.

Is this all just a farce? You decide. In the 14th century, the English word **"farce"** originally meant "stuffing," like the bready bits shoved into your turkey. It comes (via Old French) from the Latin *farcire*, meaning "to stuff, cram." But what does stuffing have to do with the comedic sense of the word? In the Middle Ages, it was a fairly common practice to fill out—or stuff—the texts of the Mass and religious plays with additional passages. Often, these took the form of impromptu comical interludes, which eventually evolved into their own genre of ludicrous satire.

This whole book, on the other hand, is almost entirely composed of comical interludes, and this last part even more so. What follows is a collection of words that might make you **giddy**, which literally means "possessed by a god," from the Old English *gydig*, meaning "insane" (from the Proto-Germanic **gudam* "god" + **-ig* "possessed").

Chatty etymology: Words for wagging tongues

As Jane Austen has her hero Henry Tilney observe in *Northanger Abbey* (1817), "Every man is surrounded by a neighborhood of voluntary spies."

Curiously, the oldest known relative of the word **"gossip"** originally meant "godparent." It evolved from the Old English term *godsibb*, literally "God relative," related to the word "sibling," which in Old English was a term for any relative or kinsperson.

Spelling was flexible at the time, and ultimately the variation "gossip" prevailed as the word expanded in Middle English to become a word for a close friend or neighbor.

Indeed, it was used most often as a word for women friends who got together on a regular basis for social occasions. And what, according to gendered stereotypes, do women friends do when they get together? They chat idly about the people in their lives.

By the 16th century, gossip had taken a negative turn, describing someone with a voracious appetite for rumors and the unfortunate habit of spreading them around.

In the 19th century, it expanded in meaning, encompassing not just the people doing the chatting but the chatting itself. Gossip soon came to refer to idle socialization—particularly of the more scandalous and rumor-driven variety.

When you're off on your own etymological investigations, you may encounter a false theory about this word—gossip about gossip, you might say. Some say that gossip comes from the phrase "go sip some ale," supposedly because politicians would tell this to their staffers, encouraging them to go to taverns to listen in on constituents' conversations in order to learn what public opinion was. This, predictably, is without evidence and does not align with the timeline of the word.

Flibbertigibbet, which dates to 1549 as a word for a person prone to gossip, is meant to fancifully echo the tittering chatter of such a person. (The same sort of judgmental, echoic energy can be found in the word **"persnickety"** and the earlier variant "pernickety," both describing someone snooty or particular.)

Similarly echoic words for people, especially women, who engage in gossip include **"bablatrice"** (1595), **"clatterfart"** (1552), **"jangleress"** (1386), **"prattle-basket"** (1602), and **"chattermag"** (1844).

Rumors tend to spread quite quietly, but the etymology of the word **"rumor"** itself speaks to how loudly they can reverberate. Although its Latin predecessor, *rumorem*, shared the same sense as the English word today, it literally meant "noise" or "clamor." This sense shows up in early French and English texts as well as a term for a commotion or a public outcry, along with the hearsay that might emerge from it.

Even in the Elizabethan era, the poet Michael Drayton wrote of "the rumorous sound" of the crashing Red Sea.

Scuttlebutt, a nautical-inspired term for gossip, rumors, and interpersonal news shared among coworkers, dates to the early 1800s and is quite literally the sailor's equivalent of "watercooler talk." A "scuttlebutt" was a cask of fresh drinking water kept aboard a ship, around which sailors loitered and chattered much as they might around the watercooler in an office break room. "Scuttle" here refers to a hole (also seen in the term "scuttling," or opening holes in a ship's hull to deliberately sink it) in the top of the cask, while "butt" is recorded as a word for a cask or barrel as early as the 14th century—indeed, before it's recorded as a word for a human rear end.

Yammer flip-flopped in meaning from "mournful" to "mildly mocking." It's ultimately from the Old English *geomor*, meaning "sorrowful," with its verb form, *geomrian*, referring to the act of lamenting or making a cry of mourning. It took on its mocking tone in the 1500s, likely because agonized wails tend to be rather loud and grating. In this way, it came to refer to any loud or annoying noise, and later blathering, annoying chatter.

Jargon, adopted from French in the 14th century, originally meant "unintelligible talk, gibberish; chattering, jabbering." It wryly took on its current meaning—"phraseology peculiar to a sect or profession"—in the 1650s due to the fact that such speech was unintelligible to outsiders.

Incidentally, the unintelligible sense of jargon also arose around the same time as the word **"jabber,"** which is from the Old English word *jablen*, meaning more or less the same thing. (Other Old English variations included *javeren*, *jaberen*, *chaveren*, and *jawin*.)

Jabber gave rise to **gibberish** in the 1550s or so as an adaptation of "jibber-jabber." In the 17th century, gibberish was used pejoratively to refer to the language of the Romany people, who were often called "gypsies."

And as you probably know, Lewis Carroll capitalized on the meaning of the word "jabber" in his nonsense poem "Jabberwocky," which first appeared in *Through the Looking-Glass, and What Alice Found There* (1871), the sequel to *Alice's Adventures in Wonderland*.

Related facts

In the early 2000s, the word **"jargonaut"** arose to refer to someone who uses too much jargon. The latter half of the word is a punny callback to the Argonauts (sailors on the *Argo*) of Greek mythology who quested for the Golden Fleece.

Much like jargon means "jabber," the word **"motto,"** which originally referred to phrases attached to heraldic designs (think *E pluribus unum*), comes from the Latin *muttire*, meaning to "mutter" or to "mumble."

Discombobulating etymology

"Discombobulate" was one of several verbs that were coined in the 18th and 19th centuries by mischievous writers who would make a game out of compiling word elements—especially Latin-sounding prefixes, suffixes, and roots—into fanciful combinations. Because these elements were typically Latin-derived or were meant to sound Latin-derived, the resulting words are sometimes called "pseudo-Latinate terms."

Discombobulated means "confused" or "disoriented" now. Its original meanings included "embarrassed," "upset," or generally thrown off.

Recorded variations include "discomboberate," "discombobricate," and "discombooberate."

If you remove the prefixes, you end up with the mostly irrelevant element *bob* or *bobule*—but that's not terribly important because the prefixes do the work of conveying the meaning of the word. The Latin prefix *dis-* means "not" or "opposite of," and the prefix *com-* means "together," giving "discombobulated" the literal sense of not being totally "with it." It may have been in part inspired by the word "discompose," meaning "to cause someone to lose their composure."

There are several other words created as part of the same Victorian brain game:

Absquatulate combines the negative prefix *ab-* and the word "squat" with a verb ending to give it the meaning "leave abruptly or run away."

Bloviate combines blow and orate to describe someone speaking nonsense or talking out their ass like a politician might.

Conflabberated is a combination of confuse and flabbergast. (By the way, **flabbergast** predates all of these, but it too is probably a silly portmanteau in a similar spirit. It's thought to be a blend of flabby or flap, as in "flapping lips," with the word "aghast," suggesting that you're surprised into speechlessness.)

Flustrate is a portmanteau of fluster and frustrate.

Obflisticate is an intentional overcomplication of the word "obfuscate," which means "to make something unintelligible or unclear."

Scrumplicate means "to eat" and is a play on scrumptious with that *-ate/-icate* verb ending, perhaps influenced by words like delicacy and delicious.

Spiflicate emerged in the late 18th century in cant dialects with the meaning "overcome" or "confounded." It may be inspired by or related to the Scottish slang term "spiffed," meaning "slightly drunk," thus lending spiflicated the meaning of "completely drunk" in many contexts.

Some of these words are first documented in both British and American literature in stretches of humorous dialogue delivered by bombastic, gregarious, or overconfident American characters (see: macaroni). These characters are often endearing but are certainly implied to be more rustic and less educated than those they share the page with.

Absquatulate is a great example. It appears in the dialogue of the strutting, buckskin-wearing character Nimrod Wildfire, a caricature of Davy Crockett, who appeared in several plays from the mid-1800s. (By the way, this cartoony character, named after the biblical Nimrod, a tyrant and great hunter, likely contributed to the ironic use of the word "nimrod" for Elmer Fudd in the *Looney Tunes* cartoons. "Nimrod" would then go on to be an insulting term for anyone who is thought to be incompetent or clumsy.)

Generally, this was all in good fun even if British writers were being a little classist when they made fun of Americans for not using "proper" English. One exception is the word **"confusticate,"** which means "to confound or confuse." Its first known appearances are in pro-slavery works including "The Cabin and Parlor," which was a response to Harriet Beecher Stowe's *Uncle Tom's Cabin* (1852). There, it's used as an example of highly exaggerated (and racist) slave dialect; it's meant to mock the speaker's intelligence.

An elocution of etymologists: Animal and professional collectives

You're likely familiar with collective nouns for animals such as a "herd of cattle" or a "murder of crows"—or perhaps even a "prickle of porcupines," a "flamboyance of flamingos," an "ambush of tigers," an "exaltation of larks," or a "dazzle of zebras."

These are called **nouns of assembly** or **terms of venery**, where venery is a word for the sport of hunting, from the Latin *venari*, meaning "to chase or pursue." "Venery" is also a word for the pursuit of sexual pleasure (hence "venereal diseases"), and it was used with great relish as a double entendre in 15th-century hunting culture.

Many terms of venery are first recorded in the 1486 *Book of Saint Albans*, or *The Book of Hawking, Hunting, and Blasing of Arms*, which was a gentleman's handbook. However, it is thought by many to have been written by a woman—Juliana Berners, a nun who wrote many treatises on hunting and field sports.

It contains about 150 collective nouns, including what may be the first recorded instances of now-common phrases like a "gaggle of geese," a "pride of lions," and "litters" of baby animals. These terms were meant to be imitative of the behavior of the animals they describe, whether through onomatopoeia, association, or more literal observation of animal characteristics. For instance, "murder" reflects the dark omens with which crows are associated; and "litter" was originally a word for straw bedding, which a domesticated animal might lie on while giving birth.

Here are a few others from the *Book of Saint Albans*:

a peep of chicks
a leap of leopards
an unkindness of ravens
a murmuration of starlings
a shrewdness of apes
a skulk of foxes
a sleuth of bears.

You may not know this, but the *Book of Saint Albans* doesn't stop at animals. It also includes human-centric terms such as:

a melody of harpers
a blast of hunters
a sentence of judges
a subtlety of sergeants
a superfluity of nuns.

If these sound funny, it's because they're meant to. They were all part of the wordplay and banter of gentlemen's hunting culture, and it was a mark of your knowledge as an experienced hunter to be able to name all the collectives.

What would your profession or hobby's collective noun be? A "revision of editors," a "launch of astronauts," a "conflagration of firefighters"?

Ruining words

Many times, learning about etymology takes you on a journey of discovery full of magic and wonder and beauty. That's not the case for these words.

At various points in your life, you've probably used the words "plethora" and "melancholy." You probably felt clever and poetic—but they are secretly disgusting.

Ever felt kinda puffy or had red patches on your skin? From the 1500s through the 1800s, doctors might have told you that you had **plethora**, a medical term referring to any number of conditions they believed were caused by an excess of blood or other bodily fluids. In fact, plethora is still a medical term describing a flushed face today. The word comes from the Greek *plēthōrē* "fullness," and it wasn't extended to refer to things other than bodily fluids until the 1700s.

In the same vein, you've probably read or heard the word **"melancholy"** and understood it to be a word for sadness—especially cinematic, romantic sadness.

But melancholy literally means "black bile." According to humoralism, a precursor to modern medicine, this fluid was one of the "four humors," which also included blood, phlegm, and yellow bile. An imbalance of any of these was thought to cause various kinds of mental instability and mood swings. An excess of melancholy or black bile was thought to cause low spirits—to the extent that melancholy came to be used as a term for depression, sullenness, gloominess, or irritability—pretty much any sort of bad mood. Which you were in because your internal juices were extra black.

The word "melancholy" does have one redeeming factor, however. The first element, *melan-*, is also the base of melanin, the polymer that gives all animals—including humans—their own unique skin, hair/fur, and eye color.

And then there's **fundament**. It means "base" or "foundation," as in "fundamental."

Fundament has also been used—both in jest and in deadly seriousness—for the buttocks or the anus since the 1300s … because you sit on it. The following is from a 16th-century animal husbandry guide, which advises putting various unspeakable things in your horse's "yarde" (penis) or soap in his "fundament" if he can't pee.

> And yf so be you see he can not stale, or staleth with paine, you must bathe hym with bath appoynted for colde, that is, oyle mingled with wine pored vpon his loynes: also a Louse put into his yarde, or Sope put into his fundament, hath been seene to helpe him. If this doo not helpe, you must squirt in Hony boyled thinne with Salt into his yarde [1]

Fundament appears in *many* 16th-century guides to horses and what to do to their buttholes.

---

[1] *Foure bookes of husbandry, collected by M. Conradus Heresbachius, counseller to the hygh and mighty prince, the Duke of Cleue: conteyning the whole arte and trade of husbandry, vvith the antiquitie, and commendation thereof. Nevvely Englished, and increased, by Barnabe Googe, Esquire*, in the digital collection *Early English Books Online*. University of Michigan Library Digital Collections. https://name.umdl.umich.edu/A03069.0001.001. Accessed March 18, 2025.

It really sucked to be Edward II, king of England from 1307 to his deposition in 1327, according to the argument of a ballad by the 16th-century writer Thomas Deloney, though whether this actually happened to Edward is disputed:

> …they locked him in a most noysome filthy place, that with the stink thereof he might be choaked; and when that prevailed not, how they thrust a hot burning spit into his fundament, till they had burnt his bowels within his body, whereof he dyed.[2]

The term "farting by the fundament"—as opposed to "belching by the stomach" or "sneezing by the nostrils"—is also recorded in an 1806 translation of Aristotle's works.[3]

---

[2] Thomas Deloney, *Works. Edited from the Earliest Extant Editions and Broadsides, with an Introduction and Notes by Francis Oscar Mann* (London: George Routledge & Sons, 1912), 405. Internet Archive. https://archive.org/details/workseditedfrome00delouoft. Accessed March 18, 2025.

[3] Aristotle, *The Works of Aristotle the Famous Philosopher: Containing His Complete Masterpiece and Family Physician; His Experienced Midwife, His Book of Problems, and His Remarks on Physiognomy* (London: John Smith, 79 High Holborn, 1830).

18

Games You Can Play with Your Words

Wordplay is a time-honored tradition—as is bending them into puzzling combinations in poetry, parlor games, jokes, puzzles, and riddles—and in this chapter we'll examine a few of the words we use to describe puzzling wordplay.

One such word is **conundrum**, whose etymology is a bit of a conundrum itself.

This word first appears in English in the late 16th century, supposedly at the University of Oxford, where it was used as an insult for an overly pedantic or studious person, which suggests it might be mock-Latin, perhaps poking fun at someone a bit too invested in their Latin studies. In other words, conundrum doesn't mean much of anything etymologically—it's more or less Latin gibberish—but it originally served the purpose of the word "nerd" (an insult that also originated on college campuses, but not until the 20th century).

In the next century or so, the meaning of "conundrum" diversified. It could mean …

> A whim, or a fanciful thought or phrase: One might be said to "have strange conundrums in one's head."[1]
> A punny quip or a stupid joke: Samuel Johnson's dictionary defines it as "a low jest; a quibble; a mean conceit: a cant word."

The spelling of this word also went off the rails—though, since it lacks a firm origin, who's to say it really had a correct spelling in the first place? Variations included "conimbrums," "qunnundrum," "conuncrums," "cunnunders," and "quadundrums." Some of these appear to be trying to connect or conflate it with quandary, which is also pseudo-Latin, possibly inspired by the Latin *quando*, meaning "when?" or "at what time?"

My personal favorite variation of conundrum is *quinombroms*, mostly because of the context in which it appears. In 1770, historian and political writer James Howell assembled a work that he called *Lexicon Tetraglotton*, ostensibly an English–French–Italian–Spanish dictionary, but more a heavily editorialized collection of words and phrases in these languages across several disciplines. In it, he wrote: "You will judge perhaps, that the Author hath some strange freaks, or quinombroms in his noddle."[2]

And indeed, that might be your judgment of his book, but given that you've made it this far into *this* book, I think you and I would both be hypocrites if we were to cast stones at people with quinombroms in their noddles.

---

[1] *The bond-man an antient storie. As it hath been often acted with good allowance, at the Cock-pit in Drury-lane: by the most excellent princesse, the Lady Elizabeth her Seruants. By Phillip Massinger*, in the digital collection *Early English Books Online*. University of Michigan Library Digital Collections. https://name.umdl.umich.edu/A07234.0001.001. Accessed March 18, 2025.

[2] James Howell, *Lexicon Tetraglotton: An English-French-Italian-Spanish Dictionary*, 1st ed. (London, 1659–60).

In the late 18th and early 19th centuries, conundrum arrived at today's meaning: It went from a punny play on words or a whimsical thought to a riddle (that might include a pun or wordplay), and from there was extended to a word for a generally puzzling or difficult, or even unanswerable, question or situation.

Dean Rivers' 1903 *Conundrums, Riddles and Puzzles* is stuffed with both punny and philosophical riddle-like conundrums, beginning with the following, which nods to the idea that "true" conundrums cannot be answered or solved: "Why is life the greatest of all conundrums? Because we must all give it up."

Read on to see if you can puzzle out the origins of more types of wordplay and riddlery.

The original charades

The name of the game of charades is interestingly a bit self-contradictory today. A singular charade is, of course, an act or an event that's obviously false, or an absurd or convoluted attempt to look like your behavior or appearance is respectable while doing or being something worse. It's a Provençal word meaning "long talk" or "chatter," implying talking or prattling on and on as part of your pretense.

As a game, though, it was originally a type of riddle, and in this type of riddle, the answer is a word with two or more syllables, and the first line or two of the charade describes the first syllable, the next one or two describe the second syllable, and the rest explains how they fit together.

They were popular during the Regency era and feature in Jane Austen's *Emma*. For example:

My first doth affliction denote,
Which my second is destin'd to feel

And my whole is the best antidote
That affliction to soften and heal.[3]

Explanation:

"My first doth affliction denote" → The first syllable is "woe."
"Which my second is destin'd to feel" → The second syllable is "man" because a man feels woe.
The best antidote to soften and heal a man's woe is a woman.

Another one from a 1791 collection is:

My first is a preposition → "for"
My next is a composition → "tune"
And my whole is an acquisition → fortune

The modern version of the game was originally called "dumb charades," or later "silent charades" or "acting charades," but instead of describing the syllables, you act out how many, and then act out each one until you get the whole word.

Puzzling out puzzles

There are two theories about the origin of the word **puzzle**. One is that it's from an Old English word, *puslian*, meaning to pick out or select something. The idea would be "to dither over selecting" or "to be bewildered" and thus unable to proceed.

The more interesting theory is that **pose** is to **puzzle** as **nose** is to **nuzzle**. The *-le* ending is frequentive, meaning it implies a repeated action, either rubbing your nose on it or

[3] Jane Austen, *Emma* (London: R. Bentley, 1886), 59.

repeatedly attempting to solve a problem. To pose also originally meant "to perplex," so puzzle could imply something that frequently poses or perplexes people. Puzzle dates back to the late 1500s, and it was a verb before it was a noun—to confuse versus the state of feeling puzzled, or for a situation that is puzzling. You could be "at a puzzle" about a problem, or you could be "in a puzzle," and in fact one of the *OED*'s earliest references to it is in Henry Porter's 1599 play *Pleasant Historie of Two Angrie Women of Abington*. One of the titular angry women says, "Swounds what a pussell am I in this night."

But a puzzle wasn't regularly used as a word for a game or test of ingenuity or knowledge until the late 18th or early 19th century, with an early reference being in Sir Walter Scott's 1814 novel *Waverley*, referring to a toy known as a "reel in a bottle," which is like one of those novelty puzzles you find where you have to disassemble it.

It was first used in the context of jigsaw puzzles in the 18th century when mapmaker John Spilsbury glued maps onto wood and cut them into pieces for educational purposes. The name *jigsaw* of course refers to the tool used to cut the wooden pieces in early puzzles—a narrow, fine-toothed saw.

Reading into riddles

The word **"riddle"** comes from the Old English *rǣdels*, which had a ton of meanings, not just the sort of wordy clever puzzles we run into today but also "counsel, consideration, debate, conjecture, interpretation, imagination, example." It's probably related to the word "read" and could even imply a frequentive sense of the word "read," suggesting that you must "read into" a riddle or read it more than once. (To be "riddled with holes" is to be like a *ridelle*, which is a Middle English word for sieve that is not related to the word "riddle" as in a puzzling question.)

The Greek word for a riddle was *ainigma*—also appearing in English as **enigma**.

The Sumerians wrote what's often said to be the world's oldest riddle; there are a few variations, but the simplest one in English is: "There is a house. One enters it blind and comes out seeing. What is it?" The solution: A school.

A 17th-century English riddle or nursery rhyme reads:

As I was going to St. Ives,
I met a man with seven wives,
Each wife had seven sacks,
Each sack had seven cats,
Each cat had seven kits:
Kits, cats, sacks, and wives,
How many were there going to St. Ives?[4]

The answer: One. Only the speaker was going to St. Ives.

Running the length of the palindrome

A palindrome, as you likely know, is a word or phrase that reads the same backward and forward (kayak, rotator, civic, madam). The word literally means "a running back" or "a running again," from the Greek *palin* "back, again" + *dromos* "a running."

Dromos is also the source of dromedary, a one-humped camel known for its speed. The Greek name for this animal was *dromas kamelos*, literally "a running camel."

The modern use of the word "palindrome" is often attributed to Elizabethan playwright and poet Ben Jonson, and it is indeed found in a 1640 collection of his poems published after his death. Here, Jonson lists many types of word

[4] Iona Opie and Peter Opie, *The Oxford Dictionary of Nursery Rhymes* (Oxford: Oxford University Press, 1951, 2nd ed., 1997), 376–7.

puzzles, including "logogriphes," "those hard Trifles Anagrams," "Esteotichs," "Acrotichs," and "Telestichs."

However, as you can see, Jonson's text implies that his reader is already familiar with palindromes. A slightly earlier text by the London official John Philipot attributes palindromes to the antiquarian William Camden, whose collected works—also published posthumously—may have predated Jonson's. Some have also suggested that the essayist Henry Peacham may have come up with the term "palindrome" when discussing the Latin phrase *Subi dura a rudibus*, which means "Endure rough treatment from uncultured brutes." Apparently, that somewhat dispiriting slogan appeared above the door of a schoolhouse in a town that—at least according to Peacham—was full of rude and uncultured people. Or, you know, children.

A palindrome from around this time by Edward Phillips reads "Lewd did I live, and evil I did dwel."

There have been some great debates about which single-word palindrome is the longest—not least because the longest ones tend to be rather fanciful. James Joyce's *Ulysses*, for instance, contains the onomatopoeic "tattarrattat." *Guinness World Records* has declared that "detartrated"—the state of a substance from which tartrates, which are related to tartaric acid, have been removed—is the longest single-word palindrome.[5] Most of the long palindromes that stand a chance at being used in conversation are mostly proper nouns, like the "Rotavator" brand of tilling machine, or "Malayalam," the South Indian language.

Palindromes are intriguing to math geeks as well as word nerds: Belphegor's prime (1000000000000066600000000000001) is a palindromic prime number named by author Clifford A. Pickover after the demon Belphegor, which is said to help

[5] Guinness World Records. "Longest Palindromic Word." https://www.guinnessworldrecords.com/world-records/longest-palindromic-word. Accessed December 8, 2024.

people make ingenious discoveries. Also, fun fact: If one squares the number 111,111,111, the result is, satisfyingly, a palindrome of the numbers one through nine: 12345678987654321.

Two books have been written as palindromes, from start to finish (and back again): David Stephens' 1980 *Satire: Veritas* (58,000 letters long) and Lawrence Levine's 1986 novel *Dr. Awkward and Olson in Oslo* (31,957 words long). It leaves one wondering how their editors managed.

Palindromes also turn up frequently in music and poetry:

- Soundgarden released a bonus CD accompanying their studio album Badmotorfinger entitled *Satan, oscillate my metallic sonatas.*
- The comedian Demetri Martin wrote a poem entitled "Dammit I'm Mad." The whole poem is a palindrome, as are its title and its last line on their own.[6]

There are also wordless musical palindromes. Joseph Haydn's Symphony No. 47, written in 1772, contains several, with parts of the Minuet and Trio written so that the second part comes first, but backwards.

Palindromes existed in Greek as well, but they were described as *carcinicos* or *karkinikos*, which is an adjective meaning "crab-like" and today is also a word meaning "cancerous," since—as you know from the zodiac—"cancer" also means "crab." But Greek palindromes are often written in mosaic-style text, such that the letters themselves are symmetrical. This means that they can be read backward and forward.

A delightful case-in-point: The Panagia Malevi monastery in the Peloponnese includes a mosaic in a washroom that reads ΝΙΨΟΝ ΑΝΟΜΗΜΑΤΑ ΜΗ ΜΟΝΑΝ ΟΨΙΝ, or "Wash your sins, not only your face."

---

[6] Demetri Martin, *This is a Book* (New York: Penguin, 2011).

Because this last palindrome can be read from left to right and from right to left, it's also a **mirror ambigram** (from the Latin *ambi-* "both, on both sides" + Greek *gramma* "letter, something drawn"). This is a typographic or lettering design that can be read from multiple directions or interpreted from multiple perspectives. (For this reason, ambigrams are also examples of visual puns.) One of the most common types of ambigram is a rotational ambigram, where a text or lettering design can be rotated and still remain legible as the same word—or as a different one. The concept is ancient (with examples popping up in Greek washrooms, Arabic calligraphy, and Hebrew art), but the term itself was coined by the computer scientist Douglas Hofstadter in the 1980s.

The artist and writer Peter Newell created an iconic series of English ambigrams, or what he called "reversible illustrations" or "ambiguous images" because they also included pictures that could be interpreted from two directions. Artists like John Langdon and Scott Kim popularized ambigrams in the 1970s, with Langdon's work gaining particular notoriety when they were incorporated into the plot of Dan Brown's novel *Angels and Demons*. (The main character, Robert Langdon, was eponymously named after John.)

A word that spells another, different word when spelled backward (BONK :: KNOB) is known as a **heteropalindrome** ("a different running back," from *hetero-* "different"), or an **anadrome**, which mashes together the *ana-* prefix from anagram and the ending of palindrome.

Although anadrome is perhaps a little more fun to say, etymologically speaking, "heteropalindrome" is the more accurate term. This is because anadrome and palindrome actually mean more or less the same thing. The prefix *ana–* also means "back" or "backwards."

Then again, the word **"anagram"** itself doesn't quite encompass what we take it to mean, because its components, *ana-* and *gramma*, give it the literal meaning "backward letter."

As we know, anagrams are words made up of letters that can be rearranged in any number of ways to make other words.

One form of anagramming used in ancient Greece and in the Middle Ages was called *themuru*, which supposedly meant "changing." The practice of *themuru*, or anagramming names, is said to have been used to find hidden meanings. For example, Cabalists rearranged the Hebrew letters of the word "Messiah" to find the meaning "he shall rejoice." These transformed anagrams were often a bit labored, aiming to find subliminal meaning where there is often none.

A more lighthearted, witty practice of playing with anagrams has been popular in Latin and English for millennia. Here are some examples:

> *Quid est veritas?* (What is truth?) <—> *Est vir qui adest* (It is the man who is here)
> William Shakespeare <—> I am a weakish speller
> anagrams <—> *Ars magna* ("the great art" in Latin)

An especially fun type of anagram is the **antigram**, which is what you get if you scramble up the letters of the word to make a new word that is a sort of sardonic commentary on the original word:

> funeral <—> real fun
> a volunteer fireman <—> I never run to a flame
> evangelist <—> evil's agent

Pangrams, meanwhile, are sentences that contain all letters of the alphabet. The classic example is "The quick brown fox jumps over the lazy dog." That's not the shortest possible pangram, though, since it contains 35 letters, including repeats. Other pangrams with fewer letters include "Jackdaws love my big sphinx of quartz" and "Pack my box with five dozen liquor jugs," both of which are documented by author Tony Augarde in *The Oxford Guide to Word Games* (Oxford University Press, 2003).

X marks the spot

Chiasmus is a rhetorical device based on a Greek word meaning "shaped like the letter X." It's when you take the grammatical structure of one sentence and reverse it but then change the words. Like this:

> Love without end, and without measure Grace.
>
> John Milton, *Paradise Lost*, 3.142

> But O, what damned minutes tells he o'er
> Who dotes, yet doubts; suspects, yet strongly loves.
>
> Shakespeare, *Othello*, 3.3.167–8

> And these tend inward to me, and I tend outward to them.
>
> *Walt Whitman*, "Song of Myself"[7]

Similarly, **antimetabole** is when you reverse the grammatical clause but keep the same words. This means that antimetabole is bit more immediately recognizable, and tends toward aphorism and cliché:

> "When the going gets tough, the tough get going."
> "I know what I like, and I like what I know."
> "If you fail to prepare, you prepare to fail."

[7] Walt Whitman, *Song of Myself* (New York: 1855).

There are a few more literary examples. Case in point:

> Fair is foul, and foul is fair.
>
> Shakespeare, *Macbeth*, 1.1.11

Admiring the paraprosdokians along the garden path

Sometimes, silly things happen to good sentences. For instance, a **paraprosdokian** is a statement in which the second half changes the way you understand the first half. The word itself was first recorded in the 1800s and is formed of Greek elements that give it the meaning "against expectations."

A classic paraprosdokian: "I've had a perfectly wonderful evening, but this wasn't it."

That one is typically attributed to Groucho Marx (without evidence; Groucho himself denied he said it), but the first known use of a variation on this quip appeared in a serialization of the 1835 movie *No More Ladies* in *The Bedford Times-Press*.[8]

Dorothy Parker was famous for her witty paraprosdokians. Here are two that she supposedly fired off in conversation with other members of the Algonquin Round Table: "You can lead a horticulture, but you can't make her think" and "The best way to keep children at home is to make the home atmosphere pleasant, and let the air out of the tires."

[8] "No More Ladies: From the Stage Play by A. E. Thomas, Adapted by Beatrice Faber from the Metro Goldwyn Mayer Picture, Chapter One: A Date with Sherry," *The Bedford Times-Press*, June 20, 1935, 7, quoted in *Quote Investigator*, https://quoteinvestigator.com/2012/07/02/wonderful-party-not/. Accessed August 24, 2024.

> Rodney Dangerfield was full of them: "My wife and I were happy for twenty years. Then we met."
> Mae West: "Marriage is a great institution, but I'm not ready for an institution."
> Winston Churchill: "You can always count on the Americans to do the right thing—after they have tried everything else."
> Zsa Zsa Gabor: "He taught me housekeeping; when I divorce I keep the house."
> Demetri Martin: "I saw a sign that said 'watch for children' and I thought, 'That sounds like a fair trade.'"

While paraprosdokians are usually funny, they don't have to be. There's one that's often misattributed to Abraham Lincoln that goes "In the end, it's not the years in your life that count. It's the life in your years."

Garden-path sentences and paraprosdokians are pretty similar in that the way you understand the statement changes when you get to the second half, often (and especially in the case of garden-path sentences) by incorporating words that could belong to more than one part of speech.

The difference is that paraprosdokians are clearly meant to be clever, while garden-path sentences tend to be more misleading and can take a minute to interpret. They get their name from the idiom "leading someone down the garden path" (or "the primrose path") which means to mislead them.

Here's a famous garden-path sentence: "The horse raced past the barn fell." When you get to "fell," you have to rethink the sentence and reinterpret the word "raced" as a passive participle: Once you do that, you come up with something like "The horse (that was) raced past the barn fell (down)."

Here's another: "The old man the boat."

Rephrased: "The old (people) man the boat." When you reread it, you realize that "the old" is a noun phrase and "man" is a verb.

Some Groucho Marx quips are also garden-path sentences. He wasn't the first to make this joke, but he popularized it: "Time flies like an arrow; fruit flies like a banana." This is a garden-path sentence because it forces you to reconsider which part of speech "fruit" is and reinterpret the second instance of the word "flies" as a plural noun instead of a verb.

"Flies" in this sentence offers an example of **antanaclasis**—a Greek word meaning "a reflection (of light, sound)" or literally "a bending back against"—which is a literary and rhetorical device in which a word is repeated but with two different meanings. Another example of antanaclasis is this quote attributed to Ben Franklin: "Your argument is sound, nothing but sound."

Garden-path sentences cause **syntactic ambiguity** or **amphibology** (from the Greek *amphi-* "both" + *ballein* "to throw", or "hitting at both ends").

Amphibology can also arise inadvertently, like in many a newspaper headline. A **crash blossom** happens when copyfitting restrictions result in word and punctuation choices that make a headline nonsensical and ambiguous. Crash blossoms are named after a 2009 headline in the newspaper *Japan Today*.[9]

"Violinist Linked to JAL Crash Blossoms"

That is: "A violinist who was linked to a Japan Airlines plane crash is enjoying a newly successful career."

At first glance, though, you'd be forgiven for wondering what a "crash blossom" is. It's this ambiguity that inspired that phrase as a neologism for confusing headlines.

---

[9] Ben Zimmer, "Crash Blossoms," *The New York Times*, January 27, 2010.

Here are a few more famous ones:

"Missing Woman Remains Found"
That is: "The missing woman's remains have been found."
"Scientists Count Whales from Space"
That is: "Scientists are counting whales using satellites," not "Scientists are counting whales that came from space."
"More Midwest Twisters: Why is Oklahoma Tornado Vexed?"
That is: "There are more twisters happening in the Midwest. Why is the state vexed by tornadoes?" (This one would have benefited from a well-placed hyphen.)
"McDonald's Fries the Holy Grail for Potato Farmers"
That is: "McDonald's fries are the Holy Grail (or a huge sales opportunity) for potato farmers."
"British Left Waffles on Falklands"
That is: "Left-wing British leaders are waffling, uncertain what their political position on the situation in the Falkland Islands should be."

19
Word Gaffes
When Words Trip Us Up

"A rolling stone gathers no moths."
"He was a man of great statue."

These are **malapropisms**, a form of misspeaking in which you mistake a word for one that sounds similar. These gaffes get their name from the character Mrs. Malaprop, from Richard Brinsley Sheridan's 1775 play *The Rivals*.

Mrs. Malaprop's name comes from the French *mal à propos*, literally "badly for the purpose," but also "inopportunely" or "inappropriately."

She tends to speak "badly for the purpose" because she aims for unnecessarily grandiloquent language, or what you might call flowery or purple prose. She says things like "*pineapple* of politeness" instead of "pinnacle of politeness" and "it gives me the hydrostatics" instead of "it gives me the hysterics."

In what may be her most egregious line in the play, Mrs. Malaprop says:

> If I reprehend anything in this world, it is the use of my oracular tongue, and a nice derangement of epitaphs![1]

[1] Richard Sheridan Brinsley, *The Rivals*, in *The School for Scandal and Other Plays* (Oxford: Oxford University Press, 2008), 46.

By which she means: "If I *apprehend* anything in this world, it is the use of my *vernacular* tongue, and a nice *arrangement* of *epithets.*"

In plainer English, that means—with a heavy dose of irony: "If I understand anything, it's the English language and descriptive words."

Malapropisms happen in real life all the time, too. Former Texas governor Rick Perry is particularly notorious for it. Some of my favorite Perryisms include "lavatories of innovation" instead of "laboratories of innovation," and "electrical votes" instead of "electoral votes."

Eggcorns vs. malapropisms

An **eggcorn** is the mistaken use of a word that sounds similar to or actually the same as the word you intend to use.

Eggcorns and malapropisms are alike, but not exactly the same. Both involve choosing a word that is close to the one you intended, but malapropisms have a few distinct features: the mistaken word is blatantly incorrect; it makes no sense in context; and the resulting statement is funny or absurd.

Eggcorns tend to be more understandable mistakes. The mistaken word is often closer to the intended word, and they're not always funny. In fact, they usually still make sense in context.

You might say or write "would of" instead of "would've"—a very common eggcorn—or "ex-patriot" instead of "expatriate," or "preying mantis" instead of "praying mantis," or "oldtimer's disease" instead of "Alzheimer's disease."

These still make logical sense, and they're common mistakes that a lot of people make, typically because they haven't seen the word they want to use in writing.

Linguistics professor Geoffrey Pullum named these minor mistakes "eggcorns" based on a case in which someone substituted the word "eggcorn" for "acorn" in a letter. Since an acorn is an egg-shaped "corn," or seed, it's a pretty logical error.

Eggcorns tend to crop up in idioms.

When you want to get to the root of a problem or put a stop to something, you might say "nip it in the butt." But the actual, "correct" phrase is "nip it in the bud," as in snipping the bud off a plant so that it won't blossom.

Another common one: "for all intensive purposes" rather than "for all intents and purposes."

Writing that something will "wet your appetite" is an eggcorn of "whet your appetite," with "whet" referring to a blade-sharpening whetstone—and therefore the idiom implies a sharpening of your hunger. "Wet" is an eggcorn rather than a malapropism because it makes perfect sense to suggest that hunger might cause your mouth to water.

You may encounter someone saying or writing "wreck havoc," rather than the older and more editor-approved term "wreak havoc." In the phrase "wreak havoc," the word "wreak" means "to cause" or "to inflict," from the Old English *wrecan*, meaning "avenge," or "drive out."

Sometimes eggcorns become so common that they overtake the original phrase in popularity. For example, the older idioms "bald-faced lie" and "barefaced lie" have been largely replaced by "bold-faced lie." The newer term is often explained away as relating to false news headlines (in a bold typeface), but there's not a lot of evidence that it was ever used that way in practice. These days it's also more common to see "chomping at the bit" rather than the original phrase "champing at the bit"; "champ" is an older term for a horse or other hooved animal's chewing or biting.

You may have noticed that eggcorns often happen with more archaic words. If you're keen to avoid them, etymology can help.

For example, you see many people use "weary," which means "tired," when they mean "wary," which means "cautious."

It helps to remember that wary is related to the word "aware," and both are from the Old English *waer*, meaning "prudent" or "cautious."

There's also "bated breath," which is often misspelled "baited breath," like fishing bait. But "bated" here is related to the word "abate," meaning "to reduce or end" something, so "bated breath" means your breath is halting or shallow.

All of that said, there is still a great deal of overlap between malapropisms and eggcorns.

A funny or absurd malapropism that is easily repeated often can enter common use and become an eggcorn.

The subreddit community /r/BoneAppleTea—itself a malapropism for "bon appétit"—has compiled lots of examples of this, like "chupacabra" instead of "capybara," "lemonade" instead of "laminate," and "roast history" instead of "rotisserie."

But some examples, such as "lie detective test," at least make some logical sense, so those could be said to be eggcorns *and* malapropisms.

One more vocabulary misstep belongs in this category: **mondegreens**. Mondegreens are malapropisms or eggcorns that result from misheard song lyrics. They were so named by journalist Sylvia Wright, who admitted in *Harper's Magazine* in 1954 that she had misheard this lyric to the Scottish ballad "The Bonnie Earl o' Moray" (written ca. 1700s):

Ye Hielands and ye Lowlands,
O, whaur hae ye been?

They hae slain the Earl o' Moray,
And laid him on the green.[2]

[2] Francis James Child, ed., *English and Scottish Ballads*, vol. 7 (Boston, MA: Little, Brown and Company, 1860).

Wright confessed that rather than the words "laid him on the green," she heard "Lady Mondegreen" and wondered who the unfortunately (ostensibly) slain lady had been.[3]

Dord: A misinterpretation that became a ghost

How does a word become a ghost?

The year is 1931. Austin M. Patterson has a recommendation for his colleagues at G. & C. Merriam Company, predecessor to Merriam-Webster. There's a list of words in their dictionary for which the letter *d* can be an abbreviation. Patterson, who specializes in words pertaining to chemistry, wants the editors to add that either the capital letter *D* or the lowercase letter *d* may be used to abbreviate the word "density."

So he submits a slip with the following note on it: "D or d, cont./density."

At the time, in the editorial department of dictionaries, when you typed up notes like this one, you'd type the headword, or the main word in the entry, with spaces in between the letters.

Patterson's first slip was lost, and when it was retyped, someone misread "D or d" and "D o r d," suggesting that "dord" was a word meaning "density."

Sure enough, in Webster's 1934 *New International Dictionary*, 2nd edition, an entry was introduced reading:

> **dord** (dôrd), n. Physics & Chem. Density.

[3] Sylvia Wright, "The Death of Lady Mondegreen," *Harper's Magazine* 209, no. 1254 (1954): 48–51.

This is how dord became a **ghost word**—a word that appears in a dictionary or other authoritative reference book but otherwise doesn't exist. Dord remained in the dictionary for five years. It was removed in 1939 after an editor noticed it, but it hung around in some print runs until 1947.

The term "ghost word" was coined in 1886 by William Walter Skeat, president of the UK's Philological Society. He collected around a hundred examples of ghost words that have appeared in dictionaries, notably the *New English Dictionary*, such as:

Feamyng: This was recorded in several dictionaries as a collective noun for a group of ferrets. The generally accepted term is a "business" or a "busyness." ("Busyness"—the state of being busy—here is distinct from "business," despite their identical etymological components.) But feamyng, as it turns out, was the result of a misreading. The *Book of Saint Albans*—the original, 15th-century hunting treatise that documents many of the names for animal collectives that we still use today, such as "pride of lions," "litter of kittens," and "murder of crows"—was written in an ornate and somewhat wobbly handwriting style. It states that a collective of ferrets should be called a "besynes of ferettis." But when 18th-century readers tried to transcribe the text, "besynes" was misread as "fesynes," which then mutated into "fesnyng" and "feamyng" in an unfortunate game of handwriting telephone (see: an elocution of etymologists).

Kime: This was added to the dictionary due to a misprint of the word "knives" in an 1808 edition of the *Edinburgh Review*, which read, "The Hindoos [Hindus] … have some very savage customs … Some swing on hooks, some run kimes through their hands."

Morse: For decades, successive editions of Sir Walter Scott's novel *The Monastery* contained the line "dost thou so soon morse thoughts of slaughter?" Footnotes were even added to explain what "morse" might mean in the context of the 1820 novel—after all, Morse code wouldn't be introduced until the 1850s—with some assuming it meant "to prime," as one might prime a musket. Only when editors consulted the original manuscript in Scott's handwriting did they discover that the original word was actually "nurse."

Abacot: a misinterpretation of the term "a bycoket." A bycoket is a medieval-era cap with a brim that comes to a point in the front and folds up in the back, much like those seen in various depictions of Robin Hood. An "abacot" is, well, nothing at all. Skeat said "there is no such word" and called its presence in the dictionary "a complete mistake… due to blunders of printers or scribes, or to the perfervid imaginations of ignorant or blundering editors."

Mountweazels, nihilartikels, and fictitious entries

Ever heard of Lillian Virginia Mountweazel? Ever tasted the dish called funistrada?

Before computers and AI made large-scale textual analysis possible, plagiarism and counterfeiting were common in printed documents.

The solution: hide fake information within a legitimate work to serve as a trap for those who might seek to steal or reproduce that information without paying for it or citing it properly.

The very publisher of this book, Chambers, included errors as far back as 1964 in *Chambers's Shorter Six-Figure Mathematical Tables*, to prevent the unwary copyist from lifting information wholesale from its pages.

When they crop up in dictionaries and encyclopedias, these are usually called "fictitious entries" or "fake entries," for obvious reasons. But there are more entertaining and specific terms as well.

Mountweazels, for example. In the 1975 edition of the *New Columbia Encyclopedia*, an entry about a person named Lillian Virginia Mountweazel described her as follows:

> Mountweazel, Lillian Virginia, 1942–73, American photographer, b. Bangs, Ohio. Turning from fountain design to photography in 1963, Mountweazel produced her celebrated portraits of the South Sierra Miwok in 1964. She was awarded government grants to make a series of photo-essays of unusual subject matter, including New York City buses, the cemeteries of Paris, and rural American mailboxes. The last group was exhibited extensively abroad and published as *Flags Up!* (1972). Mountweazel died at 31 in an explosion while on assignment for *Combustibles* magazine.[4]

Unfortunately, Ms. Mountweazel never existed. This entry was merely a trap into which potential plagiarizers could fall.

In 2005, word got out that the *New Oxford American Dictionary* contained a mountweazel of this sort beginning with the letter *e*. This sent word sleuths on a hunt to determine which word it might be. Most, including puzzle icon Will Shortz, correctly flagged **esquivalience** as the suspect term. This word, appropriately, was listed as meaning "the willful avoidance of one's official responsibilities." It was introduced into the 2001 edition of the dictionary as a copyright trap by editor Christine Lindberg, who coined it.

Five other entries from the 2005 edition of the *New Oxford American Dictionary* were incorrectly suspected of being mountweazels as well: earth loop (an alternative to the term "ground loop"), EGD (an abbreviation of "eyeglass display," an early team for the smart glasses we see today), electrofish

[4] *New Columbia Encyclopedia* (New York: Columbia University Press, 1975).

(a verb describing the process of fishing using electrocution), ELSS (an initialism for "extravehicular life support system"), and eurocreep (a term for the slow acceptance of the Euro as a common currency in the European Union). These were all real, albeit rare, terms.

In the 1970s, the U.S. Army surveyed soldiers about their preferred foods.[5] To filter out extraneous or unhelpful answers, they included **funistrada**, **braised trake**, and **buttered ermal** on the list of foods that soldiers could choose from. None of them exists—Ermal is an Albanian man's name—but respondents still ranked them over lima beans and eggplant. Since then, Funistrada has been used as the name of a racehorse and an actual restaurant in Michigan.

Another term for these words is **nihilartikel**, literally "nothing article," from the Latin *nihil* and the German *Artikel*.

One of the most notable legal cases hinging on the use of fictitious entries was the unsuccessful suit filed by author Fred L. Worth against the makers of *Trivial Pursuit*. Worth's book, *The Trivia Encyclopedia*, contained false information about the television series *Columbo* (1968–78), which was then added into the game. The suit failed because the game's creators proved that they drew from a range of sources and hadn't just copied Worth's mountweazel word-for-word.

In the world of mapmaking, false streets and fake cities have many names, including **cartographer's follies**, **phantom settlements**, **trap streets**, and **paper towns**—and in some cases these imaginary locations have become real. Agloe, a hamlet in the town of Colchester in Delaware County, New York, for example, was originally a fictional locale crafted for ExxonMobil

---

[5] Herbert L. Meiselman, Day Waterman, and Lawrence E. Symington, "Armed Forces Food Preferences" (U.S. Army Natick Development Center, 1974).

(Esso) maps. However, because of the name on the map, a general store there was named the Agloe General Store. Rand McNally created a map designating the area as a hamlet, and when Esso went after them for copyright infringement, they were able to avoid a negative judgment because Agloe had effectively been made real with the naming of the store.

20

Offbeat Origins for Word Enthusiasts

The Origins of Your Favorite Words

One of the most glorious things about English is it is so vast and so multifaceted that even those with astounding vocabularies discover new gems all the time.

Since you've nearly come to the end of this book, you must be a highly curious smarty-pants yourself and a collector of interesting words. The following are some miscellaneous favorites among logophiles everywhere—and among my readers in particular… and perhaps, in one or two cases, just among myself—and the intriguing journeys that brought them to English.

The fictional substance known as **"adamant"** or **"adamantium"** is well known to Marvel aficionados today, but it's far, far older than Wolverine and his metal-reinforced skeleton. The Greek *adamas* often referred to either real-life diamonds or the hypothetical idea of the hardest possible substance. Indeed, the word "diamond" is ultimately derived from the Greek *adamas*, altered in spelling first in Medieval Latin (*diamas*) before entering Old French (*diamant*) and then English (*diamaunt* and then diamond). Logically enough, in 14th-century English, *adamant* was a word for a variety of very hard substances, including diamonds but also naturally occurring magnetic lodestones, or exceptionally hard iron or steel.

The lodestone connection, which also appeared in Latin, may have been a folk-etymology conflation of *adamas* with the Latin *adamare* meaning "to love passionately"—an understandable association between "magnetic" emotional and romantic attraction and actual magnets. Most research suggests that these words fundamentally mean "unbreakable," but the Greek actually appears to be "unconquerable" or "untameable" (*a-* "not" + *daman* "to conquer, tame"), implying something along the lines of invincibility or indomitability.

Bombast is a word for cotton padding, ultimately from the Latin *bombax* "cotton," a variation on the Greek *bombyx*, meaning "silk" or "silkworm." Therefore, to call a person **"bombastic"** is to imply that they are puffed up, inflated, without substance. Similarly, bombastic language, or purple prose, lacks meaning and depth.

The word **"cromulent"** first appeared in "Lisa the Iconoclast," a 1996 episode of *The Simpsons*, in which Mrs. Krabappel says she had never heard the term "embiggens" before moving to Springfield, where the show takes place. A fellow teacher tells her that it's a perfectly "cromulent" word, implying that it is "acceptable" or "satisfactory." The joke, of course, is that neither embiggens nor cromulent is a commonly accepted word—though both are now in use and appear in dictionaries thanks to the episode. This joke is commonly attributed to *Simpsons* writer David X. Cohen, who almost certainly crafted the word arbitrarily for its sound rather than for any particular implied meaning or etymology. But it does have some logic to it nonetheless. The Latin ending *-ulentus* means "full of" or "with an abundance of," as in the word "flatulent" (meaning "gassy," literally "full of wind or gas") or "flocculent" (a word describing very wooly sheep, literally "abounding in wool"). The *crom* element is meaningless, but just for fun, we could still reverse-engineer an etymology, giving cromulent at least two possible faux-histories.

Crom might come from *cromlech*, a Welsh word for a megalith (Ancient Greek "big stone") like the ones seen at Stonehenge, with one horizontal stone atop two vertical ones. The first part of this word, *crom*, means "crooked" or "bent." Perhaps then "cromulent" could imply a crooked smile, and mean something like "abounding in wry humor."

Alternatively, *crom* might come from the *cro-* element in "Cro-Magnon" (rebracketed, for the sake of argument), which is an Occitan word meaning "cavity." This interpretation could imply that "cromulent" is "empty" or filling a "cavity" in English.

Crepuscular describes things and environments that are dim, indistinct, or literally "resembling twilight," from the Latin *crepusculum*, meaning "twilight" or "dusk," or perhaps "obscure" or "uncertain." Its precise root is unknown. It's found in biology texts describing creatures that emerge during twilight hours, but also in 17th- and 18th-century literature as a word describing a tentative, emerging sense of enlightenment and understanding.

Defenestrate means to throw someone out of a window, from the Latin *fenestra*, meaning "window," and it arose in English to describe three specific acts of fenestral expulsion: the three (or two-and-a-half) Defenestrations of Prague. The first Defenestration of Prague occurred in 1419, when Prague city councilors were tossed out of a window by Czech Hussites (a movement of Christian reformers), initiating the Hussite Wars. The second—which is often not considered a full defenestration because it ushered in an era of peace rather than triggering a war—occurred in 1483, when a magistrate and several dead councilors were ejected from town hall windows across the city. The final defenestration happened in 1618, when Catholic representatives were expelled—via the window—from Prague Castle by angry Protestants. Confusingly, the third Defenestration of Prague was the first to be dubbed a "defenestration," after which the word was retroactively applied to the first two.

The doldrums wasn't originally a nautical term, but earned the wind in its sails, you might say, because of its use in nautical contexts. It's probably an early 19th-century combination of the words "dull" and "tantrum," and it originally meant "low spirits" or "ennui." It was soon applied to areas of the sea near the equator known for unpleasant and baffling weather—including a sudden drop in the prevailing wind, which left ships becalmed. Many came to assume that "the doldrums" was the name for this part of the world. As a result, it became a name for a real geographical location, often used to refer to the Intertropical Convergence Zone (ITCZ), a belt around the Earth near the equator where ships are often stuck.

The word **"frolic"** comes from the Middle Dutch *vrolyc*, meaning "happy" or literally "merry-like." In the 15th century, it was common to say that a very happy person or creature was "frolicsome." The PIE root of "frolic" means "to hop," giving it the sense of "jumping for joy." It also shares this root with the word "frog." The word "rollick," meaning "to behave in a joyous way," arose in 1811 as a combination of roll and frolic. Frolic and the German word *fröhlich*, meaning "happy," are cognates, meaning they are derived from the same etymological source. Frolic also shares a root with the second part of the German word **Schadenfreude**, which is pleasure taken at someone else's misfortune, and literally translates as "damage-joy."

Related is the word **"merry,"** originally the Old English *myrge*, which comes from a Proto-Germanic word meaning "short-lasting," with the current sense arising from the notion of something pleasant making time fly. The word "mirth" is the noun form of merry; it's made in the same fashion as truth, from true; depth, from deep; and strength, from strong. The *-th* ending dates back to Old English (-*ð*) and forms nouns of action, state, or quality.

An **infinity sign** (∞) is also known as a **"lemniscate."** It's from the Latin *lemniscatus*, meaning "decorated with ribbons," from the Greek *lēmniskos*, "ribbons," or the "material used to make ribbons." In 1811, mathematician and clergyman James Booth adopted the word for the ribbon-like symbol used in algebraic geometry.

Lackadaisical is a whimsical corruption of the 17th-century term "lack-a-day" and its predecessors, including "alack the day," "alas, alack," or simply "alack"—all wails of dismay and regret. (In *Romeo and Juliet*, the Nurse cries "Alack the day! He's gone, he's killed, he's dead!" [2.3.44] in reference to her cousin Tybalt after Romeo has slain him.) The literal implication is an expression of grief over *lack*—that is, absence, loss, or, in some instances, having no other words for one's feelings. Unlike its predecessors, lackadaisical and its noun form "lackadaisy" refer not to an expression of deep care and emotional pain but to carelessness and laziness—that is, a lack of care, diligence, initiative, or motivation. Someone who is lackadaisical is either unmotivated to work or just generally unbothered, depending on the context and the speaker's tone. "Lack" itself is from the PIE **leg-*, meaning "to dribble" or "to trickle," and is thereby related to the word "leak," which is related to other Germanic words for deficiencies such as the German *lechzen*, meaning "to lust, thirst, or crave."

Limerence is a psychological term that describes a swift and intense emotional attachment to another person that then leads to hyperfixation, intrusive thoughts, and a strong desire for reciprocation. It was coined by the psychologist Dorothy Tennov who wrote about it extensively—including its origin, or lack thereof. Tennov herself wrote: "I first used the term 'amorance' then changed it back to 'limerence'... It has no roots whatsoever. It looks nice. It works well in French. Take it from me it has no etymology whatsoever."[1]

Often applied to sweet sounds and pleasant music, **mellifluous** literally means "flowing like honey." It's a hybrid word derived from the Late Latin *mellifluus*, and composed of the Ancient Greek *meli* "honey" (in Latin, it's *mel*) and the Latin *fluere* "to flow." Its relatives, therefore, include:

> **Caramel:** literally "sugar-honey," with the first part thought to be adapted from the Latin *canna* "cane," as in sugarcane.
> **Marmalade:** the honey-sweet preserve originally made from quince and later citrus fruits.
> **Mildew:** originally a word for "nectar" or "honeydew," as in the sugary-sweet excretions of decaying plants or the insects that feed on them

The second portion of mellifluous has many relatives, including:

> **Fluent:** literally "that which flows freely," applied to both water and language.
> **Superfluous:** literally "flowing over."
> **Reflux, influence, and confluence:** "a flowing back," "a flowing in," and "a flowing together" (of liquid, air, information, power).
> **Influenza:** Originally an Italian word describing any type of epidemic, implying a disease supposedly caused by the "influence" of the stars or divine forces, which incidentally also causes one's olfactory system to flow.
> **Fluctuate:** "to undulate or flow," like waves.

[1] Cited in "Will limerence take the place of love?" *The Observer*, September 11, 1977.

Petrichor is a word for the scent that emerges after rainfall, especially a light rain that slowly infiltrates the soil and releases bacteria into the air. The word is made up of the Greek *petra* "rock," and *ichor*, the fluid that flows in the veins of the gods in Greek mythology. It has also been called an "argillaceous" (clay-like) odor. Petrichor was coined in 1964 by Dick Thomas in a paper about the phenomenon. It's caused by an oil that plants secrete during dry periods, which is absorbed by soil and rock and then released along with "geosmin" ("earth-smell") and ozone when it rains. All these combine to create that distinctive smell.

A newer entry into English—but one understandably popular among word lovers—is **vellichor**, which describes the wistful contentment one finds while surrounded by old books. The parallel with petrichor suggests that it may be the smell of books that causes this feeling. Its latter half is the same *-ichor* element, while the *vell-* part comes from vellum, parchment prepared of animal skins that was used for writing. The word was coined quite recently, in the 2010s, by John Koenig, in the online collection and later book *The Dictionary of Obscure Sorrows*. It's a compendium of names for feelings we don't otherwise have words for.

Another word from *The Dictionary of Obscure Sorrows* that has taken off in logophilic circles is **sonder**, which means "the realization that each random passerby is living a life as vivid and complex as your own." But "sonder" is not a total neologism. *Sonder* also means "special" in German, though whether it influenced the English word isn't clear. In Old and Middle English, it's recorded as a different spelling of "sunder," meaning "to split apart" (also found in "torn asunder"), and in Old English it's also found as a variation of "sooner"—both apt for the neologistic sense we have today.

A **palimpsest** (from the Greek *palimpsestos*, "scraped again") is a surface that has been written on more than once.

It's typically a piece of parchment or another writing surface on which a text is written, then erased or removed, then overwritten by another text. Usually, traces of that first text remain visible under or around the new one. Its first Greek element, *palin*, "again, back," is also found in "palindrome."

The little dimple or channel in the center of your upper lip, descending from your nostrils, is called your **philtrum**. It is a Latinized version of the Greek *philtron* or *philter*, which the Greeks apparently found to be devastatingly attractive because it literally means "love charm." In fantasy fiction and board games, potions are often called "philters of healing" or "philters of ruining thine enemy's day"—but this variation of the word literally means "love potion." Both words originally come from the Greek *philein* "to love," which appears in words like philanthropy, philosophy, and Philadelphia. The human philtrum is vestigial—it doesn't do anything aside from being sexy and seductive. In dogs, cats, and some other animals, it's that line that runs down the middle of their noses, and it contributes to their sense of smell.

I'm delighted to inform you that the word **"preposterous"** is an etymological joke—and has been for millennia. The Latin *praeposterous* meant "absurd," "inverted," or "reversed," but its literal meaning—and that of the English word—is "before-behinderous" (*prae-* "before" + *post* "after, behind" + adjective ending). The word existed in Latin, where its humor would have been more readily apparent; its meaning then was quite close to the English term "topsy-turvy." That also means it's an **autological**, or **self-describing**, **word** (see: autological words).

If you've made it this far and you don't already know the word **"somnambulist"** (or **"noctambulist"**), you can probably guess its meaning based on its etymological elements. Coined in the late 1700s in a clinical context (as the condition of "somnambulism"), a somnambulist is a sleepwalker. The word is made up of the Latin *somnus* "sleep" (related to "insomnia") and *ambulare* "to walk" (related to "amble"); a similar word is "obambulation" (with the prefix *ob-* here meaning "about" or "around"), which means "a walking about." Over the next century, the romantic appeal of the somnambulist helped it venture into common use via literature and poetry. Here's a case-in-point, from Percy Bysshe Shelley's "The Witch of Atlas":

> The soldiers dreamed that they were blacksmiths, and
> Walked out of quarters in somnambulism;
> Round the red anvils you might see them stand
> Like Cyclopses in Vulcan's sooty abysm,
> Beating their swords to ploughshares.[2]

A **thaumaturge** is literally a "wonderworker," or magical miracle worker, from the Greek *thaumatos*, meaning "wondrous thing" or "a thing to look at" + *ergon*, "work." It's recorded in English in the mid- to late-1500s, notably in the work of polymath John Dee, who writes:

> Thaumaturgike, is that Art Mathematicall, which giueth certaine order to make straunge workes, of the sense to be perceiued, and of men greatly to be wondred at. By sundry meanes, this Wonder-worke is wrought.

[2] Percy Bysshe Shelley, *The Selected Poetry & Prose of Shelley* (Ware, Herts: Wordsworth Editions, 1994), 462.

21

Antiquated Words You Didn't Know You Needed

Plenty of terribly useful words have simply fallen out of regular use in English—which means they're just begging to be revived. See whether you can work some of these into your everyday conversation.

The Middle English *dight* or *dighten* meant "to adorn, dress, or make something beautiful." So, to say something was **bedighted** was a bit like the Middle English equivalent of the word "bedazzled."

In the 14th century, **meseems** was used sort of like the word "methinks," but instead of "I think" it meant "it seems to me." A very useful word, meseems.

In Middle English and early modern English, the word "**eftsoons**" was used to mean "soon afterward." So, you might say something like "I'll see you eftsoons." The adverb *eft*, meaning "afterward," shares a root with the modern word "after." After, or *aefter* in Old English, combines this root with a comparative suffix, while *eft* simply has an adverbial *-t* at its end. Indeed, the word "after" originally meant "farther off" or "more away," either in time or in physical distance, with the frequentative *-ter* ending implying extra distance.

You've probably heard the words "forego" and "foregone," as in "a foregone conclusion," but what about **fordo** and

fordone? In Middle English, *fordone* was used euphemistically to mean "killed" or "destroyed." In some English dialects, fordone is still used to mean "overcome with fatigue," like "I'm fordone with the heat after working in the sun." A similar sense appears in today's phrase "We're done for," which characters in books and movies say when they're in grave danger.

The word **"dern,"** meaning "hide" or "conceal," is still used in some English dialects—most often as the past participle "derned"—but it's based on an Old English word meaning "secret" or "hidden," and it shares a root with the word "dark."

In the 1500s, the word **"gratulate"** meant "to give thanks" or "to show joy," from the Latin *gratulari*, also meaning "to give thanks" or "to show joy." We don't usually use it on its own anymore, but of course we do use "congratulate," literally meaning "to show joy together."

One of the more entertaining Middle English words to be found is *balter* also recorded as *balteren*, *baltyre*, and *bauter*, and it means to dance or move in a goofy, graceless way. It appears in several poems and prose works in the late 1300s and early 1400s, including the *Alliterative Morte Arthure*,[1] and is found as recently as the 19th century in a glossary of words used in the town of Whitby in Yorkshire with the definition "to tread in a clownish manner."[2]

A useful and remarkably relatable archaic word recorded first in the 1600s, **latibulate** means "to hide oneself (in a corner)," from the Latin *latere* "conceal, hide, lie hidden" and the suffix *-bulum*, which implies a "vessel" or "place."

---

[1] *The Allierative Morte Arthure*, in the digital collection *Corpus of Middle English Prose and Verse*. University of Michigan Library Digital Collections. https://name.umdl.umich.edu/AllitMA. Accessed April 10, 2025.

[2] Francis Kildale Robinson, *A Glossary of Words Used in the Neighbourhood of Whitby* (Periodicals Service Company, 1876).

Brægnloca was an Old English word for "head." It literally means "brain-locker" or "brain-stronghold." The first element, perhaps obviously, is the predecessor to the word "brain," while the second element is from the Old English *loca*, implying "locked space" or "enclosure." This is an example of a **kenning**, a metaphorical compound used to replace an everyday noun, sometimes out of superstition, other times to avoid repetition, many of which are found in Old English and Old Norse poetry. For instance, in *Beowulf*, the sea is variously called the *seġl-rād* ("sail-road"), *hron-rād* ("whale-road"), and *hwæl-weġ* ("whale's way").

A few other ideas drawn from other famous works of early Northern European literature: a ship can be called a *gjálfr-marr* or an *unnsvín* ("sea-steed" or "wave-swine"), the sun can be called *heofones ġim* or *eofon-candel* ("heaven's jewel" or "heaven-candle"), and fire can be called *grand viðar* ("wood's bane").

Dumfungled is a 19th-century word that means "worn out." I've seen some less than reliable sources saying that it's been around since Old Scots but lexicographer Susie Dent says it's an American invention and indeed I've found most written references to it in 19th-century American contexts.

Gubbertushed means "having large projecting teeth." Why it means this is a mystery. *Gubber* is not a part of any other words relating to large or projecting things, as far as we know, and *tushed* is not related to the word "tush," as in a person's posterior, which is from the Yiddish *tokhes*, meaning "beneath." The first known appearance of gubbertushed is in the 1688 manuscript *Academy of Armory* by Randle Holme. Holme's grandfather's job was to arrange funerals for those entitled to official coats of arms, and he also made funerary hatchments and memorial boards, which showed the crest and achievements of the deceased. The book covers symbolism in heraldry and armor design—as well as heavily editorialized lists of body parts, emotions, diseases (so many diseases), and vocabulary words. Gubbertushed, which, Holme says, "is when teeth stand out, and not in order," appears in a section dedicated to terms describing "outward shapes of the body"—and it's not the only insulting attribute he lists. In fact, it reads like a third-grade bully's guide to insulting people for things they can't control. He writes that you can be "wry-necked" (having a crooked neck). You can have "chuffe," "puff," or "blob" cheeks. You can have "blopper" lips, "loll" ears, or a "beckle" brow, which appears to be a word for a unibrow.

Other, older words for what we might call a hullabaloo, brouhaha, or kerfuffle include **hubbleshubble**, **bobbery**, and **foofaraw**. There are many words in English that are imitative or onomatopoeic, from words for actions and sounds to the names of birds and other animals that make distinctive sounds. It seems we also tend to gravitate toward words for disturbances that conjure up the sound of a ruckus.

What do you think a **bellibone** is? If you guessed "beautiful woman," throw yourself a figurative bone—though the word "bone" has nothing to do with it. It's found as early as the 16th century and is probably a fanciful mashup of words like the French *belle* and the word "bonny," which is related to the French *bonne*, or "good." It might also be an intentional inversion of the term "bonnibelle," which has a similar meaning.

Jactation sounds naughtier than it actually is. It's from the Latin *jacĕre* "to throw" and has a few meanings, all of which suggest swaggering or throwing out one's chest, such as "boasting," "bragging," or "putting on an ostentatious display."

Eructation is a word for a belch or the act of belching, from the Latin elements *ex* "out" and *ructare* "to belch." The verb form is eruct.

A **rampallion** was the female equivalent of a **rapscallion** in 17th-century English. A *ramp* was a Middle English word for an ill-behaved woman, likely drawing on the notion of a woman "run rampant." This word was used in parallel to rascal, which was more commonly applied to men.

Balbutient was an adjective describing a state of stuttering or stammering, from the Latin *balbutire* "to stammer."

Stertorous was an adjective describing someone who is snoring deeply, from the imitative Latin word *stertere* "to snore," which is also related to *sternuere* "to sneeze."

A **threnody** is a song of lamentation or a dirge, from the Greek *thrēnōidia,* from *thrēnos* "wailing" + *ōidē* "ode." *Thrēnos* is thought to be related through its PIE root to the English word "drone."

Persiflage was a noun for the practice of engaging in casual and flippant banter, especially about a subject that others would treat with more gravity. Its components are ultimately the Latin *per* "through" and *sibilare*, meaning "to hiss," with the frivolity implied in the word introduced via one sense of the French derivative *siffler*, "to whistle."

Stridulous was an adjective describing a quiet though shrill sound, like that which grasshoppers make on a summer night (stridulation). It's ultimately an imitative word, brought into English from the Latin *stridere*, "to make a shrill or grating sound." This means it's related to the word "strident," which describes harshness and insistence, echoing the use of the word "shrill" itself as a word for someone speaking vehemently.

Although its origin is unknown, **mulligrubs** is a word for a fit of the blues or nonspecific abdominal pain. It appeared (also as "mulliegrums") rather commonly from the 1500s onward. In his 1823 sportsmen's slang dictionary, John Badcock proposed this fanciful, *Iliad*-inspired example sentence—though whether he drew it from elsewhere or penned it himself is unclear:

Hector suggested that if he went not to the battle, the Trojan dames would:

Cry, "Bless us! What is come to Hector,
He used to maul the Grecian scrubs:
Pray, has he got the mulligrubs?"[3]

Mumpsimus is a word for someone who stubbornly insists they're right despite being wrong. Its origin is a bit of a Mrs. Malaprop situation (see: malapropisms). Mumpsimus was popularized because it was found in one of the letters of the Dutch priest and writer Erasmus. In it, he told a story about a Catholic priest who was conducting communion where, instead of writing *Quod ore sumpsimus* (What we have received by the mouth), he wrote *Quod ore mumpsimus*. The friend he was writing to corrected him, but Erasmus continued to stubbornly use the incorrect term—and thus mumpsimus became a word for anyone with a similar tendency.

In the Victorian era, there were many slang and fanciful terms for liars, such as **pseudologist** (with that *pseudo-* element meaning "false"). There was also **wrinkler**, implying someone who adds figurative wrinkles into the truth, **gabber**, **mogger**, and **canter gloak**. A word for a little white lie was evidently a **taradiddle**, first attested in Sir Francis Grose's 1811 *Dictionary of the Vulgar Tongue*.

Ventosity is a Latin-derived coinage first found in the 14th century, but in use at least as recently as the 19th century. The root here is the Latin word *ventus*, meaning "wind." It's first found in medical writings describing someone who is afflicted by either belching or flatulence. Understandably, it's also recorded describing the empty but grandiloquent speech of someone who you might describe as a "windbag." Washington Irving included that sense in a few of his works about the culture of New York City. The same kind of punnery is sometimes found in descriptions of Chicago, which is famously windy and also famously home to many "windbag" politicians.

[3] John Badcock, *Slang: A Dictionary of the Turf, the Ring, the Chase, the Pit* (London: T. Hughes, 1823).

22

Extralongitudinal Linguistifabulations

The Longest Words You Never Knew

Let us end this etymological journey with some excessively, ridiculously, absurdly long words—parting words for the most extravagant philologists.

By assembling a variety of roots and affixes, one can achieve words of tongue-tripping length. Some of the longest words in English that might actually come up in conversation are **incomprehensibilities**, **counterproductiveness**, **inapplicableness**, **unintelligibleness**, and **incontrovertibleness**. (That *-ness* ending does quite a bit of heavy lifting if you need to extend a word for, say, *Scrabble* purposes.)

Other epically long words might turn up in the list of ingredients on your "fruit" snacks or eczema medication. That is, many of the longest words emerge in scientific contexts, such as **pseudopseudohypoparathyroidism**, an inherited condition that affects the thyroid; **dichlorodifluoromethane**, a gas used as a fire repellant for submarines and aircraft; and **electroencephalographically**, an adverbial form of **electroencephalograph**, a device that records brain waves.

And then, of course, there's Mary Poppins, whose film persona popularized the term **supercalifragilisticexpialidocious**—though it was Syracuse University student writer Helen Herman who first penned the elaborate word in 1931, originally spelling it *supercaliflawjalisticexpialidoshus* in a column called "A-muse-ings" in *The Syracuse Daily Orange*. The 1964 film's songwriters, Richard and Robert Sherman, also faced a copyright infringement suit from the writers of a 1949 song, "Supercalafajalistickespeealadojus," but the suit ultimately failed because Herman's variation on the term—and a few others besides—predated the writing of either song.

Beyond chemicals, medical conditions, and magical nannies, the longer words get, the more they tend to veer into the absurd or intentionally cheeky. (Mary Poppins' excellent word doesn't fall into this category because she is, of course, "practically perfect in every way.")

One nonscientific long word many discover early in their life as word nerds is **antidisestablishmentarianism**, a double negative that emerged in 19th-century England. But the reason many people know it as one of the longest words in English—and the reason we often learn this as early as grade school—is thanks to a 12-year-old girl named Gloria Lockerman.

Antidisestablishmentarianism is unique for being a long word with a practical, unfanciful, and nonscientific use. It was, in short, a reaction to 18th-century disestablishmentarianism, which was a movement calling for churches to remove (disestablish) themselves from the Church of England (the "establishment," so to speak) so that it would no longer continue the default, official church. This was in many cases due to abuses of power and absurdly inflated salaries for Church of England officials. Slap an *anti-* on disestablishmentarianism to describe the position that churches should not be disestablished and should continue to receive government funding and be subject to its influence. Proponents of antidisestablishmentarianism believed that disestablished churches might descend into partisanship and ethnic nationalism.

The word itself was not well known outside of this historical context until 1955.

On an episode of the U.S. game show *The $64,000 Question*, 12-year-old Gloria Lockerman correctly spelled the word, winning $8,000—a sizeable chunk of change at the time. She became a sensation, and her winning word became known to a wide audience. She would return for another episode of *The $64,000 Challenge* (same show, different night) and correctly spell the sentence "The belligerent astigmatic anthropologist annihilated innumerable chrysanthemums." She was up against a boy named David Douglass, competing for a $32,000 prize. The result was a tie, and they split the money.

Gloria could have come back and gambled her winnings to take a shot at still more, but on her grandmother's advice, she took the money she had already won and said it would go toward college. She told *Jet* magazine, "I'd rather be Gloria the undefeated champion than Gloria the girl who lost."[1]

According to later reporting by the *Chicago Tribune*, one of the reasons Gloria gained such wide acclaim was because she was Black.[2] Her show of spelling aptitude defied the expectations of racist viewers, who held to negative stereotypes about Black people's intelligence. Even supposedly impartial news coverage emphasized her race.

Gloria became an instant celebrity after her on-air triumph. She was declared an honorary schoolteacher in her hometown; she met celebrities; she was invited to appear in parades; the National Pickle Packers Association reportedly sent her 16,000 pickles;[3] she appeared on the popular variety program *The Martha Raye Show* (famously drawing complaints from bigoted viewers, which may have led to the show's later

[1] *Jet*, November 1955.

[2] "Has Anyone Seen Gloria Lockerman?" *Chicago Tribune*, November 24, 1987. https://www.chicagotribune.com/1987/11/24/has-anyone-seen-gloria-lockerman/

[3] *Marshall Evening Chronicle*, September 1, 1955, p. 1.

cancellation). Gloria is even referenced in the 2005 comedy film *The Honeymooners*.

All this hype resulted in the previously obscure word "antidisestablishmentarianism" becoming one that everyone had heard of, even if they weren't well versed in the 19th-century politics of the Church of England. Which makes Gloria Lockerman a true icon among word nerd influencers.

How about a few more long-ass words before we go?

One might call **pneumonoultramicroscopicsilicovolcanoconiosis** a pseudo-scientific word since it's not actually used by the scientific community but is meant to look like it is. It's an invention of Everett M. Smith, who, during his reign as president of the National Puzzlers' League, opened the organization's 103rd semiannual meeting by introducing the word.[4]

It's an extension of the real medical term "pneumoconiosis," a lung condition caused by the inhalation of dust, which is composed of the Greek elements *pneúmōn* "lungs," *kónis* "dust," and the ending *-osis*, which is often used in the names of medical conditions. Smith also added the Latin *ultra* "beyond," the Greek-derived "microscopic" (*smikros* "small, little" + *skopein* "to look at, examine"), and the English word "volcano" (from the Latin *Vulcanus*, Roman god of fire).

The result is a word that could describe a real condition—but isn't, because shorter, slightly less specific terms exist. It means "a lung disease caused by inhaling very fine ash and dust from a volcano."

If you don't care much for etymology, and yet you're still reading this book, you might feel yourself slipping into a state of **floccinaucinihilipilification**: the impression that something is worthless. It's said that students at Eton College coined it based on this quote:

---

[4] "Puzzlers Open 103rd Session Here by Recognizing 45-Letter Word," *New York Herald Tribune*, February 23, 1935.

> Flócci *of a lock of wool*, náuci *of a nut-shell*, níhili *of nóthing*, píli *of a hair*, ássis *of a pénny*, hújus *of this*, terúncii *of a fárthing*, addúntur *are ádded*, peculiáritèr *pecúliarly or véry próperly* vérbis *to verbs* æstimándi *of esteéming*.[5]

This passage and similar ones appear in versions of and responses to 16th-century grammarian William Lily's *Eton Latin Grammar*, a formative work on classical grammar.

Each of the Latin items in the sequence represents a worthless or negligible part of the already-insignificant whole that follows: a *floccus* is a "wisp," so we have "a small tuft of a lock of wool"; *naucum* means "a trifle," so we have "a trifle of nut shell"; *nihilum* means "nothing," so we have "nothing of nothing"; *pilus* means "hair," so we have a "hair of a hair." The Latin-inspired *-fication* ending makes it a noun.

Honorificabilitudinitatibus appears in Shakespeare's *Love's Labour's Lost* (5.1.39–40), but it's actually a bit older even than that, just not in English. It's a real medieval Latin word—sort of. Was it used in conversation? Not so much. But its existence is grammatically justifiable. It's the dative and ablative plural of *honorificabilitudinitas*, meaning "the state of being able to achieve honors." But in practice it's mostly tossed around among scholars and poets for being pretentious or just too darn long. (Shakespeare puts the word into the mouth of the clown Costard, who is making fun of two pedants who have just been holding forth using ridiculous Latinate words; see: nonce words.)

And, of course, there are James Joyce's linguistic monstrosities from *Finnegans Wake* (1939). This one is meant to capture the sound of the thunderclap that accompanied the fall of Adam and Eve:

---

[5] *Eton Latin Grammar*, ed. T. W. C. Edwards (Eton College, 1826).

> Bababadalgharaghtakamminarronnkonnbronntonnerronntu onnthunntrovarrhounawnskawntoohoohoordenenthurnuk.

It contains allusions to several words for thunder in different languages, including the French *tonnerre*, Italian *tuono*, Greek *bronte*, and Japanese *kaminari*, as well as approximations of Hindi and Irish words for "rumble" and "crack."

Here's a bonus one, transliterated from Greek. This is the ridiculously elaborate fictional dish mentioned in Aristophanes' 391 BCE comedy *Assemblywomen*:

> Lopadotemachoselachogaleokranioleipsanodrimhypotrim matosilphiokarabomelitokatakechymenokichlepikossypho-phattoperisteralektryonoptekephalliokigklopeleiolagoiosir-aiobaphetraganopterygon

It is made up of more than 25 different Greek words ranging from food preparation methods such as *katakhéō*, "pour over," to flavors and textures such as *drīmús* "sharp, pungent" and *traganós* "crunchy," to ingredients such as shark, pigeon, blackbird, hare, crab, honey, and laserwort.

Hippopotomonstrosesquipedaliophobia is a fanciful word for the fear of long words. *Sesquipedalia* was a Latin word for something "a foot-and-a-half long," and was used in English as "sesquipedalian" starting in the 1600s to describe words that were very long. I assume this was hyperbolic in almost all cases, unless you were writing very big. *Phobia*, of course, refers to fear, and *hippopoto* and *monstro* are elements modeled after large things such as hippos and monsters, just for scale. This is a pretty recent word, found no earlier than the 1990s, though the less hyperbolic variation, sesquipedaliophobia, is recorded a decade or so prior.

And on that monstrous note, let's ride these words into the etymological sunset.

EPILOGUE

Goodbyes and Whys

Much as we began with "hello," we shall end with "goodbye."

Goodbye is a contraction of older parting terms like "god be with ye" (with some influence from "good day" and "good evening" and such). It's first recorded in the 1500s as *godbwye*, a shortened signoff found at the ends of correspondence.

And, unfortunately, it's time to sign off with a *godbwye* of our own.

This was quite a ride. What should you do with all this new information? How will you apply your newfound knowledge in the real world? My strategy has been to write books and record podcasts and make games, but beyond that, learning about etymology has provided me with a lens through which to peer into careers, histories, intellectual journeys, and creative pursuits I may never have time to pursue in depth.

Here's some parting advice.

Play. Words are meant to be bent and blended and diced and reassembled. Whatever you do to the words you write and speak is okay. You come by it honestly. So go ahead and verb nouns and adjective verbs just like Shakespeare did.

The more you study etymology, linguistics, and the development of language, the more you realize that language is always changing. It does have rules of a sort—literally all languages do—but those rules evolve, so I've found that being prescriptive about colloquialisms and emerging language patterns isn't productive. The rules were meant to be broken. Wordplay is as old as language itself.

Stay curious and, when in doubt, look up your words. Be voracious about collecting new words for your lexical toolkit. Always look up words you've never met before.

Whatever words you choose to use, try to understand enough of their story so that you don't cram them in uncomfortable places. Learning more about words before you use them may help you avoid unintended shades of meaning.

(For what it's worth, at least at the time of this book's writing, conversational AI tools will not give you accurate or reliable etymological information. Indeed, they'll often parrot common myths and folk etymology. Start with the *Oxford English Dictionary*'s online etymology tools instead. They're sourced.)

But this isn't just a cautionary tale. Learning the origins of words can provide you with creative inspiration. New words unlock imagination and opportunity.

Above all, though, here's a piece of advice I've given before and will stand by for the rest of my life: **Wield your words for good, for creativity, and for the cultivation of knowledge.**

Each word holds within it a book's worth of discovery waiting for you to examine, unfurl, and unravel.

If you learn to look beyond its cover and take words for more than granted, you might find etymology quite useful after all.

BIBLIOGRAPHY

*When it arrived in English in the 1600s, "bibliography" (*biblion *"book" +* graphos *"a thing drawn or written") was a word for the practice of writing books: One could be a bibliographer and practice bibliography, much in the same way a calligrapher practices calligraphy or a photographer practices photography. It then evolved to mean "the study of books and authors," then a list of books and/or authors collected for a particular purpose—like, for example, assembling a book of whimsical etymology facts.*

Augarde, T. *The Oxford Guide to Word Games*. 2nd ed. Oxford: Oxford University Press, 2003.

Ayto, J. *Dictionary of Word Origins*. New York: St. Martin's Press, 1990.

Barnhart, R. K., ed. *Barnhart Dictionary of Etymology*. H. W. Wilson Co., 1988.

Baugh, A. C., and T. Cable. *A History of the English Language*. 6th ed. New York: Routledge, 2012.

Beekes, R. *Etymological Dictionary of Greek*. Leiden: Brill, 2010.

Blount, T. *Glossographia: Or a Dictionary Interpreting All Such Hard Words*. London: Thomas Horne, 1656.

Buck, C. D. *A Dictionary of Selected Synonyms in the Principal Indo-European Languages*. University of Chicago Press, 1949; reprinted 1988.

Cambridge History of the English Language. Vol. 1, edited by R. M. Hogg. Cambridge: Cambridge University Press, 1992.

Crystal, D. *The Stories of English*. New York: Overlook Press, 2004.

Crystal, D., and B. Crystal. *Shakespeare's Words: A Glossary and Language Companion*. London: Penguin Books, 2002.

Dent, S. *Word Perfect: Etymological Journeys Through the English Language*. Oxford: Oxford University Press, 2023.

De Vaan, M. *Etymological Dictionary of Latin and the Other Italic Languages*. Vol. 7 of Leiden Indo-European Etymological Dictionary Series, ed. Alexander Lubotsky. Leiden: Brill, 2008.

Dobson, E. J. *The Origins of the Modern English Language*. London: Routledge & Kegan Paul, 1968.

Farmer, J. S. *Slang and Its Analogues Past and Present*. London, 1890.

Flexner, S. B., and H. Wentworth. *A Dictionary of American Slang*. New York: Macmillan, 1960.

Fowler, H. W. *A Dictionary of Modern English Usage*. Oxford: Oxford University Press, 1926.

Gordon, E.V. *A History of the English Language*. Boston: Houghton Mifflin, 1951.

Greene, H. *French and English Lexical Borrowings*. New York: Holt, Rinehart and Winston, 1971.

Grose, F. *A Classical Dictionary of the Vulgar Tongue*. London: S. Hooper, 1811.

Grose, F. *Dictionary of the Vulgar Tongue*. London: S. Hooper, 1785.

Hall, R, *Snig'Lit: Any Word That Doesn't Appear in the Dictionary, But Should*, 8th printing ed. New York: Macmillan, 1984.

Hoad, T. F. *The Concise Oxford Dictionary of English Etymology*. Oxford: Oxford University Press, 1993.

Horne, P. *A Comprehensive Etymological Dictionary of the English Language*. New York: Harper & Brothers, 1825.

Johnson, S. *A Dictionary of the English Language*. London: 1755.

Klein, E. *A Comprehensive Etymological Dictionary of the English Language*. Amsterdam: Elsevier Scientific Publishing Co., 1971.

Krebs, C. *Historical Linguistics and Language Change*. Edinburgh: Edinburgh University Press, 1985.

Levy, E. *A New French Dictionary*. London: J. M. Dent & Sons Ltd, 1917.

Linnaeus, C. *Systema Naturae*. 10th ed. Stockholm: Laurentius Salvius, 1758.

Lyovin, A.V. *An Introduction to the Languages of the World*. Oxford University Press, 1997.

MacLeod, R. *The Etymology of Medieval English Terms*. New York: Columbia University Press, 1948.

Martin, R. C. *Encyclopedia of Islam and the Muslim World*. New York: Macmillan Reference USA, 2004.

Merriam-Webster, Inc. *Merriam-Webster's Encyclopedia of Literature*. Springfield, MA: Merriam-Webster, 1995.

Mills, A. D., and D. Crystal. *A Dictionary of British Place Names*. Oxford: Oxford University Press, 2011.

Morgan, J. *The History of English Vocabulary*. London: Routledge, 1979.

Murray, J. A. H. *A New English Dictionary on Historical Principles*. Oxford: Clarendon Press, 1888–1928.

Murray, J. A. H. *The Oxford English Dictionary*. Oxford: Oxford University Press, 1933.

Partridge, E. *Origins: A Short Etymological Dictionary of Modern English*. London: Routledge, 1958.

Pope, M. K. *From Latin to Modern French with Especial Consideration of Anglo-Norman*. Manchester: Manchester University Press, 1934.

Rajan, K. *A Comparative Study of the Lexical Borrowings in English*. London: Routledge, 1991.

Reaney, P. H. *The Origin of English Words*. London: Longmans, Green and Co., 1958.

Richardson, H. *A Dictionary of American Slang*. Macmillan, 1960.

Ringe, D. *From Proto-Indo-European to Proto-Germanic*. Oxford: Oxford University Press, 2006.

Roud, S. *A Dictionary of English Folklore*. Oxford: Oxford University Press, 2004.

Sampson, M. L. *The Origins of Common Words*. Cambridge: Cambridge University Press, 1965.

Shipley, J. T. *The Origins of English Words: A Discursive Dictionary of Indo-European Roots*. United Kingdom: Johns Hopkins University Press, 2001.

Simpson, J. A., and E. S. C. Weiner, eds. *The Oxford English Dictionary*. 2nd ed. Oxford: Clarendon Press, 1989.

Skeat, W. W. *A Concise Etymological Dictionary of the English Language*. Oxford: Clarendon Press, 1901.

Skeat, W. W. *An Etymological Dictionary of the English Language*. Oxford: Clarendon Press, 1888.

Smith, C. J. *Synonyms and Antonyms*. United States: Creative Media Partners, LLC, 2022.

Smith, E. *The English Language and Its Origins*. Cambridge: Cambridge University Press, 1932.

Smith, W., ed. *A Dictionary of Greek and Roman Antiquities*. London: John Murray, 1878.

Tulloch, H. *The Etymology of English Words*. London: Edward Arnold, 1922.

Turner, W. *Latin Language and Its Influence on English*. Oxford: Oxford University Press, 1927.

Vallins, M. *English Word Origins*. London: Macmillan, 1951.

Watkins, C. *The American Heritage Dictionary of Indo-European Roots*. Boston, MA: Houghton Mifflin Harcourt, 2000.

Wedgwood, H. *A Dictionary of English Etymology*. 3rd ed. New York: Macmillan & Co., 1878.

Weekley, E. *An Etymological Dictionary of Modern English*. John Murray, 1921; reprinted 1967. Dover Publications.

Wells, S. *Shakespeare: For All Time*. New York: Oxford University Press, 2003.

Whitney, W. D., ed. *The Century Dictionary and Cyclopedia*. New York: The Century Co., 1895.

ACKNOWLEDGMENTS

I could offer gratitude for this work to a list of people far longer than the book itself, but among those to whom I owe the most:

Drew Zafarris, my lover, best friend, and partner—and our pets Ranger, Ladybird, Wolf, and Artichoke for the necessary cuddles whenever I needed a breather.

My sister, Melissa Farris, and my best friend, Emily Hightower, who have supported this journey every step of the way.

Joshua Williams and Robert Tuesley Anderson, this book's life-saving surgeons.

Sarah Cole, the fairy godperson who gifted me with the opportunity to write this book and its wicked sister—and guided me to professorhood.

Rob Watts, the person who best understands why anyone would write a book like this in the first place, and who, through the podcast he trusted me to co-create, has helped me workshop much of its content.

Emma Green, Carolyn Farnham, and Jen Campbell at Chambers, who have invested an enormous amount of time, patience, and thought into my word-nerdy work and scattered ideas.

Marian Allen for the endless encouragement.

Mom, Dad, Grammy, Gramps, Aunt B, Tim, Jacki, Shelby, Albert, Robin, Danielle, Libby, Chris, and Farrises, Garretts, and Zaferises all.

My brain trust of former colleagues, which is extensive and includes Shannon Miller, Mollie Cahillane, Jameson Fleming, Al Mannarino, Luz Corona, Kai Deveraux Lawson, Doug Zanger, Zac Petit, David Griner, and Alexia Marrache.

My book club: Christina Garnett, Jiya Jaisingh, and Sonia Baschez.

The Writer's Digest team and all who have been there before.

And, of course, the fellow creators and writers who have inspired, supported, and educated me in myriad ways, including but by no means limited to: Mignon Fogarty, Dexter Sorenson, Gretchen McCulloch, Danny Hieber, Maxwell Smith, Charlotte Moore-Lambert, Mattie Wechsler, Laurie Knox, Joshua Blackburn, Matthew Watson, Emily Moyers, Kyle Imperatore, Anne Merrow, and Hank Green.

INDEX